Praise for
The Amazing Infant

"*The Amazing Infant* is a fabulous book. Beautifully crafted, written by one of the most creative figures in the field of infancy, this book will charm both college students and parents wanting to learn about the wonders of the baby's mind. Who needs dinosaurs or astronomical Big Bangs when we have babies to explore? The infant is the keeper of many, many mysteries, and this book engages us in exploring quite a few of them."

Joseph J. Campos, University of California, Berkeley

"Tiffany Field is without question our leading researcher and writer on the role of touch in infant development and behavior. *The Amazing Infant* is an excellent primer on infant behavior and development, utilizing her personal experiences with her own daughter's development. An exceptional aid for new parents as well as students."

Lewis P. Lipsitt, Brown University

"This book is a very good read. The writing style is engaging and easy to follow. It is also truly unique in the field of infant development . . . a field in which far too little attention has been paid to the obvious fact that infants' development involves learning and that specific patterns of maternal behavior are essential for successful child behavioral outcomes."

Martha Pelaez, Florida international University

The Amazing Infant

Tiffany Field, PhD

Touch Research Institute
at the University of Miami School of Medicine

Blackwell Publishing

BLACKWELL PUBLISHING
350 Main Street, Malden, MA 02148-5020, USA
9600 Garsington Road, Oxford OX4 2DQ, UK
550 Swanston Street, Carlton, Victoria 3053, Australia

The right of Tiffany Field to be identified as the Author of this Work has been asserted in accordance with the UK Copyright, Designs, and Patents Act 1988.

First edition published 2007 by Blackwell Publishing Ltd

1   2007

Library of Congress Cataloging-in-Publication Data

Field, Tiffany.
    The amazing infant / Tiffany Field. — 1st ed.
       p.   cm.
    Includes bibliographical references and index.
    ISBN 978-1-4051-5391-1 (hardcover : alk. paper) — ISBN 978-1-4051-5392-8 (pbk. : alk. paper)   1. Infant psychology.   2. Infants—Development.   I. Title.

    BF719.F525 2006
    155.42′2—dc22

                                                                    2006036881

A catalogue record for this title is available from the British Library.

Set in 10 on 12 pt Sabon
by SNP Best-set Typesetter Ltd, Hong Kong
Printed and bound in the United Kingdom
by TJ International Ltd, Padstow, Cornwall

The publisher's policy is to use permanent paper from mills that operate a sustainable forestry policy, and which has been manufactured from pulp processed using acid-free and elementary chlorine-free practices. Furthermore, the publisher ensures that the text paper and cover board used have met acceptable environmental accreditation standards.

For further information on
Blackwell Publishing, visit our website:
www.blackwellpublishing.com

Contents

Foreword
by Michael Lewis

Research in infancy, at least in the latter half of the twentieth century, put to rest William James's claim that the newborn and very young infant was a mass of confusion, with poorly developed senses. In fact this surge of research led to the publication of such edited volumes as *The Competent Infant*, which implied that the old view of the very young infant was wrong and needed to be revised. Work on the mother–child interaction, as well as society's commitment to intervene in the life of infants and parents who needed help, promoted the growth of "intervention" studies.

The research interest from both a basic science perspective as well as from a desire to promote healthy development has continued to the present day, with laboratories all over this country as well as all over the world studying infant abilities. Tiffany Field has been a leader in this effort, focusing her considerable skills not only on studying basic processes in early development but by putting into practice what she and her colleagues have uncovered. Her work on massage therapy, both as a basic need and as a way to intervene in the life of preterm infants, stands as a model of how science and practice can be connected.

In this delightful and informative book, Tiffany Field leads us through the exciting last 20 years of research on infant development. The range of her knowledge and her commitment to turning research into practice make this an invaluable book for parents, clinicians, students, and anyone interested in what has been happening in the study of infants.

Preface

Every day, as I perform neonatal assessments, I am truly amazed by the responsive eyes, ears, and skin of newborns. Their senses of smell and taste are also impressive, as they scrunch up their faces to my rubber-gloved fingers while engaging in the sucking reflex. And sometimes, they "look straight through me" as if seeing something in their reveries from their days in utero or from the minutes spent passing through the birth canal or from recent hours in their parents' arms. Infants are fascinating, from their very first movements as fetuses until they "walk out of infancy" into their terrible twos and continue – though they think they are just beginning – to command their worlds.

I had a fascinating infant of my own once – I wrote a book about Tory years ago (*Infancy*, 1990), and I am doing it again many years later as she is turning thirty – not only because her infancy is still alive in my memory, but also because many fascinating phenomena about infants have recently come to light. We know more than the basics now. We understand the nuances and subtleties and the very sweetness of every baby's development. We also know how influential we can be in helping them navigate their way through those early years.

I am not reviewing the basics of infant development here. You can find those in my earlier work and in many other authors' books. Instead, this book brings together some of the fascinating new studies from the past few years by my young, middle-age, and older-than-middle-age colleagues. I felt it was important that these new findings be collected somewhere for students of infant development and for the parents we are always trying to reach. In response to the many people who have asked me over the years just how we know what we know about infancy, I have tried to detail how these studies were conducted. Infants are truly inspirational and never cease to amaze us, and, hence, this book.

Acknowledgments

Several infants inspired this book, starting with my own, Tory Lana, and with others I have cared for or watched grow and develop, including Loren, Garrett, Will, and Jes. Their adorable photos can be found throughout these pages. All photos are my own, except for figure 5.5b by Regina Yando and figure 7.6a by Sandy Conde. I also want to acknowledge my collaborators on many of the studies described, namely Maria Hernandez-Reif and Miguel Diego, and the invaluable help I received with this manuscript from Angela Ascencio.

1

How Infancy Research
is Conducted

Infancy literally means "without language" – which is one of the reasons why the infant poses problems for the parent, student, and researcher and the reason why we have known very little about infants until the last few decades. The challenge is finding measures to determine what an infant knows and can do. Until recently, when people described infancy research, they said that the field "was in its infancy." With the development of increasingly sophisticated methods and measures, we can now say that the field of infancy is no longer in its infancy but perhaps in its childhood. This chapter is about some of those methods and measures that help us to understand infant development.

Methods and Measures

In a book I published in 1990, *Infancy* (Harvard University Press), I appealed to my colleagues for more natural-observation research, such as that of Piaget and Darwin. With such research, interesting phenomena that had not yet been studied – such as the exploration of objects by mouth and "container" behaviors (i.e. putting objects inside boxes or drawers and then removing them and repeating these actions) – could be documented. More than 15 years later, those interesting behaviors have still received very little attention. Laboratory methods continue to be the most widely used to study infant development, although these methods have become more sophisticated. The most popular measures now include looking (or the visual-preference model), facial expressions, tracking (or head turning), nonnutritive sucking, habituation/dishabituation, operant conditioning, heart rate, vagal tone, electroencephalograms, event-related potentials, magnetic resonance imaging, cortisol, and genetic studies. Let's examine some of these measures.

Looking behaviors/visual preference

Infants' looking behavior can be recorded reliably through peepholes or using infrared photography of corneal reflections. Looking, a measure of an infant's visual preference, varies with the nature of the stimulus provided. Differential looking (or a change in infants' visual preference) occurs depending on the novelty, complexity, and other qualities of the stimulus. Visual fixations are difficult to interpret because longer fixations can indicate a preference, but they can also be interpreted as slow learning or failure to learn. It is important to observe an infant's behavior when recording physiological measures such as heart rate, in order to know how the infant is reacting. In one heart rate study, for example, we were perplexed that no heart rate changes occurred. When we looked at the infants, we found that they were asleep. The dancing lights moving across a stage, which was the stimulus we had provided, were not interesting enough to keep them awake.

Facial expressions

Facial expressions are also used to measure infants' perception and discrimination of stimuli. Elaborate facial expression coding systems have been developed to identify different movements in infant faces. Typically the coding is done at slow-speed video playback. Although facial expressions would seem to be a particularly logical response for indicating perception and discrimination, and can now be accurately measured by muscle movements in the face, researchers are still debating whether facial expressions are as informative as other measures such as looking behavior.

Tracking/head turning

Getting infants to follow or track moving objects with their eyes is easy. But, as with head turning, it is necessary to position the newborn's head to the center before trying to get them to follow a moving object because as most newborns have a right head-turning reflex. Tracking can be readily seen in the first examination given in a newborn's life, the Brazelton Neonatal Behavioral Assessment Scale (Brazelton, 1973), in which the newborn is prompted to track an object and other stimuli – a red ball, a ringing bell, a human face and voice – by turning his head in their direction. These behaviors are signs of the newborn's being able to see and hear.

Nonnutritive sucking

Sucking starts in the womb and is, therefore, well developed by birth. The problem with sucking is that it seems to cease when something else attracts the infant's attention. This is called the Bronshtein Effect. It is difficult to elicit sucking in breastfed babies. Also, sucking may affect other measures being recorded. For example, it can confound the measurement of heart rate because heart rate invariably increases during sucking (Nelson et al., 1978). In addition, when infants are sucking, it is sometimes difficult to get them to pay attention to anything else.

Newborns can be easily trained to suck on a pacifier more or less rigorously in response to hearing or seeing something interesting such as the mother's voice. For example, the newborn's sucking behavior can be reinforced by the sound of his mother's voice, either when he sucks for longer periods, or when he pauses for longer periods, or when he sucks less or more intensely. This procedure was used to demonstrate that a newborn recognized his mother's voice from having heard her read Dr. Seuss stories to him during her pregnancy (De Casper & Fifer, 1980).

A variation on shortening or lengthening sucking in response to reinforcement is found with the two-stimuli operant discrimination learning procedure. In this procedure, two isolated stimuli are presented and the newborn is required to alter his nonnutritive sucking patterns to receive a reinforcer, such as his mother's voice reading a nursery rhyme. As the session proceeds, the newborn shows bursts of sucking in response to his mother's voice.

Habituation/dishabituation

Habituation is the most primitive form of learning. When an infant is repeatedly exposed to a meaningless stimulus, she gradually shows a reduced response to it as she learns that it does not signal anything. For example, a rattle is shaken, and a newborn startles. Then, after subsequent trials, she learns that nothing happens when the rattle is shaken, so she goes back to sleep. If a new sound is presented, however, such as a bell, then the newborn will show startles again. This is called dishabituation, or recovery of response.

Heart rate

Heart rate has been frequently recorded in infants since the classic experiment conducted by Graham and Clifton (1966) showing that heart rate slows down when an infant is attending to interesting stimuli, and speeds up in response to uninteresting or adverse stimuli. One of the reasons heart rate is the most frequently used physiological measure is that it can indicate what is being perceived and learned during sleep, an activity newborns engage in most of the time. (See figure 1.1.)

Unfortunately, an accurate measure of an infant's heart rate can be confounded by other behaviors, such as sucking, and certain kinds of movements, including fussing, crying, and gaze averting, which cause movement artifacts or heart rate increases (Nelson et al., 1978). Heart rate is also affected by changes in an infant's state, such that heart rate is higher during an active (versus quiet) alert state and during an active (versus quiet) sleep state.

Heart rate has also been an effective measure of individual differences among infants. For example, 4-month-old infants who fix their attention on something for short periods maintained higher heart rate variability than long-looking infants across an habituation session. Long-looking infants had greater heart rate acceleration in response to stimuli than short-looking infants (Maikranz et al., 2002).

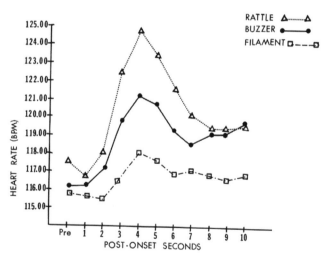

Figure 1.1 *Heart rate accelerations to different stimuli*

In another example from the same group of investigators at the University of Kansas, 4-month-old infants were exposed to sequences of light stimuli of 2 seconds' duration, alternated with a dark period 3 to 5 seconds long (Colombo & Richman, 2002). For eight trials, a predictable on/off pattern was used, but for the ninth trial, the light stimulus was omitted. On the ninth trial, the infants showed heart rate responses that were closely synchronized with the expected recurrence of the stimulus. These patterns were observed predominantly in infants who had previously shown sustained attention with visual stimuli.

Vagal tone

Vagal tone, a measure of heart rate variability (Porges, 1995), is controlled by the vagus nerve (one of the 12 cranial nerves) and is thought to indicate central nervous system functioning. The sinus arrhythmia component of heart rate (a component affected by respiration), vagal tone can be derived from heart rate recordings via a vagal tone monitor or with computer software developed for that purpose.

Vagal tone is considered a stable biological marker of an infant's ability to sustain attention (Richards & Cronise, 2000) and regulate emotion (Stifter & Fox, 1990). Typically, infants who show higher vagal tone show superior performance on cognitive tasks and developmental assessments. In one experiment, vagal tone was recorded in 6-month-old infants during mother–infant interactions (Porter, 2003). The videotaped interactions were then coded to demonstrate symmetrical behavior between the mothers and infants. The infants' vagal tone was correlated with symmetrical behavior.

In another example, infants' ability to recognize objects they have already seen, or recognition memory, was related to individual differences in looking duration and heart rate variability. In a recognition memory study on 5- and 6-month-old infants (Frick et al., 2001), those with high levels of heart rate variability showed greater ability to recognize or remember visual stimuli that had been briefly presented to them.

Neonatal heart rate and the heart rate associated with respiration (vagal tone) have been found to be better predictors of 3-year outcomes than birth weight or medical risk factors. Higher heart rate variability was associated with better social skills, mental processing, and gross motor skills (Doussard-Roosevelt et al., 1997). Lower heart rate (which usually is correlated with or related to higher heart rate variability) was associated with better behavior regulation and social skills.

Decreased vagal tone (also called vagal withdrawal), on the other hand, may indicate an infant's ability to control his behavior during stress. For example, in a study in which mothers were asked to show a still-face (no movement) to their 3-month-old infants (Moore et al., 2004), the infants demonstrated increased negative affect and higher heart rate, and decreased vagal tone, indicating physiological self-regulation of distress. Infants who did not show decreased vagal tone during the mother's still-face (called nonsuppressors) demonstrated less positive affect and higher reactivity during normal play with their mothers. And, in another study on 6-month-olds (Porter et al., 2003), marital conflict in an infant's household was associated with lower vagal tone in the infant. Porges (1995) described a "vagal brake," which slows down the heart (i.e., increases vagal tone) during situations that are not stressful. During stress, however, the vagal brake is turned off, and heart rate increases. Thus, the vagal brake allows infants to self-regulate.

Electroencephalogram or EEG Recordings

An electroencephalogram, or EEG, measures brain wave activity as it is transmitted through electrodes that are taped directly to the infant's scalp, or imbedded in an electrode cap placed on the infant's head or in a net of electrodes surrounding the head. (See figure 1.2.) In the infancy literature, EEG is often measured in the frontal region. Greater relative right-frontal EEG activation is typically associated with emotions such as sadness (called "withdrawal emotions" in infancy research). Greater relative left-frontal EEG activation often accompanies emotions such as happiness (known as "approach emotions"). Low-frequency EEG wave-forms are associated with relaxation and sleep, and high-frequency EEG waveforms are associated with alertness.

In a study by our group (Field et al., 2004), the frontal asymmetry of the newborn was positively correlated with the mother's frontal asymmetry and negatively correlated with the mother's prenatal depression and anxiety scores (left frontal is positive and right frontal is negative). That is, neonates of high depression/high anxiety mothers had greater right-frontal EEG activation. In another sample (Field et al., 2005), EEG was monitored in pregnant women, who were then divided into two groups: greater relative right- and left-frontal EEG activation. The newborns of the right-frontal EEG mothers (e.g. depressed/anxious mothers) showed greater relative right-frontal EEG, had lower levels of dopamine and serotonin (neurotransmitters that play a role in regulat-

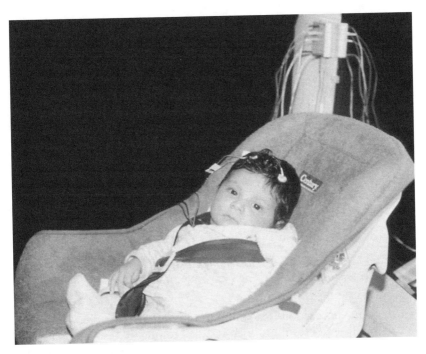

Figure 1.2 *Newborn with EEG electrodes*

ing mood), spent more time in indeterminate (disorganized difficult-to-code) sleep, and had inferior Brazelton scores (Brazelton, 1973).

In a sample of newborns (Field et al., 2002), those with greater relative right-frontal EEGs were found to have mothers with lower prenatal and postnatal serotonin and higher postnatal cortisol (stress hormone) levels, greater relative right-frontal EEG activation, and lower vagal tone. These newborns had elevated cortisol levels, showed a greater number of changes in their alertness and drowsiness during behavior observations, and performed less optimally on the Brazelton Neonatal Behavior Assessment Scale, including on the habituation, motor, range of state, excitability, and depressive symptoms scales. These data suggest that newborns with greater relative right-frontal EEGs may be at a greater risk for developmental problems than newborns with greater relative left-frontal EEG activation.

In a study on the relation between frontal EEG asymmetry and cortisol and withdrawal-related behaviors (fear and sadness) in 6-month-old infants, higher cortisol levels were associated with extreme

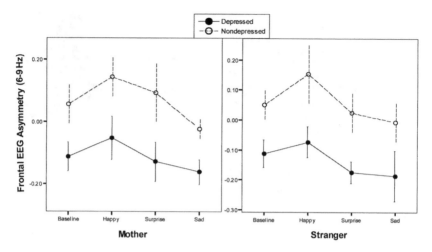

Figure 1.3 *EEG responses to mother and stranger faces by infants of depressed and nondepressed mothers*

right-frontal EEG asymmetry (Buss et al., 2003). Reactive cortisol is that which occurs in reaction to a stimulus, rather than the cortisol level that occurs when one is resting, which is called resting or baseline cortisol. A withdrawal negative-affect task (designed to elicit withdrawal away from a task and elicit negative emotion) was also associated with extreme right-frontal EEG asymmetry. EEG during the withdrawal negative-affect task was associated with fear and sadness. Similarly, 4-month-old infants of depressed and non-depressed mothers showed right-frontal EEG during the surprise and sad expressions of their mothers and a stranger (Diego et al., 2002). (See figure 1.3.)

In research on the development of brain waves from 5 months to 4 years of age (Marshall et al., 2002), a peak emerged in the 6–9 Hz range (i.e., the power of the brain wave). Coding of peaks in the power spectra of individual infants showed a clear developmental increase in the frequency of this peak. The relative amplitude of this central rhythm peaked in the second year of life, when major changes are occurring in locomotor behavior, particularly the development of walking.

In a twin study on the heritability and "environmentability" of EEG in infants (Orekhova et al., 2003), EEG was recorded in pairs of monozygotic (identical) and dizygotic (fraternal) twins aged 7 to 12 months during (1) visual attention and (2) darkness. The influence of shared environment was shown to be greatest for the amplitude of the theta waves (the relaxation waves). For many of the EEG parameters, heritability increased during the second half of the first year of life, thus supporting the hypothesis about an increasing influence of genetic effects and a decreasing influence of common environmental effects across early development.

The environment can still have powerful effects. The negative effects of environment on EEG were recently reported in a sample of institutionalized infants in Bucharest, Romania. When compared with children of the same age who were living with their families (Marshall et al., 2004), the institutionalized group showed a pattern of increased low-frequency waves (theta) and decreased high-frequency waves (alpha and beta, the waves associated with attentiveness) in the frontal region. Cognitive development was adversely affected in these children as late as 11 years of age (Beckett et al., 2006). This finding is consistent with EEG studies on children facing environmental adversity and children with learning disorders. The institutionalized group also showed less marked hemispheric EEG asymmetries than the at-home group. According to the authors of the study, the pattern of EEGs in the institutionalized children reflected a lag in nervous system development.

Event-related potentials

Event-related potentials, or ERPs, are the positive and negative peaks in brain waves seen in response to stimulation. As with EEGs, they are recorded with the use of electrodes placed at different sites on an infant's scalp. A group in Finland examined the maturation of auditory event-related potentials from birth until 12 months of age (Kushnerenko et al., 2002). All the ERP peaks observed at 12 months had already been identified at birth. As in previous studies, ERP peaks increased and the latencies shortened with increasing age. In addition, the time courses were different for the amplitude growth of each of the peaks.

In a study on face perception in 4-month-olds, the different faces could only be perceived when the faces were presented in an upright position. (Farroni et al., 2004). In a study on ERPs in response to words (Thierry et al., 2003), 11-month-old infants shifted their attention automatically to familiar words within 250 milliseconds of those words' being presented to them. The first negative peak, which indicates change detection in adults, occurred when familiar words were presented.

Mismatch negativity (MMN), a form of ERP, is thought to represent a neurophysiological index of auditory information processing that is independent of attention. Because this measure does not require an overt behavioral response, MMN has the potential to evaluate higher-order perceptual abilities in infants, young children, and difficult-to-test populations. Mismatch negativity is a negative component of the auditory ERP, reflecting the brain's automatic change-detection process (Kushnerenko et al., 2002). A Finnish group investigated the development of pitch change detection, as indexed by the MMN, in the same infants from birth until 12 months of age. The MMN was identified in approximately 75% of infants at each age, and it was relatively stable in latency and amplitude at the group level across the ages studied. However, within the same subjects, the MMN substantially varied from age to age.

Sound perception can be studied in sleeping neonates using the MMN component of auditory ERPs because it is not contingent on conscious perception or response. Again, a group from Finland (Ceponiene et al., 2002) presented harmonic tones of different duration and frequency. MMN was elicited in 81% of the newborns exposed to sounds of varying frequencies and in 78% of the newborns exposed to sounds of varying duration. The majority of neonates demonstrated an ability to discriminate between various sound frequencies and between sounds of various duration.

Magnetic-resonance imaging

Magnetic resonance imaging (MRI) and functional magnetic resonance imagining (fMRI) can localize and convey an image of activity in specific areas of the brain by tracking the flow of blood and oxygen. Although MRIs are rarely used with infants, because infants are rarely inactive, studies on brain development have used MRI and fMRI equipment designed for infants. (See figure 1.4.) For example, an evaluation of normal brain development looked at the relationship between cerebral cortical function and white matter myelination (insulation of the nerves) in the visual pathway. MRI and fMRI were used in neurologically normal infants (aged 0 to 5 months) (Yamada et al., 2000). A gradual increase in signal intensity was observed in optic radiation as the infants got older, indicating progression of white matter myelination or healthy brain development.

In a study on reward development, MRIs were performed on infants with different physiological development rates at 6 weeks of age (Morgan et al., 2002). Postnatal physiological development was assessed by measuring age-related deep body temperature patterns during sleep. Neuronal development was assessed by analyzing the MRI images. The normal group acquired the adult temperature pattern, and the normal group had a significantly higher myelination score.

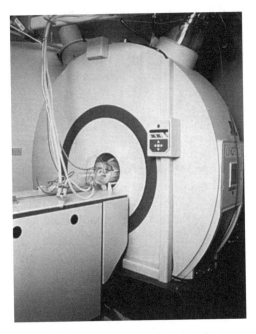

Figure 1.4 *MRI equipment adapted for preterm newborns*

Cortisol

Cortisol is a stress hormone that can be found in blood, urine, and saliva. With infants, it is typically measured in saliva, as this is a noninvasive, easy way to collect it, particularly now, with the development of the litmus-paper-like test (Laudenslager, 2005). Salivary cortisol is correlated with plasma cortisol, making it a relatively reliable measure. Elevated cortisol is typically interpreted as a stress response. The saliva is usually collected before the stress-inducing event (stressor) and then again 20 minutes after the event ends, since cortisol levels reflect what was happening 20 minutes earlier. Some investigators have suggested that due to variations in cortisol stress response time across stressors, cortisol should be sampled beyond 30 minutes (Goldberg et al., 2003), but 20 minutes is usually the "gold standard." In another methodological study on the timing of the cortisol response, considerable variation in the timing of the peak cortisol response suggested that obtaining only a single poststressor cortisol sample does not provide a sensitive enough measure of cortisol reactivity.

Between 5 and 8 months of age, infants' cortisol levels decreased with age. The levels were also negatively related to sleep, and did not show adult-like circadian (daily) rhythm decreases from early morning to mid-afternoon (de Weerth & Geert, 2003). Finally, the individual infants' cortisol levels changed across assessments, suggesting variability within an individual's cortisol level.

Developmental decreases in cortisol have also been noted across infancy, with levels being higher among 12-, 18-, and 24-month-old infants than among 30- to 36-month-old children (Watamura, 2004). For all five age groups, cortisol levels were highest upon waking up in the morning and lowest upon going to bed in the evening. Unlike with adults, the infants' levels did not decrease from early morning to mid afternoon. In another study, a correlation was noted between the appearance of the sleep–wake circadian rhythm and the cortisol circadian rhythm in infants 2 to 5 months old (de Weerth et al., 2003).

Most of the infant cortisol studies have focused on cortisol responses to stressors. In one study on the association between cortisol and behavioral reactivity, infants were pricked in the heel and given a neuro-behavioral exam. Both behavioral distress and cortisol reactivity occurred in response to both stressors (Keenan, 2003). In another example, 2-month-old infants with higher cortisol levels required more time to calm down after their immunizations (Wilson, 2003).

In a frustration study (Lewis & Ramsay, 2005), 4-month-old infants were involved in a contingency learning procedure in which their learned responses could no longer reinstate an event. And 6-month-old infants were presented with a still-face mother, and the infants' negative reactions to their mothers' still-face could not reestablish a normal interaction. In both frustration situations, sadness was related to the cortisol response, although anger was not. The greater the sadness, the higher the cortisol response.

Genetic studies

Genetic studies are conducted mostly on infant temperament. Temperament has been noted to vary as a function of genotype (genetic makeup). A longitudinal study, for example, investigated the relationships between genotype and temperament at 2 weeks of age, 2 months of age, and 12 months of age (Auerbach et al., 1999; Ebstein et al., 1998). At 2 weeks, infants carrying a long form of the dopamine-activating gene had higher Brazelton orientation, motor organization, range of state, and state-regulation scores than infants with the short form of that gene (Ebstein et al., 1998). Those infants having the short form of the dopamine gene scored significantly lower on the orientation scale if they also possessed the serotonin-inhibiting gene. Infants of this group also displayed more negative emotionality, suggesting an interaction between the dopamine-activating and the serotonin-inhibiting genes.

At 2 months of age, the same genotypes were investigated in relation to infants' temperament measures (Auerbach et al., 1999). Consistent with the results at 2 weeks of age, a significant interaction was found between the dopamine-activating and the serotonin-inhibiting genes. Those infants possessing the genotype had more negative emotions and distress as a result of experiencing limitations, but only in the absence of the long form of the dopamine-activating gene. This suggests that the infants were inclined to explore their environment, but the inhibitory effects of the serotonin-inhibiting gene stopped them.

Similar results were noted again at 12 months (Auerbach et al., 2001). Temperament was assessed using observational methods exploring interest, fear, pleasure, anger, and activity level. Infants with the dopamine-activating gene showed less anger-related negative emotionality than the infants with the serotonin-inhibiting gene. These results indicate that the serotonin-inhibiting gene is related to fear and pleasure, while the dopamine-activating gene is related to interest and activity.

In another study by a different research group, 1-month-old infants with the dopamine-activating genotype exhibited significantly less difficulty in modifying their reactions to a change in stimuli such as objects, food, or clothes than those with the serotonin-inhibiting gene (DeLuca et al., 2001). Infants carrying the long allele of the dopamine-activating gene also displayed shorter attention spans than those with the short allele form of the dopamine-activating gene at 1 year of age (Auerbach et al., 2001). There, too, an interaction occurred between the genotypes of dopamine and serotonin. Those infants with both the long allele of dopamine (activating) and the short allele of serotonin (inhibiting) had the shortest looking times or attention span, suggesting that the long allele of dopamine may be exacerbated by the short allele of serotonin. These results highlight the importance of looking at multiple genes. (See figures 1.5a, 1.5b, 1.5c.)

Arousal Effects on Infant Studies

The big problem of finding infants in the right state to be studied has been called the "culprit variable" or "disrupting variable." For example, an infant may fall asleep or go into a crying jag right in the middle of a study. Before concluding this chapter, it is important to highlight those

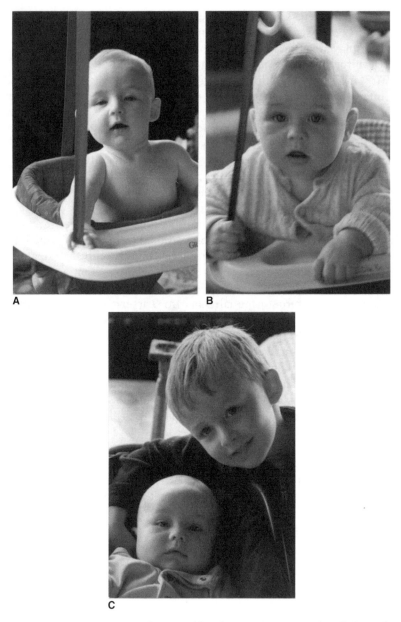

Figures 1.5a–c *Genetic similarities of brothers Garrett (a) and Will (b) in their jolly jumpers at 5 months and when Garrett is the big brother (c)*

culprit variables that make infant research so challenging. Examples are irregular sleep cycles, feeding cycles, fussiness, and drowsiness.

Sleep cycles

An infant's state of arousal, or where he is on his feeding and sleep–wake cycle, affects his perceptions. Many studies are conducted during sleep because infants spend a lot of time in sleep. In a study using EEG and behavioral responsiveness to auditory stimulation, infants were found to be more responsive during active sleep than during deep sleep, and they gave more behavioral responses to stimuli of lower intensity than they did EEG responses (Trinder et al., 1990).

In a similar observation study on sleep, behavior observations and activity monitoring found that newborns spend more time in quiet (or deep) sleep on the day of birth than 24 hours later. The author suggested that this was a "temporary adaptive response to the stress of the birth process." This finding challenges the more frequently reported observation that newborns are most awake during their first day of life, and that the first day is the most optimal time for testing them. In today's nurseries, with 24-hour hospitalizations (called "drive-in deliveries"), much of the testing would need to occur on the first day. However, the above data suggest that on this day, the thresholds would be higher because the newborns were spending more time in quiet sleep.

Sleep observations are a very important area of newborn research in their own right. Sleep patterns during the newborn period have been noted to predict temperament as late as 8 months of age based on activity monitoring (Novosad et al., 1999). In a similar study, several sleep variables on day 1 and day 2 were significantly related to mental and motor scores at 6 months of age (Freudigman, 1996).

Feeding cycles

In a visual recognition memory study (Geva et al., 1999), newborns tested before and after a feeding shifted from preferring familiar objects before feeding to preferring novel objects after feeding. Thus, state of arousal significantly affects visual attention, and is certainly one of the important considerations when conducting newborn research.

Over the years, infancy researchers have moved from studying infants with the use of one-dimensional stimuli (e.g., tones and checkerboards) to studying infants' perceptions of voices and faces, perhaps because the latter are more real-world stimuli and because they are more interesting and more likely to get the infants through the experiment. Some researchers have claimed that in between feedings is an optimal time to study infants because it is at that time that they are most alert. Others, as just noted, have reported that the period following feedings is optimal for the infants' state of arousal. Thus, before feeding, infants may be more alert, but are often fussier because they are hungry. Immediately after feeding they may be less fussy, but they may also be sleepier because they have just been fed. However, as has been pointed out, infants learn in their sleep, so a sleepy state might be preferable to a fussy state.

Fussiness and drowsiness

Despite all our efforts to find optimal states for infant study, the dropout rate in infancy research approximates 80%, probably biasing the results of studies, since the infants who remain in the studies tend to be more alert and less fussy than those who drop out. The problem with fussiness is that while you can give an infant a pacifier, sucking affects many measures, including heart rate. Also, as has been noted, sucking may reduce the infant's interest in other stimulation, given that sucking is one of the more interesting forms of stimulation for an infant.

One effective method for reducing infant fussiness and drowsiness is the doll's-eye reflex. The infant is positioned facing the experimenter. The experimenter does a few deep knee bends and makes some tongue-clicking sounds. The combination of moving and auditory stimulation can help the infant reach an alert state. Infants are also more alert when they are held upright on an adult's shoulder or in a face-to-face position.

Summary

These, then, are brief descriptions of the most popularly used methods/measures in infant research. With new technology, the methods are becoming more sophisticated and are increasingly showing us the impressive skills of the amazing infant. If we could only read their minds, we could know how truly amazing they are.

2

Being a Fetus (Prenatal Growth and Development)

This chapter will give you an overview of key factors that influence prenatal growth and development. We know that early fetal development plays an important role in the long-term growth of a child. From early on, we see how an infant learns and how the environment can play a critical role in development. Mothers and fathers influence an infant's cognitive and emotional development in many ways. From their own emotional states to their socioeconomic status, parents can unknowingly create stress on the fetus. Further, when parents engage in more risky behaviors such as drug abuse, smoking, and drinking, we observe even greater negative effects on the physical, emotional, and cognitive development of the infant. This chapter reviews research on prenatal influences on the infant, and what factors may play a role in creating developmental problems.

Fetal Learning

The newborn can discriminate her mother's voice from that of a stranger (DeCasper & Fifer, 1980). This finding led several researchers to the conclusion that learning occurs prenatally. A series of studies then presented various kinds of stimulation to the fetus, including vibratory, auditory, and vibroacoustic stimulation. Typically, these forms of stimulation were presented in an habituation paradigm, and fetal heart rate and movement were used as response measures. The studies of DeCasper and his colleagues in the United States, Lecanuet and his research team in France, and Kisilevsky and her group in Canada provided models for this research.

The mother's voice

In a program of several studies, DeCasper and his colleagues documented discrimination of the mother's voice by neonates and fetuses. In the first study, they showed that newborn infants sucked on a nonnutritive nipple more often to produce their mother's voice than the voice of another female (DeCasper & Fifer, 1980). Shortly after delivery, neonates reportedly discriminated their mothers' voices reading Dr. Seuss's *And to Think That I Saw It on Mulberry Street*. Following a period of baseline sucking (5 minutes of sucking observed prior to testing), the neonates were required to either suck longer or shorter than their baseline sucking period to produce their mother's prerecorded voice. A preference for their mother's voice indicated that the neonates met that requirement. During the first third of the testing session, the neonates did not show a preference for their mother's voice. However, by the last third of the session, they sucked during stimulus periods associated with their mother's voice 24% more often than those periods associated with a stranger's voice. The authors concluded that the perceptual preferences shown in this study might have derived from prenatal experience.

DeCasper and his colleagues suggested that because the maternal voice is audible in utero, and because third-trimester fetuses can hear, perhaps the neonatal preference for the mother's voice results from this exposure. They also presented data from another study to bolster their argument, which was that neonates do not show a preference for their father's voice (DeCasper & Prescott, 1984). Male voices are not very audible in utero, and thus the lack of preference for the father's voice may derive from this lack of prenatal experience. This led the DeCasper group to study the neonatal discrimination of passages of speech that had been recited during the last trimester of pregnancy.

Newborn discrimination of stories heard in utero

In the pregnancy study, pregnant women tape-recorded their voices reading passages, again from Dr. Seuss (this time, *The Cat in the Hat*) and from the author's variation on that story, called "The Dog in the Fog" (DeCasper & Fifer, 1980). The mothers recited those passages aloud each day during the last 6 weeks of pregnancy. The passage that had been read to the fetus and a new passage were recorded, and those passages served as the reinforcers. For some infants, sucking bursts that were equal to or greater than the infant's baseline sucking bursts produced the mother's voice reading the familiar passage. The second group was reinforced for shorter bursts. Infants sucked more or less to hear their mother's voice (depending on their assigned condition). Thus, the sounds of the passage that had been recited to the fetuses (familiar passage) were compared with the sounds of the new passage. The newborns discriminated the new from the familiar passages. DeCasper and his colleagues concluded that the third-trimester fetuses' experience with their mothers' speech sounds had influenced their preferences at the neonatal stage.

Fetal discrimination of maternal speech

To then determine the fetal response to maternal speech, DeCasper collaborated with the Lecanuet fetal research group in Paris (DeCasper, Lecanuet, Busnel, & Maugeais, 1994). In this study, pregnant women recited one of the passages to the fetus during the last trimester. The fetuses were then presented with tape recordings of the familiar passage and a new passage, and their heart rates were recorded. Heart rate decelerations showed that the fetuses had become familiar with the passages that had been read to them.

Lecanuet and his colleagues had shown that when fetuses were presented repeatedly with the syllables bi and ba, and then ba and bi, at 95 decibels in utero, heart rate decelerations occurred to the initial stimulation, and then again as the stimulus was changed (Lecanuet, Grainier-Deferre, & Busnel, 1989). The researchers also showed that the onset of these syllables would elicit cardiac decelerations (Lecanuet, Grainier-Deferre, & Busnel, 1992). These data, combined with the data presented by DeCasper and his group suggest that the fetuses are attending to and discriminating their mother's voice. (See figure 2.1.)

Prenatal learning of the mother's voice might enable the infant to locate the source of his mother's voice after birth. Orienting to the mother's voice might also facilitate the infant's learning his mother's face, since the source of the voice is the mother's moving lips. In turn, focusing on the mother's face might reinforce the mother's desire to engage her infant in interaction, thus potentially strengthening the mother–infant bond, or perhaps increasing the mother's physical attention or closeness to her infant. In contrast, an infant who does not discriminate his mother's voice from other objects in the environment would not be expected to look for the source of her voice.

Research by our group suggests that the fetuses and newborns of depressed mothers may show inferior performance in the maternal speech discrimination studies performed by DeCasper et al. because of their elevated activity in utero (excessively active fetuses are less attentive) (Dieter et al., 2001). Data showing that newborns of depressed

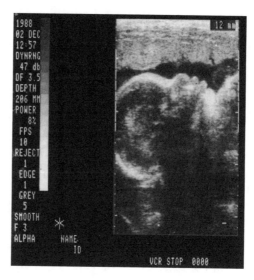

Figure 2.1 *Profile face of a fetus from ultrasound*

mothers fail to show a preference for their mother's face and voice (Hernandez-Reif et al., 2004) suggest that these newborns would also show less optimal performance on the DeCasper paradigms.

Fetal Habituation

Several studies provide examples of fetal habituation (i.e., the rate at which a fetus becomes accustomed to, and doesn't respond to, stimuli) to various forms of stimulation. Fetal habituation to vibroacoustic stimulation, for example, was studied in relation to fetal states and fetal heart rate (Van Egeren et al., 2001). According to these authors, the reduced response by the fetus to repeated stimulation can be used to assess the fetal condition and the function of the fetal central nervous system. However, the effect of fetal activity on habituation remains to be clarified. The authors studied habituation and the effects of fetal sleep states and fetal heart rate on habituation in healthy term fetuses. Vibroacoustic stimuli were applied to the maternal abdomen above the fetal legs for a period of 1 second every 30 seconds. Fetal trunk movement within 1 second after stimulation was defined as a positive response. The habituation rate was defined as the number of stimuli applied until four consecutive stimuli failed to elicit a response. Fetal heart rate was recorded for a 10-minute period before and after the test. Fetal sleep states were also recorded. Of the 32 fetuses that responded normally during the first test, 26 habituated (that is, became accustomed to the stimuli and stopped reacting to them) and six had persistent responses (that is, they continued reacting to the stimuli).

Fetal Responses to Music

Fetuses also discriminate low-pitched musical notes (Lecanuet et al., 2000). Heart rate responses of 36- to 39-week-old fetuses suggested that fetuses could discriminate two low-pitched piano notes. Seventy percent of the fetuses in the study reacted to the onset of the first note with the expected heart rate decrease. After their heart rates had returned to their baseline level, the other note was played. Ninety percent of the fetuses who reacted to the note change did so with another cardiac deceleration. Control fetuses, for whom the note did not change, displayed fewer cardiac decelerations. Thus, fetuses detected and responded to the note and its subsequent change regardless of which note was presented first. Because the loudness of the notes was controlled, it seems that the differences in frequency were responsible for the fetuses' detecting the change. Fetal discrimination of piano notes that lie within the narrow range of voice tones may play an important role in the early stages of speech perception.

In a slightly different approach to acoustic stimuli, temporal pattern and spectral complexity were explored as stimulus parameters for eliciting a heart rate orienting response or a heart rate deceleration in fetuses (Groome et al., 2000). Term fetuses were exposed to four sounds formed from four different combinations of temporal (e.g., pulsed, continuous) and spectral complexity. The pulsed sounds elicited a significantly greater heart rate deceleration than continuous sounds. However, the heart rate response was relatively unaffected by spectral complexity. The results indicate that temporal characteristics were more effective at eliciting attention in human fetuses than spectral complexity.

To examine whether prenatal exposure to a musical stimulus alters fetal behavior (within 3 days prior to delivery), and whether this continues into the newborn period, music was played to fetuses via a headphone placed on the maternal abdomen. A control group also had headphones but without sound (James et al., 2002). Subsequently, the test subjects were exposed as newborns to the same music on days 3 to

5. Fetal heart rate and activity were recorded, and neonatal behavior states were coded. Fetuses had a higher mean heart rate (FHR) and spent more time exhibiting high FHR variation during the first hour of the study. By the fourth hour, the fetuses not only showed a higher mean heart rate, but also had more state changes and higher FHR variation. These effects were carried over into the neonatal period, with newborns exposed to music prenatally showing more state changes and spending more time in awake states. Newborns, then, have music preferences, for example preferring vocal versus instrumental music, although this discrimination was not shown by newborns of depressed mothers in a recent study by our group (Hernandez-Reif et al., 2006). The infants' responsiveness to music has, in turn, been related to developmental age in a Japanese study (Matsuyama, 2005).

Fetal brain activity in response to an acoustic stimulus has been recorded using magnetic encephalography (magnetic fields) (Holst et al., 2005) and by functional magnetic resonance imaging (Moore et al., 2001). In the Moore et al. study, pregnant women were scanned at between 37 and 41 weeks' gestation. Twelve had an auditory stimulus applied to their abdomens (study group) and four had an auditory stimulus applied to their ears (control group). Two of the 12 study-group patients experienced back pain, so the experiment was abandoned. Four fetuses showed significant activation in one or both of the temporal lobes (which is the sound-processing lobe).

Fetal Activity

Fetal activity is typically measured during ultrasound examinations. In ultrasounds, high-frequency sound waves are bounced off the fetus to form an image called a sonogram. Fortunately, in a longitudinal follow-up at 8 years of age, no deleterious effects were noted for multiple ultrasounds given at any age (Newnham et al., 2004). Fetal activity can simply be observed or stimulated by a vibroacoustic stimulus (after about 28 weeks' gestation) or by massaging the mothers feet (but not her hands) as early as 20 weeks (Diego et al., 2005).

Using fetal movement as a variable in these studies is complicated by the fact that movement decreases across gestation, and gender differences are also apparent, with males showing greater movement. In a recent study, for example, leg movements were recorded prenatally (ultrasonography at 30, 34, and 37 weeks' gestational age) and postnatally (at birth and 6 weeks of age). The fetuses and neonates displayed decreasing numbers of leg movements per minute during prenatal development

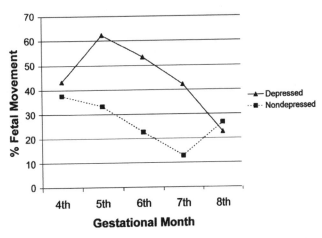

Figure 2.2 *Activity of fetuses of depressed and nondepressed mothers*

(30 to 37 weeks), followed by increasing numbers of leg movements per minute during postnatal development (birth to 6 weeks of age). Males displayed more leg movements per minute than females during both the prenatal and postnatal period. Fetal-to-neonatal continuity was found for leg movements between 37 weeks' gestation and the neonatal period. Females displayed a stronger movement continuity pattern than males. In a study by our group, fetal activity was significantly greater in fetuses of depressed mothers from 4 to 7 months' gestation (Dieter et al., 2001). (See figure 2.2.)

Patterns of fetal activity and habituation are predictors of obstetric complications, anthropometric measures, and neurobehavioral outcome, according to a longitudinal study on fetal activity and habituation (Israelian, 2000). In the study, fetal movement in response to a repeatedly presented vibroacoustic stimulus were studied in fetuses between 34 and 38 weeks' gestational age. Fetuses were classified as "habituators" or "nonhabituators." Habituation was defined as five consecutive trials in which the fetus did not respond to the vibroacoustic stimulus. The fetal movement response to the repeated stimulus was found to be sensitive to pre- and perinatal risk factors and predictive of obstetric complications. The ability of the fetus to exhibit habituation of the movement response was associated with more optimal maternal health, greater birth weight, and fewer obstetric complications. Levels of motor activity were predictive of obstetric complications and

Apgar scores at birth. Although fetal movement and habituation were not predictive of scores on the Brazelton Neonatal Behavioral Assessment Scale, there was a positive correlation between the number of trials to habituation and the number of abnormal reflexes on the Brazelton Scale.

Fetal activity is also predictive of motor activity and temperament in neonates, infants, and toddlers (DiPietro et al., 2002). Three measures of fetal activity (activity level, amplitude, and number of movements) were collected at 24, 30, and 36 weeks' gestation in healthy fetuses. Individual stability was noted in fetal activity. Fetal activity at 36 weeks and neonatal irritability and motor activity were correlated with each other. Fetal activity level at 36 weeks was also associated with maternal reports of infants' activity level at 2 years. Fetal activity was correlated with distress at 1 year and behavioral inhibition at 2 years.

Prenatal Predictors

Fetal activity and fetal heart rate are increasingly used as prenatal indicators of nonoptimal outcomes. In a study on the antecedents of infant temperament, more active fetuses became more difficult, unpredictable, unadaptable, and active infants (DiPietro et al., 1996). Higher fetal heart rate was associated with lower emotional tone, activity level, and predictability. These data were based on fetal heart rate and movement recordings of fetuses at six gestational ages, beginning at 20 weeks. Maternally reported temperament data were later collected at 3 and 6 months. By 36 weeks' gestation, fetal behavior accounted for between 22% and 60% of the variance in temperament scores, suggesting that infant activity and heart rate can be used to predict infant temperament.

Sleep and circadian rhythms are developed during the prenatal period. Both quiet and active sleep are distinguishable during the last 10 weeks' gestation (Mirmiran et al., 2003). The circadian rhythm of fetal heart rate is synchronous with maternal rest–activity, heart rate, cortisol, melatonin, and body temperature rhythms during the last 10 weeks of gestation. The prenatal circadian rhythm (24-hour cycle) becomes ultradian (less than 24-hour cycle) at birth. In research on developmental changes in information processing during quiet sleep during the perinatal period, infants were tested as fetuses at 36 to 40 weeks and again as neonates at 2 weeks (Groome et al., 2001). Quiet sleep was defined in the same way for fetuses and neonates, and the same sound was used for fetal and neonatal testing. Stimulation elicited sustained heart rate deceleration in the majority of fetuses. However, the response was more heterogeneous when these infants were tested after birth, with approximately half the 2-week-old infants exhibiting prolonged heart rate deceleration and half exhibiting heart rate acceleration.

Stress Effects on the Fetus

Prenatal stress comes in many forms, including the daily hassles, depression, anxiety, anger, panic disorder, posttraumatic stress disorder, and even optimism/pessimism experienced by the pregnant woman. These emotional states seem to stimulate stress hormones and excessive activity in the fetus and, in turn, contribute to fetal growth delays, obstetric complications, and undesirable neonatal outcomes, including prematurity, low birth weight, and less optimal motor and mental development – both short-term and long-term effects. Maternal stress has been increasingly associated with fetal stress.

In one study, stress during laboratory tests and word tasks led to significant increases in maternal systolic blood pressure and respiratory rate and to significant heart rate increases in the fetus (Monk et al., 2000). To assess the placental transfer of maternal antibodies following prenatal stress, squirrel monkeys were exposed to different pregnancy conditions (Coe & Crispen, 2000). A condition of chronic disturbance significantly lowered the antibody levels in the mothers and the fetus. Gender differences were found, with males being born with lower antibody levels than females.

Long-term effects of prenatal distress have been noted. For example, in one study (Martin et al., 1999) maternal distress during the first trimester was associated with ratings of negative emotionality at age 5, with a stronger correlation for males.

Anxiety and depression

Other types of stress have been assessed, including prepartum anxiety in mothers. In one study, high-anxiety mothers manifested more psychological and social pathology than moderate- and low-anxiety mothers, and their children showed signs of poorer adaptation (Barnett et al., 1991). Depressed adults have been noted to have histories of being reared by prenatally depressed mothers and having experienced short gestation and low birth weight outcomes (Preti et al., 2000).

These prenatal stress data are disconcerting inasmuch as large numbers of women experience prenatal depression, and many of these have elevated levels of cortisol (Field et al., 2004). In a recent sample of African American and Hispanic women, more than half showed elevated depressive symptoms and had less social support and more negative life events than found in previous studies (Zayas et al., 2002). African Americans had more practical social support and more people in their support networks than did Hispanics. Over a third of the sample had lost an important person in the past year, and depressed women reported more negative events than nondepressed women.

In a Swedish sample of depressed/anxious women (Anderson et al., 2004), significant associations were found between depression and/or anxiety and increased nausea and vomiting, prolonged sick leave during pregnancy, and increased number of visits to the obstetrician, specifically visits related to early contractions and fear of childbirth. Planned cesarean delivery and the use of epidural analgesia during labor were also significantly more common in women with prenatal depression and/or anxiety. Increased risk of epidural analgesia use, operative deliveries (cesarean sections and vaginal deliveries using instruments such as forceps), and admission to the neonatal intensive care unit have been more frequent in samples of depressed pregnant women, likely because of the increased incidence of premature births among that group (Chung-Tony et al., 2001).

Pregnancy-specific anxiety has been associated with attention and behavior problems in the infant at 3 months and 8 months (Huisink et al., 2002). It has also been associated with maternal reports of "difficult" temperament in the infant at 4 to 6 months (Austin et al., 2005). These effects appear to persist inasmuch as greater levels of prenatal stress have been associated with difficult temperament and behavior problems at the toddler stage (Gutteling et al., 2005), and at 6 years, when there is a significant correlation between prenatal stress, the child's temperament, and his school grades (Niederhofer et al., 2004). Anxiety in mid-pregnancy has also predicted lower mental and motor development scores at 8 months. In that study, early morning cortisol levels during late pregnancy were negatively related to both mental and motor development at 3 months and motor development at 8 months (Buitelaar et al., 2003).

In another study (Gutteling et al., 2005) done in the Netherlands, pregnancy stress was a predictor of restless/disruptive temperament, behavioral problems, and especially externalizing behavioral problems in the child at 2 years of age. High maternal anxiety levels during late pregnancy have also been associated with lower mental development scores in the child at 2 years (Brouwers et al., 2001).

Anger

Anger also affects the fetus. For example, in one of our studies (Field et al., 2002), fetuses of high-anger women were noted to be more active and to experience growth delays. The high-anger mothers' high prenatal cortisol and low dopamine and serotonin levels were mimicked by their neonates' high cortisol and low dopamine levels. The high-anger mothers and infants were also similar in measures of their greater relative right-frontal EEG activation and their lower vagal tone. Finally, the newborns of high-anger mothers had disorganized sleep patterns (greater indeterminate sleep and more state changes) and less optimal performance on the Brazelton Neonatal Behavioral Assessment Scale.

Optimism/pessimism

Optimism is another emotional state found to affect fetuses (Lobel et al., 2000). In one sample, women who were the least optimistic delivered infants who weighed significantly less (controlling for gestational age). Optimists were more likely to exercise, and exercise was associated with lower risk for preterm delivery. The combination of prenatal optimism and pessimism also seems to be a prenatal stressor (Devicent, 2002). In this large sample study, women high in both optimism and pessimism were more likely to deliver preterm infants than women who were high in optimism but low in pessimism.

Type-A behavior

Another characteristic that appears to influence infants is type-A behavior in pregnant women. Women who were classified as more type A for "job involvement" on the Jenkins Activity Survey, rated their infants as more intense and less predictable (Parker & Barret, 1992). The women were also more likely to be breastfeeding their infants at 3 months. Type-A behaviors during pregnancy were measured in a self-selected group of healthy, middle-class women carrying their first child. Their newborns were assessed at 48 hours of age, and the women completed an infant temperament questionnaire when their babies were 3 months old. Women classified as type A on the "job involvement" scale had infants who cried more during a standardized neurobehavioral assessment as compared with infants of women who were type B on the same scale.

Confounding Variables

The combination of different prenatal moods or emotional states have been noted to differentially affect fetal and infant development including different types of depression, called "withdrawn" versus "intrusive" depression, and different combinations of stress, anxiety, anger, and even combined optimism and pessimism. Because many of these states exist simultaneously with prenatal depression, the depression effects would appear to be confounded.

Infants of withdrawn mothers are noted to perform less optimally on the Bayley Scales at 1 year. Their mothers' prenatal profiles are different, as are their infants' profiles. In a study conducted by our group (Field et al., 2001), depressed mothers who could be classified as withdrawn or intrusive were compared with nondepressed mothers on their prenatal cortisol and catecholamine levels and on fetal activity and neonatal outcome variables. The data suggested that the withdrawn mothers had lower dopamine levels during pregnancy. The infants of withdrawn mothers also had the highest cortisol levels and the lowest dopamine and serotonin levels as well as the most asymmetrical EEG patterns and lower Brazelton Scale scores.

In another study by our group (Field et al., 2003), women were classified as experiencing high or low anxiety during the second trimester of pregnancy, but the high-anxiety women also had high scores on depression and anger scales. In a follow-up across pregnancy, the fetuses of the high-anxiety women were noted to be more active and to experience growth delays. The high-anxiety mothers' high prenatal norepinephrine and low dopamine levels were followed by their neonates having low dopamine and serotonin levels. The high-anxiety mothers' newborns also had greater relative right-frontal EEG activation and lower vagal tone. Finally, the newborns of high-anxiety mothers spent more time in deep sleep and less time in quiet and active alert states, and showed more state changes and less optimal performance on the Brazelton Neonatal Behavioral Assessment Scale (motor maturity, autonomic stability, and withdrawal). In a similar study on simultaneous prenatal anxiety and depression (Davis et al., 2002), maternal anxiety and depression during the prenatal, but not the postnatal, period were related to infant negative behavioral reactivity to novelty at 4 months.

Corticotropic-releasing hormone and cortisol effects

The corticotropic-releasing hormone (CRH), a precursor of the stress hormone cortisol, and cortisol pass through the placenta and can precipitate preterm labor, reduced birth weight, and slow growth rate in prenatally stressed infants (Wadwha, 2005; Wadwha et al., 1998). CRH and/or cortisol have also been associated with impaired fetal habituation to stimuli and temperamental difficulties in infants (Weinstock, 2005). Excess amounts of CRH and cortisol reaching the human fetal brain during periods of chronic maternal stress could alter personality and predispose an infant to attention deficits and depressive illness through changes in neurotransmitter activity. In one study, these infants were more likely than those in the control group to be small for their gestational age. They were also more likely than the control infants to have suffered at least one obstetric complication (Preti et al., 2000).

Elevated cortisol may be the culprit variable that leads to premature birth, difficult temperament, and other nonoptimal outcomes for prenatally stressed women. For example, in a study done in the Netherlands, (de Weerth et al., 2003), infants were divided into two groups based on their mothers' late-pregnancy cortisol levels, into high and low prenatal cortisol groups. High-cortisol infants were delivered earlier than those in the low-cortisol group. Furthermore, the behavior observations showed that the higher prenatal cortisol group displayed more crying, fussing, and negative facial expressions. Supporting these findings, maternal reports on infant temperament also showed that these infants had more difficult behavior. Similarly, in a study done in Italy (Cianfarani et al., 2002), high cortisol levels were inversely related to birth weight and birth length. Infants with elevated cortisol also showed growth failure.

In studies by our group (Field et al., 2004; 2005; 2006), cortisol was the strongest predictor of prematurity and low birth weight (See figure 2.3). Cortisol in late pregnancy has also been negatively related to both mental and motor development in infants at 3 months and motor development at 8 months (Huizink et al., 2003). This relationship may be predicted by prematurity.

On the other hand, lower cortisol levels were observed both in mothers and in babies of mothers who developed posttraumatic stress disorder (PTSD) in response to 9/11, compared with mothers who did not develop PTSD (Yehuda et al., 2005). Lower cortisol levels were most apparent in the babies born to mothers with PTSD who were exposed in their third trimester.

Neurotransmitters

Neurotransmitters have also been implicated in prenatal stress effects. For example, in our studies (Field et al., 2004; 2006), we reported that

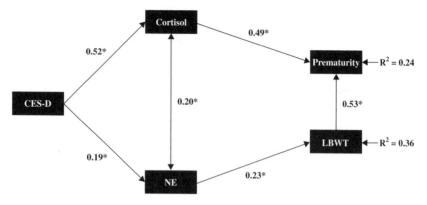

Figure 2.3 *Path analysis for relationship between cortisol and prematurity*

depressed mothers had higher cortisol and norepinephrine and lower dopamine levels which were stable across pregnancy and across pre- and postnatal assessments. The prenatal biochemistry predicted the mother's postnatal biochemistry. Specific relationships occurred between prenatal cortisol, dopamine, and serotonin and postnatal cortisol, dopamine, and serotonin. Analyses of the neonatal biochemistry, with the mother's prenatal biochemistry entered as predictor variables, also suggested specific continuity between the mother's and the newborn's neurotransmitter/neurohormone profiles.

Low progesterone has also been implicated in pregnancy. In an Australian study, women who received progesterone were less likely to give birth before 37 weeks (Dodd et al., 2005).

Ethnic and socioeconomic status differences

Ethnicity and socioeconomic status (SES) also appear to have differential effects on the fetus, and therefore, may be confounding variables. For example, African Americans are noted to deliver prematurely more than any other ethnic group. In a comparison between African American and Hispanic pregnancies (Field et al., 2002), the Hispanic mothers were older and had higher SES and higher prenatal norepinephrine levels. Their fetuses were also more active. At the neonatal period, the mothers had higher anger scores, but also higher serotonin levels. Their infants had higher dopamine and lower cortisol levels, and spent less time in deep and indeterminate sleep. The comparison by middle/lower SES revealed that the middle SES group was older, had more social support, and showed less depressed affect, but had higher norepinephrine levels prenatally. At the postnatal period, the middle SES mothers had lower depression, anxiety, and anger scores and lower norepinephrine levels. Their infants also had lower norepinephrine levels, fewer postnatal complications, and were less excitable on the Brazelton Neonatal Behavioral Assessment Scale.

Interventions for Prenatal Stress

Serotonin reuptake inhibitors

These data highlight the need for pregnancy interventions to lower stress and stress hormones. In the case of prenatal depression, medications have been studied, typically serotonin reuptake inhibitors (SSRIs), such as Prozac (Lattimore et al., 2005). The critical issue of whether the depression or the drugs have worse effects on the fetus has not yet been evaluated. In one recent study (Laine et al., 2003), SSRI-exposed infants had lower concentrations of cord blood serotonin. In another study (Moses-Kolko et al., 2005) late SSRI exposure carried a risk for neonatal behavioral syndrome. The most severely affected infants displayed central nervous system, motor, respiratory, and gastrointestinal signs that were usually mild and disappeared by 2 weeks. A review of studies on SSRIs during pregnancy suggested many methodological problems (Gentile, 2005).

Psychotropic medications

When used during pregnancy, psychotropic medications are thought by many to be teratogenic, that is, related to developmental malformations in the fetus, although the literature is mixed on this. In a recent study, 98% of women discontinued their medication for fear of harming their fetus. Of those, 70% reported adverse physical and psychological effects (Einarson et al., 2001). A very large body of literature has continued to debate the efficacy of psychotropic medications for prenatal depression.

Although some have concluded that there is no efficacy (Gentile, 2005), others have reported negative effects on the neonates, including lower Apgar scores and lower Bayley developmental scores (DeCasper et al., 2003; Misri et al., 2004).

Alternative therapies

Alternative therapies as interventions for prenatal stress have also been tried, for example, virtual fetal touch (Severi et al., 2005). In this study, a three-dimensional image was made by a computer of segmential two-dimensional ultrasound images of the fetus. The mothers' stress was measured before and after these images were presented. After the experience, a significant reduction was observed, in the mothers' anxiety as well as their salivary cortisol levels.

Massage therapy has been successfully used by our group (Field et al., 2005; 2006). Depressed pregnant women were recruited during the second trimester of pregnancy and randomly assigned to a massage therapy group, a progressive muscle relaxation group, or a control group that received only standard prenatal care. The massage therapy group participants received two 20-minute therapy sessions by their significant other each week for 16 weeks of pregnancy, starting during the second trimester. The relaxation group provided themselves with progressive muscle relaxation sessions on the same time schedule. Immediately after the massage therapy sessions on the first and last days of the 16-week period, the women reported lower levels of anxiety and depressed mood and less leg and back pain. By the end of the study, the massage therapy group had higher dopamine and serotonin levels and lower levels of cortisol and norepinephrine. These changes may have contributed to the reduced fetal activity and the better neonatal outcome for the massage therapy group (i.e., lesser incidence of prematurity and low birth weight), as well as their better performance on the Brazelton Neonatal Behavioral Assessment Scale. Moderate versus light pressure massage was more effective for neonatal outcomes (Field et al., 2006). (See figures 2.4 and 2.5.)

Giving stress-reduction instructions to pregnant women has resulted in lower stress levels, fewer symptoms of depression and negative affect, and lower cortisol levels (Urizan et al., 2004). Acupuncture is another effective therapy (Mauber et al., 2004). Following acupuncture treatments, depression scores were reduced in pregnant women.

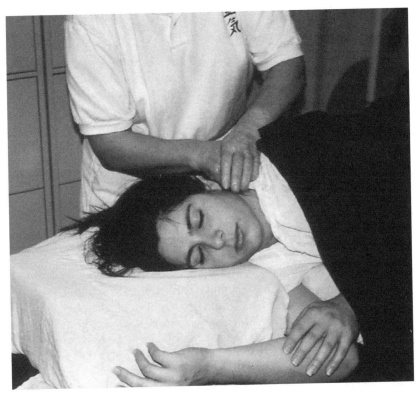

Figure 2.4　*Pregnant woman receiving massage therapy*

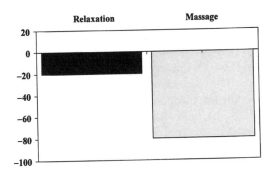

Figure 2.5　*Cortisol level decrease following massage therapy*

Prenatal Drug Exposure

Drug exposure is another significant risk factor for the growth and development of the fetus. Years ago, heroin was the culprit drug. Ironically, the methadone that was used to treat the mother resulted in worse symptoms for the newborn than the heroin itself. More recently, cocaine has been the most popularly used illicit drug. But its effects are typically confounded by the other drugs taken by cocaine users, including alcohol, with the effects of coca-ethylene (cocaine combined with alcohol) being more severe than those from cocaine alone. Other high-use, negative-impact drugs are cigarettes and caffeine. Paradoxically, chocolate (albeit less loaded in caffeine) has positive effects.

Cocaine exposure

For many years, parents have complained about their irritable, difficult infants who were exposed to cocaine prenatally. Neonatal researchers did not find significant problems, suggesting that symptoms of the cocaine exposure were not emerging until later in the newborn period. Current findings suggest that the newborn does not experience withdrawal symptoms until several weeks later. The effects also seem subtler than, for example, the deformed features noted in fetal alcohol syndrome. Other symptoms of cocaine exposure are problems regulating arousal which influence attention and, thus, learning (Mayes, 2002). In a study assessing the effects of combined tobacco and cocaine exposure during pregnancy on fetal responses and habituation to vibroacoustic stimulation, the authors observed what appeared to be the fetal counterpart of crying (Gingras et al., 2005).

Several studies on rats have concluded that adolescent and adult cocaine-exposed rats were more aggressive (Wood & Spear, 1998). Human infants exposed through the third trimester have been noted to be at increased risk for motor dysfunction (Swanson et al., 1999). This association between motor dysfunction and cocaine exposure was related to the timing and duration of gestational exposure. The effect of prenatal cocaine exposure on the motor development of full-term infants was examined in this study, controlling for maternal characteristics and exposure to other substances. Intrauterine cocaine exposure was determined at birth by maternal self-report and was verified by hair analysis. At 4 months, cocaine-exposed (COC) and noncocaine-exposed (NON-COC) infants were assessed by "blinded" examiners using a standard evaluation of neuromotor function, the Movement Assessment of Infants (MAI). Relative to NON-COC infants, COC infants had significantly higher full-scale MAI total risk scores for both total risk and Volitional Movement, and when compared with infants exposed only within the first two trimesters, they had significantly more deficits in Volitional Movement. Although MAI scores for the majority of exposed infants were within the normal range, infants exposed through the third trimester were at significantly increased risk for motor dysfunction. Intrauterine cocaine exposure had an adverse effect on infant motor development after the neonatal period. This association was related to the timing and duration of gestational exposure.

Other studies link prenatal exposure to cocaine to impaired information processing and language development (Harvey, 2004; Morrow et al., 2003; Singer et al., 2001). The weight of research evidence indicates that children born to mothers who use cocaine are likely to have neurological and cognitive deficits (Mayes, 2003; Noland et al., 2005).

Any chemical effects on the fetus and young infant are, of course, confounded by cocaine effects on the mother's behavior. For example, in a study on the effects of prenatal cocaine/polydrug use on maternal–infant feeding interaction during the first year of life (Minnes et al., 2005), women who used cocaine during pregnancy were less sensitive to their infants than noncocaine-using women. In infants, prenatal cocaine exposure was related to poorer clarity of cues. Controlling for covariates, concentration of cocaine metabolites was inversely related to maternal sensitivity to infant cues and infant clarity of cues at 1 year.

Mother's perceptual responses to infant distress signals were also distorted (Schuetze et al., 2003). Cocaine-using mothers (a) rated tape recordings of infants' cries as less arousing, aversive, urgent, and sick; (b) indicated that they were less likely to pick up or feed their infants; and (c) indicated that they were more likely to give the crying infants a pacifier or to just "wait and see." These ratings indicated that cocaine-using mothers found their infants' cries to be less perceptually salient and less likely to elicit nurturant caregiving responses.

In animals, oxytocin (the hormone that induces labor) enhances maternal behavior and lowers blood pressure, while prenatal cocaine disrupts oxytocin activity and increases maternal neglect and aggression (Light et al., 2004). These authors compared oxytocin, blood pressure, maternal behavior, and affect in mothers who used cocaine. The cocaine-using group had lower oxytocin levels, greater hostility and depressed mood, less support from others, and higher blood pressure and norepinephrine levels (a stress neurotransmitter), while cortisol and epinephrine responses were blunted.

Toddlers who have been exposed to cocaine are less sensitive or less empathetic. In a study we conducted, toddlers were monitored for affect and EEG activity during different conditions, including an infant crying, simulated maternal distress, and a mildly frustrating task (Jones et al., 2004). The children who had been exposed to cocaine had greater relative right-frontal EEG activity, showed fewer empathetic reactions to a crying infant as well as to their own mothers, and were also less proficient in completing a cooperative task.

Alcohol

Alcohol also affects fetal development and can lead to fetal alcohol syndrome (Barr & Streissguth, 2001; Caley et al., 2005). Drinking during pregnancy continues to be associated with increased risk of miscarriage, decreased fetal growth, morphologic abnormalities, and central nervous system impairment. Infants displaying the latter three symptoms and having certain facial characteristics (e.g., small eye openings, smooth skin over upper lip, thin upper lip), are believed to have what is called fetal alcohol syndrome. These data have been derived from large epidemiological samples (Little & Wendt, 1991; Weiner & Morse, 1990). Evidence has implicated alcohol in the disruption of retinoic acid synthesis, which appears to play a crucial role in the development of the limbs and the central nervous system (Paullarkat & Azar, 1992).

In at least one study, the combination of exposure to alcohol plus caffeine produced an additive effect in reducing birth weight and synergistic effects in increasing postnatal mortality (Hannigan, 1995). The author used an animal model of alcohol-related birth defects to assess the teratogenic potential of caffeine as a risk factor in fetal alcohol syndrome. Rats exposed prenatally to alcohol with or without caffeine had reduced maternal weight gain during pregnancy and reduced birth weight of the offspring. Prenatal alcohol exposure had a significant negative impact on development.

In a longitudinal follow-up study on a large sample of women (Sood et al., 2001), low levels of alcohol use were reported in 64% and moderate/heavy use in 13% of pregnancies. Increasing prenatal alcohol exposure was associated with lower birth weight and lower gestational age. Children with prenatal alcohol exposure were more likely to have higher externalizing (aggressive and delinquent) and internalizing (anxious/depressed and withdrawn) syndromes.

A wide range of neuropsychological deficits have been found in children prenatally exposed to alcohol, including deficits in visuospatial function, verbal and nonverbal learning, attention, and executive function (Riley and McGee, 2005). These children also exhibited a variety of behavioral problems that further affected their daily functioning.

The level of fetal cocaine exposure is also associated with developmental precursors of speech/language skills at 1 year of age (Singer et al., 2001). More heavily exposed infants had lower auditory comprehension scores than nonexposed infants and lower total language scores than lightly exposed and nonexposed infants. Prenatal alcohol exposure during the first trimester also predicted deficits in learning and short- and long-term memory, specifically in the verbal domain as late as 14 years into development (Willford et al., 2004).

One recent study found that prenatal exposure to binge drinking was linked to a greater likelihood of having IQ scores in the mentally retarded range and a higher incidence of acting-out behavior at 7 years of age (Bailey et al., 2004). Also, a recent study found that moderate alcohol drinking by pregnant women (three or more drinks a day) was linked with increased risk of preterm birth (Parazzini et al., 2003).

Paternal alcohol consumption has also been implicated in the development of the offspring. Alcohol may be a direct toxicant to sperm and may alter the chemical composition of semen (Cicero, 1994). Paternal alcohol consumption effects on fetal development, as distinguished from genetic heritability of alcoholism, may impact later cognitive and biochemical disturbances and possibly lead to future addiction. In animal studies with proven nondrug-using females who produced normal offspring, male alcohol consumption affected their ability to produce normal progeny, suggesting that alcohol may be a direct toxicant to sperm. Similarities have been found on progeny produced by males exposed to morphine and males exposed to alcohol. Paternal alcohol consumption may directly affect the sperm, may select out a specific population of functionally intact sperm that survived the alcohol, or may alter the chemical composition of semen so as to influence the sperm.

Fetal alcohol syndrome (FAS) is the most severe form of alcohol exposure and is a common cause of developmental disability, neuropsychiatric impairment, and birth defects. The disorder is identified by the presence of growth impairment, central nervous system dysfunction, and a characteristic pattern of craniofacial features. Prevalence of the disorder varies widely, and recent estimates approach 1% of live births. People with FAS have high rates of comorbid conditions, including attention deficit hyperactivity disorder (40%), mental retardation (15–20%), learning disorders (25%), speech and language disorders (30%), sensory impairment (30%), cerebral palsy (4%), and epilepsy (8–10%) (Burd et al., 2003).

Smoking

Smoking during pregnancy is also noted to have negative effects on the fetus. Preterm births and low birth weights, fetal and neonatal deaths, respiratory problems, and sudden infant death syndrome (SIDS, also known as "crib death"), are all more common among the offspring of mothers who smoked during pregnancy (Godding et al., 2004; Moore & Davies, 2005). Prenatal exposure to heavy smoking has been linked in one study to nicotine withdrawal symptoms in newborns (Godding et al., 2004), and to excessive crying in another study (Reijneveld et al., 2005).

In a large questionnaire study (Kelmanson et al., 2002), the infants of smoking mothers were more often born prematurely with a lower birth weight, they had lower Apgar scores at 5 minutes (a scale that evaluates breathing and heart rate), and they were less frequently breastfed at birth and at the time of the study. The infants born to smoking mothers also had more frequent fussy periods, and paid less attention to their parents during parent–infant interactions. Smoking during pregnancy is also predictive of higher heart rates in newborns, lower heart rate variability, and an increased number of tremors and changes in behavioral states (Schuetze et al., 2001). Heart rate variability was significantly lower even in the fetuses of mothers who smoked cigarettes during pregnancy (Zezkind and Gingrass, 2005).

Fathers' smoking is also noted to affect developing fetuses and newborns via passive smoke effects. Despite this reality, in a recent study (Blackburn et al., 2005), news of the birth of a new baby was not associated with a majority of the fathers' attempting or successfully quitting smoking. Fewer than 20% had tried to quit, and only 4% had successfully quit smoking since the birth of their babies. Half of the participants reported that they had not changed their cigarette consumption since their babies' births. Not smoking in the home appeared to be a more achievable behavior for many fathers; 78% had attempted and 60% had successfully achieved not smoking in the home. In a large sample study, women who quit early in pregnancy had lower stress levels and fewer depressive symptoms (Ludman, 2000).

Caffeine

Several studies have documented the negative effects of caffeine use on the fetus and neonate, including one from our lab (Diego et al., 2004). In this study the mothers reported sleep problems and obstetric complications. Their newborns had a lower birth weight and showed more stress-induced behavior, including tremors and jerkiness, during sleep observations. In another study, the severity of caffeine use predicted poorer neurobehavioral outcomes and was associated with altered sleep–wake state organization (Brandon et al., 2005). It is paradoxical, then, that chocolate, which also has some caffeine, could have positive effects. In a recent study (Raikkonen et al., 2004), mothers who reported daily consumption of chocolate rated their infants' temperament more positively at 6 months.

Licorice, on the other hand, despite being popular like chocolate, has negative effects, possibly because it inhibits cortisol metabolism. As already mentioned, cortisol is a strong predictor of low birth weight and prematurity. A group in Finland studied birth outcome in relation to licorice consumption during pregnancy (Strandberg et al., 2001). Babies with heavy exposure to licorice were not significantly lighter at birth, but they were significantly more likely to be born earlier.

Hormones

Several hormones affect fetal development. For example, gonadal hormones are thought to affect whether a baby becomes right- or left-handed. In one study, the mean grasp reflex of the right hand was significantly higher than that of the left hand in females, in contrast to males. The mean grasp reflex strength of the left hand was higher in males than in females (Tan et al., 1992). For males only, the grasp strength of the right and left hands was positively correlated with body weight. The authors examined the grasp reflex with regard to sex-related differences in female and male newborns within the second day after birth. In 10 trials, infants closed the fingers of both hands on a balloon placed in their palms. The balloon was connected to a pressure-measuring device. The sex-related difference may be associated with the influence of hormones on brain development in the fetus.

Others have argued that left-handedness is a result of increased levels of testosterone during fetal development and have suggested that it is related to immune-system dysfunction and certain learning-disability subtypes (Bryden & Steenhuis, 1991). In addition, handedness has been thought to be related to language functions in the brain, and thus might help one predict the pattern of language development in an individual. The authors argued that if these hypotheses are to be evaluated properly, there must be some consistency in the way hand preference is measured.

HIV

A high incidence of sudden, unexplained deaths in infants born to HIV-infected mothers has been noted (Starc et al., 1999). Children born to HIV-infected mothers may be at risk for traumatic or sudden, unexplained, non-HIV-related death. These children seem to be at risk regardless of their own HIV infection status. Furthermore, four of the deaths in the Starc et al. study (1999) occurred within the first few months of life, suggesting that this is a period of increased vulnerability. Studies to identify associated risk factors for non-HIV-related death are needed to identify these high-risk infants. Children born to HIV-infected mothers may be more vulnerable than was recognized previously and may be in need of increased social services, especially in early infancy.

Summary

These, then, are examples of signs and predictors that can be used for identifying infants at high risk for developmental problems. The way the mother feels and what she consumes can significantly affect the growth and development of her infant. Fathers, too, via their behavior and their sperm, affect fetal development. Because so much is learned prenatally, it is not surprising that cognitive and emotional development would be affected.

As more sophisticated ultrasound equipment is developed, we may see even more signs of fetal learning and be able to detect the effects of certain substances on the fetus. Most of the teratogenic effects have been reported for the neonate, not the fetus. Having the mother observe her fetus on ultrasound as she smokes or drinks may be a good intervention. We reported, for example, greater birth weights after mothers received positive feedback during prenatal ultrasounds (Field et al., 1985).

Many other less obviously harmful activities, such as sleep deprivation, overeating, and excessive exercise have yet to be studied. The fetus has earned more respect as we have learned more about fetal learning. Some have even come to call the fetus a prenate.

3

Coming into the World (The Perinatal Period)

The perinatal period including labor, delivery, and the neonatal stage (first month) is both exciting and frightening. Fear of childbirth, labor pain, operative delivery, and the newborn's need of special care are among the concerns of a pregnant woman.

Fear of Childbirth

Some women dread and avoid childbirth despite desperately wanting a baby. This is called tokophobia. In a study on women noted to dread childbirth (Hofberg & Brockington, 2000), an analysis of their psychiatric interviews suggested that avoidance of pregnancy often starts in adolescence, and sometimes is a symptom of a traumatic delivery or a symptom of prenatal depression. In this analysis, the pregnant women with tokophobia had worse symptoms if they were not able to choose their delivery method.

A prenatal questionnaire on fear of childbirth given to more than 8,000 pregnant women revealed that the most frequent fears were fear for the child's health (50%) and fear of pain (40%) (Geissbuehler & Eberhard, 2002). Fears related to medical interventions, such as cesarean delivery and anesthesia, were reported by only 10% of the sample.

Labor Pain and Alternative Therapies

A large literature suggests obstetric medications have side effects. Thus, several alternative therapies have been researched for their pain-alleviating effects, including acupuncture, music therapy, hypnosis, and massage therapy.

Acupuncture

Acupuncture has been effective as an analgesic during labor. In one study, meperidine was given to only 11% of the acupuncture group versus 37% of the no-acupuncture group (Nesheim et al., 2003). The use of other analgesics was also lower in the acupuncture group.

Music therapy

Music therapy has also been effective. When women who had a coach/partner along with music therapy during labor were compared with a group who had a coach but no music therapy (Browning, 2001), the music therapy group were more relaxed during the 3 hours prior to delivery, and they also experienced more feelings of personal control during their labor.

Hypnosis

Hypnosis has also been used for pain relief during labor and childbirth (Cyna et al., 2004). Comprehensive analyses of several databases revealed that fewer patients receiving hypnosis required analgesia. Also, those using hypnosis had less labor pain and used fewer opioids. In another study using hypnosis (Melh & Lewis, 2004), women receiving prenatal hypnosis had significantly better birth outcomes than women who did not.

Massage therapy

Massage therapy has also been effective in lowering labor pain (Field et al., 2000). In our study, the significant others massaged the mothers for the first 15 minutes of every hour of labor, concentrating on the lower back and legs while the mothers lay on their sides. The massaged women had significantly shorter labor by an average of 5 hours and less need for labor medication. (See figure 3.1.)

Sitting position

Using a sitting position, versus lying down, has also been noted to reduce the intensity of labor pain. Pain intensity was rated on a visual analogue

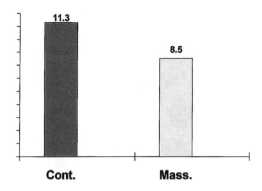

Figure 3.1 *Shorter labor (hours) following massage therapy*

scale by women, who alternately assumed sitting and supine positions (i.e., lay on their backs) for 15 minutes each during labor (Adachi et al., 2003). The pain scores were lower for the sitting position. The largest decrease occurred in lower back pain.

Delivery Methods

Cesarean section

The use of cesarean section is increasing in the United States, where the cesarean rate in 1994–5 was 16%, and in 2002–3 had increased to 58% (Ryan et al., 2005). During the same time period 23% of babies in England were delivered by cesarean section (Mayor, 2005).

The benefits and risks of cesarean section continue to be debated (Ben-Meir, Schenker, & Ezra, 2005; Lee et al., 2005; Sheiner et al., 2005). Some critics believe that too many babies are delivered by cesarean section in the United States. More cesarean sections are performed in the United States than in any other country in the world. The cesarean delivery rate jumped 6% from 2002 to 2003 in the United States to 28% of all births, the highest level since 1989, when these data began to be reported on birth certificates (Martin et al., 2005).

One of the advantages of cesarean delivery is lower cortisol levels. In a study from Ireland, those infants delivered by elective cesarean section

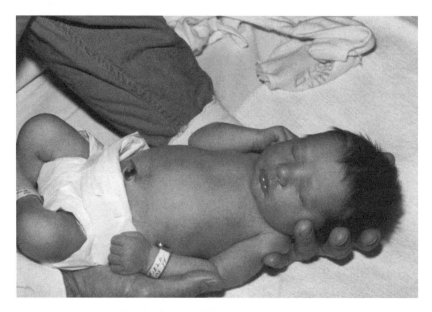

Figure 3.2 *Tory in her dad's hands following cesarean*

had the lowest cortisol levels, while the highest levels were recorded in those infants following instrumental delivery (Mears et al., 2004). One of the disadvantages of cesarean section is the increased risk of the mother's readmission to the hospital after the cesarean versus after a vaginal delivery (Liu et al., 2005).

Vaginal delivery

Vaginal deliveries with analgesia also have their disadvantages. For several years, the negative effects of obstetric medications have been reported. The most frequently reported effects are the newborn's reluctance to feed and his fussiness. For example, in a study assessing the effects of analgesia during labor on the development of spontaneous breastfeeding movements, crying behavior, and skin temperature in healthy term newborns, those with more analgesia showed a lesser incidence of making licking movements, sucking the breast, or touching the nipple with their hands before sucking (Ransjo et al., 2001). Nearly half of the infants exposed to analgesia did not breastfeed within the first few hours of life. Those infants also had higher temperatures and cried more than infants whose mothers had not received any analgesia.

Waterbirth

Many forms of natural childbirth have been tried, including the Lamaze method (breathing exercises), the Leboyer method (a warm and quiet delivery room and placement of the newborn in warm water), and the increasingly popular waterbirth. Both negative and positive effects have been noted for waterbirths. A recent review of 74 papers on waterbirth (Pinnette et al., 2004) described complications associated with waterbirth. These included drowning, infectious disease, cord rupture with neonatal hemorrhage, and death.

In contrast, another study found no negative effects when comparing deliveries in water with deliveries in bed (Thoni et al., 2005). The positive effects were the shorter duration of labor (first stage) and the lower rate of episiotomies in water compared with other delivery types. Also, there were no differences in the duration of the second stage of labor and arterial umbilical cord blood pH. Postpartum maternal hemoglobin levels remained unchanged, analgesics were required, and infections after waterbirths did not occur more frequently than after traditional births.

Still another study on 2,939 women noted positive effects for waterbirth (Cluett et al., 2004). Less use of epidural/spinal/paracervical analgesia/anesthesia occurred in the group who experienced water immersion during the first stage of labor compared with those who did not. Women who used water immersion during the first stage of labor also reported less pain. No differences were noted for Apgar scores, neonatal unit admissions, or neonatal infection rates.

Postbirth Events

Apgar test

The first experience of the newborn following delivery is the Apgar test. In 1953, Virginia Apgar, MD, published her method for evaluating the newborn (Finster & Wood, 2005). She selected five signs that could be evaluated and taught to delivery room personnel without difficulty. Those included heart rate, respiratory effort, reflex irritability, muscle tone and color. At 1 minute, 5 minutes, and 10 minutes after delivery, each sign is rated 0, 1, or 2, depending on whether it is absent or present. Infants in poor condition typically score 0–2, infants in fair condition score 3–7, while scores of 8–10 are usually given to infants in good condition.

Skin-to-skin contact

Skin-to-skin contact, or placing an infant on the mother's bare skin is desirably the next thing that occurs immediately after birth. This practice has led to many positive effects, including a greater incidence of breastfeeding. In one study (Mizuno et al., 2004), infants receiving skin-to-skin contact were breastfed an average of 2 months longer than others. In another sample (Mikiel-Kostyra et al., 2002), infants who remained with their mothers for at least 20 minutes were weaned 2 months later than those who had no skin-to-skin contact after delivery.

Breastfeeding

Breastfeeding happens very naturally following skin-to-skin contact. Breastfeeding constitutes a major focus of research in international health because of its impact on child survival. Five million infants a year in developing countries have fatal cases of diarrhea, and in most cases, breastfeeding provides an effective defense against infant diarrhea (McDade & Thomas, 2001). A recent demographic study on breast-feeding mothers suggested that those who chose to breastfeed were more educated, more often employed before birth, married, and used contraception postnatally (Sharps et al., 2003). Breastfeeding mothers also had higher scores on empathy toward their infants as well as fewer perceived hassles on the Parenting Daily Hassle Scale.

A study in Argentina suggested that at discharge, 1 month, 4 months, and 6 months, the frequency of exclusive breastfeeding was 97%, 83%, 56%, and 19%, respectively (Cernadas et al., 2003). The median duration was 4 months. A longer duration of exclusive breastfeeding was significantly associated with positive maternal attitudes toward breast-feeding, adequate family support, good mother–infant bonding, appropriate suckling techniques, and no nipple problems.

A large sample questionnaire study in Japan asked mothers to choose one out of five defined types of breastfeeding infants, including barracudas, ineffectives, procrastinators, gourmets, and resters (Mizuno et al., 2004). The mothers who described their infants as "barracudas" had the highest breastfeeding rate. The "procrastinators" had the lowest rate of breastfeeding. Sucking behavior during the neonatal period affected the breastfeeding rate at 3 and 6 months of age. The reasons for ceasing breastfeeding were perceived shortage of milk volume and elder children's anger and jealousy.

Breastfeeding has several advantages for babies, including that they find the odor of human milk more attractive than formula. In one study,

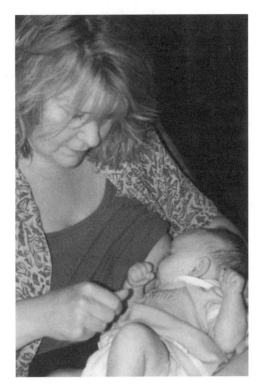

Figure 3.3 *Breastfeeding mother and infant*

for example, behavioral responses of 3- to 4-day-old newborns to the aroma of human milk and formula milk were recorded (Marlier & Schaal, 2005). When both types of milk were unfamiliar, breastfed as well as bottlefed infants oriented their head and mouthed more vigorously to human milk than to formula. These results demonstrate that the aroma of human milk is more attractive to newborns than is that of formula, and that this preference is independent of postnatal feeding experience.

Early behavior and physiology are also affected. For example, breastfeeding behavior was correlated with performance on neonatal behavioral assessments in one study (Radzyminski, 2005). Newborns who had higher breastfeeding scores on rooting, latch-on, sucking, and swallowing also had higher neurobehavioral scores.

Temperament and EEG were affected in another study (Jones et al., 2004). Depressed mothers who had stable breastfeeding patterns were less likely to have infants with highly reactive temperaments, and their infants did not show the frontal asymmetry patterns that are reported for infants of depressed mothers. Breastfeeding can be predictive of development outcomes. In a developmental outcome study, feeding behavior was rated as (1) no sucking and weak expression, (2) arrhythmic alteration of expression/suction and weak pressure, (3) rhythmic alteration, but weak pressure, and (4) rhythmic alteration with normal pressure (Mizuno & Ueda, 2005). Feeding classification was correlated with neurodevelopmental outcome at 18 months. The feeding classification was more predictive of 18-month outcome than an ultrasound assessment.

Higher cognitive scores (except memory) have been observed among children who were breastfed (Clark et al., 2006; Smith et al., 2003). Differences on the test scores of the breastfed children versus those who did not receive breastfeeding were four IQ points for overall intellectual functioning and two IQ points for verbal ability. Neonatal feeding performance (in terms of expression and sucking pressures) has also been related to late infancy Bayley developmental scores (Mizuno & Veda, 2005). In an even larger longitudinal study (Richards et al., 2002), breastfeeding was positively associated with reading ability as late as 15 and 53 years.

Breastfeeding has also been associated with better health and a reduced risk of obesity as compared with formula feeding in several small studies (Oddy et al., 2006; Owen et al., 2005). In formula-fed infants, weight gain during the first week of life was associated with adulthood overweight (Stettler et al., 2005).

The only apparent negative aspect of breastfeeding is the potential harm that could come from ingesting breast milk that has expired or breast milk that has been spoiled by drugs or bad food. One study suggested that infants limit their consumption in these cases. In this study, infants consumed significantly less milk during the 4 hours immediately after exposure to alcohol in their mother's milk as compared with the control condition (Mennella, 2001). Compensatory increases in intake were then observed during the 8 to 16 hours after exposure, when mothers refrained from drinking alcohol.

Holding the infant

Holding the infant, and on which side, when comforting and rocking is also an early caregiving consideration. In 1962, psychologist Lee Salk noted that 80% of mothers held their infants on the left side of the body. New studies also suggest that the left-side bias is only for holding infants (or infant dolls), not for books, packages, or other objects (Harris, 2002). Although the discovery of the left-sided bias has been credited to Salk, Salk himself claims that he only rediscovered what had been noted at least 200 years earlier.

In one empirical study on the question of side preference, college students were asked to imagine holding an infant, and then to report their foot preference when standing on one foot (Erber et al., 2002). Right-handed college students were given this exercise along with questions about their foot preference for posture and balance. Sixty-five percent of the students reported a left-side preference for infants.

In another empirical study, college students were asked to imagine holding in their arms first an object (either an "expensive vase" or an "old shoebox") and then a young infant (Almerigi et al., 2002). Eighty-one percent of the students reported holding the imagined vase in their right arm, 64% reported holding the imagined shoebox in their right arm, and 66% reported holding the imagined infant in their left arm. These results further supported the hypothesis that the left-side bias is unique to holding infants.

Swaddling

Swaddling is an old caregiving practice. It has been used primarily to induce sleep and to reduce crying among irritable infants. In a recent study, swaddling was associated with increased sleep efficiency and decreased time spent in non-REM (rapid eye movement) sleep (Franco et al., 2005). When swaddled, the infants also awakened less often.

Co-sleeping

Co-sleeping (parent–baby) is another important early caregiving decision. The incidence of co-sleeping is very high, and it increases across infancy (Jenni et al., 2005), despite the fact that some mothers and fathers were initially afraid that they would squash or suffocate their baby in their sleep, and others were concerned that the infant's presence would negatively affect their own sleep (Ball, 2000).

In the United States, co-sleeping is controversial. Proponents suggest advantages such as increased bonding and breastfeeding, and opponents suggest potential increased risks of suffocation and sudden infant death syndrome. In a large sample at age 3–7 months, 51% usually slept alone and 48% usually slept in a bed with a parent or other adult (Brenner et al., 2003). Similarly, at age 7–12 months, 51% usually slept alone, and

47% usually slept in a bed with a parent or other adult. In another sample, 50% of the infants slept with their mothers in body contact in the same bed (Gorman, 2002), while 23% of the infants slept in their mother's bed, but not in body contact. Breastfeeding in bed was a common practice, and the mothers who breastfed their infants in bed breastfed them for a longer duration.

Sleep behaviors of mother–infant pairs have been compared under both solitary and co-sleeping conditions (Barone, 2002). Infants sleeping alone showed more large limb movements, small limb movements, head rotations, vocalizations, crying, self-soothing behaviors, and spontaneous startles. Mothers used more vestibular soothing with their infants when they were sleeping alone.

In a longitudinal study at 5 weeks and 6 months, co-sleeping infants differed from non-co-sleepers on a number of measures: (1) at 5 weeks, the co-sleepers showed more quiet sleep and longer bouts of quiet sleep, and (2) at 6 months, co-sleepers also showed less active sleep, fewer arousals in active sleep, and less wakefulness (Hunsley & Thoman, 2002). The differences suggested a lower arousal level in the co-sleeping infants. In contrast, over the long term, co-sleeping infants may have more trouble sleeping.

In another longitudinal sample, co-sleepers (who began co-sleeping early in infancy) were compared with reactive co-sleepers (children who began co-sleeping at or after age 1) and solitary sleepers. They were compared on night wakings and bedtime struggles, and children's self-reliance and independence in social and sleep-related behaviors (Keller & Goldberg, 2004). Solitary sleepers fell asleep alone, slept through the night, and weaned earlier than the co-sleepers. However, early co-sleeping children were more self-reliant (e.g., more able to dress themselves) and exhibited more social independence (e.g., made friends by themselves). Reactive co-sleepers had more frequent night wakings.

A cross-cultural study in Norway, comparing Norwegian and Sami infants (an indigenous group), also found that children who were co-sleepers (the Sami infants) were more socially independent (Javo et al., 2004). Nonetheless, when sleeping patterns were videotaped and coded, the co-sleeping infants appeared more stressed (Hunsley, 2002).

Concerns of Parents

Baby switching

Baby switching is one of the biggest fears soon after birth, but recognizing your baby helps allay those fears. In a recent questionnaire study

(DiPasquale et al., 2001), 10% of women reported anxiety about baby switching, but 66% recognized their babies from their recorded cry sounds and 52% recognized their babies by their smell.

Preterm infants

Maturation and health of the baby are also a significant concern. Inasmuch as 13% of infants are born prematurely in the United States (as contrasted with 1% in China), this is a real concern. The preterm birth rate in the United States increased 27% from 1982 to 2002 (National Center for Health Statistics, 2004). Approximately 13% of US births are now preterm. In the United States, there has also been an increase in low-birth-weight infants in the last two decades, and the US low-birth-weight rate of 7.6% is considerably higher than that of many other developed countries (Cuevas et al., 2005; National Center for Health Statistics, 2004; UNICEF, 2001).

Entire books have been written about preterm babies and their development. In this chapter, we discuss some of the recent findings on follow-ups of preemies and on caregiving interventions for infants who need intensive care.

In a study on physically attractive preterm infants, those rated as physically more attractive by nurses caring for them in the neonatal intensive care unit (NICU), thrived better as measured by weight gain and by length of hospital stay. Presumably this finding relates to the infants' receiving more nurturing (Badr & Abdallah, 2001).

As neonates, preterm infants have more perceptual problems. For example, premature newborns, unlike full-term newborns, do not show maternal voice recognition (Therien et al., 2004).

In later infancy, body rotation, spontaneous reaching out, and manipulation during parts of the Bayley Developmental Test were inferior in 2-year-old preterm infants (de Vries & de Groot, 2002). Most preterm infants showed nonoptimal body rotations and nonoptimal arm and hand movements in contrast with most full-term children. In one very large follow-up study (Klassen et al., 2004), NICU children had problems in many areas, including sight, speech, getting around, using hands and fingers, taking care of themselves, learning and remembering, thinking and solving problems, pain and discomfort, general health, and behavior.

Cognitive delays have also been noted for preterm infants. At 4 and 5 years, samples of preterm infants had lower Stanford–Binet IQ scores and lower Stanford–Binet subscale scores, except in short-term memory and quantitative reasoning (Caravale et al., 2005; Kilbride et al., 2005). They also had lower spelling scores on the Wide Range Achievement Test and lower Peabody motor quotients (Kilbride et al., 2004). And, in another sample, NICU graduates in late childhood and early adolescence had shorter spatial memory spans and made more forgetting errors on a spatial working memory tasks (Curtis et al., 2002). Learning difficulties have also been reported in at least 18 studies on very low-birth-weight infants (Rodrigues et al., 2006).

NICU Interventions

Our recent survey of 84 NICUs suggests that 10% are using incubator covers, 65% co-bedding of multiple-birth infants, 98% kangaroo care, 72% music, 38% massage therapy, and 100% treatments for painful procedures (Field et al., 2005).

Incubator covers

The simplest of the intervention procedures has been incubator covers. These were first designed to reduce retrolental fibroplasia (a kind of blindness from too much light). Recently they are also being used to enhance sleep. For example, in one study on sleep patterns, a positive correlation was noted between postnatal age in days and the mean duration of quiet sleep periods when incubator covers were used (Hellstrom-Westas et al., 2001).

Co-bedding multiple-birth infants

Co-bedding multiple-birth infants (twins, triplets, quadruplets) is another very simple intervention, but a very controversial one for "cross-contamination concerns" – the effects the infants have on each other can be difficult to assess. In one study, co-bedding multiple-birth infants reputedly boosted growth and development and enhanced bonding (Gannon, 1999). In contrast, another group's findings showed no differences in clinical and developmental outcomes between the traditionally bedded and the co-bedded groups (Polizzi, 2003). (See figure 3.4.)

Kangaroo care

Kangaroo care (in which the parent carries the baby in an upright position underneath her clothing) is a cost-effective intervention. Preterm

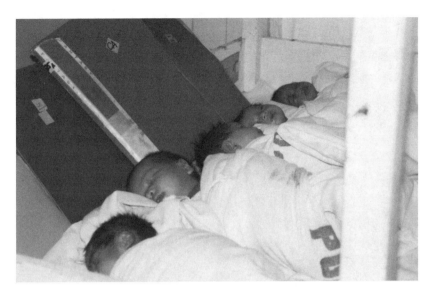

Figure 3.4 *Co-bedding newborns in China*

infants often have difficulty coordinating their breathing and heart rate, and the close physical contact with the parent provided by kangaroo care can help stabilize the preterm infant's heartbeat, temperature, and breathing (Dodd, 2005; Feldman & Eidelman, 2003; Ferber & Makhoul, 2004). Further, researchers have found that preterm infants who experience kangaroo care have longer periods of sleep, gain more weight, decrease their crying, have longer periods of alertness, and experience earlier hospital discharge (Lehtonen & Martin, 2004; Ludington-Hoe et al., 2004; Worku & Kassir, 2005). Increasingly kangaroo care is being recommended for full-term infants as well (Johnson, 2005).

Dozens of studies have been conducted on kangaroo care, but only a few are reviewed here. In a study conducted in Israel, infants receiving kangaroo care showed a more rapid maturation of vagal tone between 32 and 37 weeks (Feldman & Eidelman, 2003). In addition, they showed more rapid improvement in state organization (longer periods of quiet sleep and alert wakefulness and shorter periods of active sleep) as well as better scores on neonatal habituation and orientation. (See figure 3.5.)

In another study on the effects of kangaroo care on preterm infants (Dodd, 2004), the daily weight gain in the kangaroo care group was 5

Figure 3.5 *Kangaroo care Bill and Jes*

grams greater than in the group practicing traditional holding. A randomized, controlled trial of kangaroo care (Charpak et al., 2001) suggested that head circumference was also greater in the group given kangaroo care. That group also spent less time in the hospital, they had fewer severe infections, and a greater number of the kangaroo care infants were breastfed. Neonatal performance was also superior for the kangaroo care infants, including higher scores on the Brazelton Orientation and State Regulation Scales. At 6 months, they had lower "intensity" scores and higher "mood" scores as well as higher Bayley Scale scores at 12 months (Ohgi et al., 2002).

Another comparison of kangaroo care and traditional care (Feldman et al., 2002) suggested that after kangaroo care, interactions were more positive at 37 weeks. Mothers showed more positive affect, touch, and adaptation to infant cues, and infants showed more alertness and greater looking at their mothers. The mothers also reported less depression, and they perceived their infants as being less abnormal. At 3 months, mothers and fathers of kangaroo care infants were more sensitive and provided a better home environment. At 6 months, kangaroo care mothers were more sensitive, and their infants scored higher on the Bayley Mental Scale.

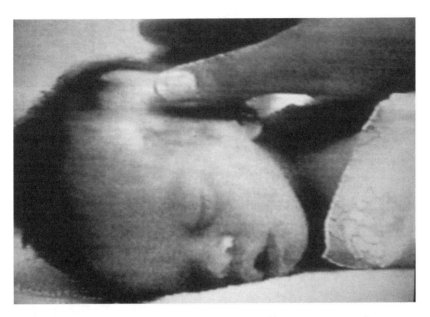

Figure 3.6 *Preterm newborn receiving massage therapy in Neonatal Intensive Care Unit*

The only negative findings were that kangaroo care was associated with bradycardia (slow heart rate) and hypoxemia (lower oxygen) and with less regular breathing (Bohnhorst et al., 2001). These changes were unexpected and may have been related to heat stress. The authors suggested that body temperature, heart rate, and oxygenation should be monitored during kangaroo care.

Massage therapy

Massage therapy has been one of the most effective NICU treatments. In an Israeli massage therapy study, preterm infants received massage therapy in the NICU by their mothers (Ferber et al., 2004). The mothers experienced less postpartum depression, and when the massaged infants were 3 months old, the mothers were less intrusive, their interactions were more reciprocal, and the massaged infants were more socially involved. (See figure 3.6.)

Many studies have shown greater daily weight gain (up to 49% greater) and earlier hospital discharge (on average 5 days) for preemies receiving massage therapy (see Field, 2004, for a review). Other studies have noted greater bone density and head circumference (Moyer-Milleu,

Figure 3.7 *A cartoon by a massage-loving neonatologist*

2005). A recent study by our group suggests that these growth effects are mediated by increased vagal activity that facilitates food absorption and bone growth (Diego et al., 2006). The massage-induced growth is significant inasmuch as growth velocity during an NICU hospitalization has an independent effect on neurodevelopmental and growth outcomes at 18–22 months (Ehrenkranz et al., 2006).

Massage has also been combined with music in interventions for premature infants. In one study, mothers of premature, low-birth-weight infants received training on overstimulation and techniques for its avoidance (Whipple, 2000). Length of hospitalization was shorter, and average daily weight gain was greater for infants whose parents received the training.

Painful procedures

Painful procedures are always a problem for infants in the NICU. A recent Medline Internet search on neonatal pain suggested that the main topics of the articles were pain related to colic (20%), general neonatal pain issues (14%), and procedural pain (13%) (Banos et al., 2001). In an empirical study on neonatal pain (Grunau et al., 2005), higher cumulative neonatal procedural pain exposure was related to a lower cortisol response to stress and to lower facial reactivity to pain.

Having the preterm infant suck on a sugar-coated pacifier is one of the simplest procedures to lower procedural pain. In one study (Greenberg, 2002), newborns pricked in the heel were randomly assigned to one of four groups: (1) those given a water-moistened pacifier, (2) those given a sugar-coated pacifier, (3) those given an oral sucrose solution, or (4) a control group. The sugar-coated pacifier group cried less than the group given a water-moistened pacifier and the control group. In addition, the sugar-coated pacifier group had lower vagal tone when pricked in the heel than the group given an oral sucrose solution and the control group.

In a study by our group, newborns were given a water or sucrose solution before a heelstick procedure (poking the heel) (Fernandez et al., 2003). Infants who received water showed increased relative right-frontal EEG activation from baseline to the post-heelstroke phase, a pattern that typifies negative affect. (See figure 3.8.) The EEG of infants in the sucrose group did not change. Heart rate increased rapidly in both groups during the heelstroke phase. However, after the heelstick, the heart rate of infants who received sucrose returned to their original levels. These findings add to the growing literature showing that sucrose lessens newborns' negative responses to painful stimuli.

Glucose has been similarly effective in reducing heelstick pain. Endogenous opioids were always considered the underlying mechanism, but when opioid antagonists were administered, no decrease in analgesic effect was noted (Gradin & Schollin, 2005).

Early Caregiving Problems

In the early months after birth, parents also worry about caregiving problems, including colic or excessive crying, sleep disturbances, and sudden infant death syndrome (SIDS). As a result, a large body of literature has built up around each of these problems.

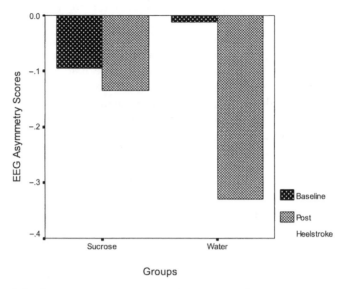

Figure 3.8 *Sucrose versus water EEG responses by neonates to aversive heelstroke*

Colic/excessive crying

Crying has been viewed as evolutionarily adaptive. An evolutionary argument has been made that crying is adaptive because infants are born into an uncertain parenting environment, which can range from indulgent care of offspring to infanticide (Soltis, 2004). Infants' cries are adaptive because they keep parents close and providing care. During crying, for example, neural input to the vocal cords increases cry pitch. Caregivers may use this information to guide their caregiving behavior. Cry analysis has also been used to diagnose neurological and medical status. A stimulus is typically used to elicit 30 seconds of crying, which is submitted to a computer for digitizing (LaGasse et al., 2005).

Increased crying during the first few months of life is universal. Excessive crying, or colic, represents the upper end of this normal increase. In a recent study by one of the leading cry research teams (Roberts et al., 2003), unexplained crying in infants 1 to 3 months old was a common concern for parents. These investigators examined the hypothesis that excessive crying is due to high infant responsivity. Eight-day-old infants were tested for their response to two standard, mildly challenging, procedures, including a neurobehavioral test involving undressing, putting down, and handling, and a painful heelstick to obtain a blood sample. The infants' crying over 24 hours was recorded in parental diaries. Newborns high on responsivity during the neurobehavioral assessment were also those infants who cried a lot and met a definition of "colic" as excessive crying.

To describe the behavioral and physiological responses associated with colic, the responses of 2-month-old infants with and without colic were studied during a physical examination (White et al., 2000). Parents kept a diary of infant behavior for 3 days following the visit. Colic was defined as fussing/crying for 3 hours or more on each of the 3 days. Behavioral data coded by "blind" observers showed that during the physical exam, colic infants cried twice as much, cried more intensely, and were more inconsolable than control infants. Despite these behavioral differences, heart rate, vagal tone, and cortisol measures indicated no difference, and the colic and control infants did not differ on daily average cortisol level. According to the mothers' diaries, they also slept about 2 hours less per day.

In a study on the frequency of crying (McGlaughlin & Grayson, 2001), mothers who attended child health clinics with their infants (up to 12 months of age) were interviewed on their perceptions of the amount of time their infants cry at six different periods of the day. Crying peaks were concentrated in the latter part of the afternoon and early evening. To investigate the accuracy of the mothers' reports, infant crying (5–16 weeks old) was recorded by means of a miniature wireless microphone worn by the baby (Salisbury et al., 2001). Crying was transmitted to a voice-activated recorder while, at the same time, the mothers kept a log of their babies' crying. The number of minutes of crying and the number of bouts of crying obtained from the two procedures were highly correlated, although the amount of crying reported by the mothers was less than that obtained from the recorder.

Parents who reported excessive infant irritability were more likely to report sleep difficulties (Salisbury, 2001). In this study, sleep state organization differed between the irritable infants and the comparison infants who were the same age at both 5 weeks and 6 months of age. The irritable infants showed disrupted state organization, specifically less mature state patterns of sleep behaviors and wakeful behaviors.

Crying has been noted to affect later control of emotions. In one study (Stifter et al., 2002) cry diaries were used to categorize excessive cries and typical criers at 6 weeks of age. At 5 and 10 months of age, infants and mothers participated in procedures to elicit infant reactivity and regulation during a frustration task and in response to maternal sensitivity and intrusiveness during a free-play session. Results showed that the excessive criers had higher levels of negative reactivity than the typical criers. Excessive criers also demonstrated lower self-regulation. Boys in the group of excessive criers exhibited the lowest level of self-regulation.

Excessive early crying has also been noted to affect parent–infant interactions. In a study on interactions (Raiha et al., 2003), both parents of colicky infants had less optimal parent–child interactions. Problems were most pronounced between the fathers and infants in the severe colic group. This may relate to their infants' having the highest arousal levels following crying. In a study on parents' reactions to crying (Seifritz et al., 2003), functional magnetic resonance imaging was used to record the brain responses to infant crying and laughing in mothers and fathers of young children and in women and men without children. Parents showed stronger activation to crying, whereas nonparents showed a stronger activation to laughing.

In a study on infants who were referred for persistent crying and were assessed later at 4 years, excessive crying beyond the first 6 months was associated with a greater prevalence of eating and sleeping difficulties at 4 years (von Kries et al., 2006); the children who had shown persistent crying as infants also had more hyperactivity problems and more conduct problems (Wolke et al., 2002). Parents rated the temperament of their children to be more negative, and teachers reported lower academic achievement. Persistent crying also contributed to maternal sleep problems in an American sample (Thomas & Foreman, 2005) and to maternal depression in an Australian sample (Wake et al., 2006).

The Breathing Bear has been an effective tool for excessive fussiness. Originally used as a source of rhythmic stimulation for preterm infants and fussy full-term infants (Novosad & Thoman, 2003), the stuffed teddy bear is set to make "breathing" movements like a normal infant at a rate matching that of the infant. Previous studies have indicated that preterm infants prefer a Breathing Bear over a similar bear that does not make "breathing" movements, and they show neurobehavioral benefits from having one in their crib. A Breathing Bear has also been provided for fussy full-term infants, from 5 weeks to 6 months. After 6 months, the mothers in the Breathing Bear group rated their infants' temperament as being less negative, and rated themselves as being less depressed and stressed than the mothers in the non–Breathing Bear group.

Sleep disturbances

Sleep problems and excessive crying are related. It is not clear when in development crying first occurs, but sleep is well organized as early as the prenatal period.

Several sleep states have been identified by many investigators to describe infants' sleep–wake activity:

- **Deep or quiet sleep** (also called nonrapid eye movement, or NREM, sleep). In this state, the infant is not moving, he is breathing evenly, and his eyelids are firmly closed and show no movement.
- **Active sleep** (also called rapid eye movement, or REM, sleep). In this state, the infant is showing some movements, including occasional startles and limb movements. His breathing is somewhat irregular, and his eyelids are closed but may show movement.
- **Drowsiness.** In this state, the infant's eyelids are often open but close intermittently, and the limbs may be moving.
- **Quiet alert** (or alert inactivity). In this state, the infant is awake, looking wide-eyed or alert, and is relatively inactive.
- **Active alert.** In this state, the infant is actively moving about, not very attentive, and sometimes may become fussy.
- **Crying.** In this state, the infant's facial expressions and vocal expressions are distressed, and there are considerable limb movements.

At the newborn period, infants often sleep (about 75% of the time). They also show periods of alertness (about 10% of the time), and these alternate with drowsiness (about 10% of the time). About half of the newborn's sleep time is spent in the less mature REM sleep (sleep in which rapid eyelid movements can be observed). As infants develop, they approximate the more mature sleep state (NREM sleep) and spend about the same time as the adults' 20% time in REM sleep.

Other sleep disturbances include:

- **Snoring and noisy breathing** during sleep may interrupt sleeping infants. In a study on 2- to 4-month-old infants (Klemanson, 2000) 5% were habitual snorers, 24% had noisy breathing during sleep, and 70% had both snoring and noisy breathing. These infants were also rated as having difficult temperament, particularly those infants who had both snoring and noisy breathing during sleep.

- **Elevated sleeping temperatures** might also disrupt sleep, as was shown in 2- to 4-month-olds (Franco et al., 2003). In these infants, elevated temperatures were accompanied by higher heart rate, and lower vagal activity in REM and NREM sleep.

Sleep Interventions

Several interventions have been tried for sleep disturbances including adjusting bedtime routines, and using white noise, sleep aids, and a parent intervention called "controlled crying." Few objective data are available regarding infant's night waking behaviors and the development of self-soothing during the first year of life. A cross-sectional study examined 80 infants at 3, 6, 9, or 12 months for four nights by using video-somnography to code nighttime awakening and parent–child interactions (Goodlin et al., 2001). A large degree of variability was observed in parents' putting the infant to bed awake or asleep and in responding to crying during the night. Even in the 12-month-old group, 50% of the infants typically required their parents' intervention to get back to sleep.

Bedtime routines and white noise

Bedtime routines and white noise were tested in one study (Borkowski et al., 2001). Schedules and positive bedtime routines combined with white noise were effective, reducing bedtime struggles and night wakings. Scheduled bedtimes, scheduled naptimes, white noise, and co-sleeping have been commonly employed procedures for sleep problems. Sleep schedules are an important example of parents helping their infants self-regulate. Sleeping through the night is considered a developmental milestone by most parents. In one report (Adams et al., 2004), 50% of babies slept through the night by 8 weeks, and 75% by 12 weeks. Relevant underlying factors for sleep problems in one sample (in order of importance) were problems setting limits for the infant, fussy/difficult infant temperament, maternal anxiety–depression, ambivalent attachment, and the use of physical comforting (cuddling to sleep, settling on sofa or in parental bed, and giving a feed) (Morrel & Steele, 2003).

Sleep aids

Another report suggested that sleep aids (pacifier, teddy bear, etc.) during the night reduced the occurrence of sleep disorders, whereas prolonged breastfeeding and co-sleeping interfered with normal development of sleep (Benhamou, 2000). Although most infants (64%) lost their pacifier within 30 minutes of falling asleep (Franco et al., 2004), sucking periods were associated with increased vagal activity. Even during non-sucking periods, in both REM and NREM sleep, infants using a pacifier had lower heartrate and higher vagal activity compared with those who did not have a pacifier.

Controlled crying

Controlled crying, or the practice of parents responding to their infant's crying at increasing time intervals, appears to be the most effective parental intervention. In at least one study, controlled crying effectively facilitated the infants' falling asleep by themselves (Hiscock & Wake, 2002).

Sudden infant death syndrome

SIDS is another major worry for parents. Rates have declined 55% between 1992 and 2001 (Malloy & MacDorman, 2005). Much of the decline has been related to the change from prone to supine (facedown to faceup) sleeping positions in infants, as now recommended by the American Academy of Pediatrics. Placing infants in a prone sleeping position has been an issue, since many SIDS infants were found sleeping on their stomachs. Pediatricians now recommend the supine position. In one survey, parents claimed to prefer (Borkowski, 2002) back or side sleeping positions for their infants at all ages. Results have shown (Gibson et al., 2000) that 72% of infants slept nonprone in 1997 compared with 32% in 1993 and 59% in 1994. Other risks for SIDS (Blair et al., 2005) have been associated with the infant's being "small at birth," being placed in the side position for sleeping, co-sleeping, or being a routine pacifier user and not having one for the last sleep.

One of the problems relating to SIDS, despite parent positioning, is that infants change position while sleeping. For example, in one study (Togari et al., 2000), the number of infants who rolled over from the back to the stomach position was greater than those from the stomach to the back.

Another problem related to the prone position is elevated heart rate. In at least one study, reported baseline heart rate was elevated in the prone compared to the supine position in quiet sleep at 2 to 3 weeks and 5 to 6 months, and in active sleep at both time periods (Tuladhar et al., 2003). The prone sleeping position is also associated with a shift in EEG activity toward slower frequencies (Sahni et al., 2005). These changes may be related to decreased arousal in the prone position and, in turn, increased risk for SIDS.

Another potential explanation for the incidence of SIDS at 4 months is the waning of the respiratory occlusion reflex. Present at birth, this reflex serves as an initial defense against smothering (Lipsitt, 2003). Infant reflexes wane after learned responses are acquired. During this transition, for the first couple of months some babies may be especially vulnerable if they do not have the defensive behaviors needed to prevent occlusion (obstruction), such as turning the head away or swiping at any occluding material. In a study using computed tomography (CT) scans, airway occlusion was noted behind the base of the tongue in 89% of infants when placed prone with the head down, in 84% when placed prone with the head rotated to the side, and in 18% of infants in the supine position (Rambaud et al., 2004).

Still another possibility is the overheating experienced during co-sleeping. A higher rectal temperature has been reported for infants who were monitored sleeping with their parents versus those sleeping alone (Ball, 2002). Despite this problem and the problem of suffocation already noted, the prevalence of co-sleeping in a recent large sample was 47% (Alexander & Radisch, 2005).

Brazelton Neonatal Behavioral Assessment Scale

Soon after birth, typically on the first or second day, newborns, at least in research hospitals, are given the Brazelton Neonatal Behavioral Assessment Scale. This test involves showing the infant, or exposing him to, a number of items, including habituation items (primitive learning), orientation items (social interaction), motor maturity items (or motor tone or motor movement), autonomic stability and state regulation items (which involve the newborn's ability to remain or return to calm, alert states), reflex items (which reflect nervous system integrity), and depression and excitability items (which tap the newborn's mood states and activity level). The order in which these are administered can be seen in Table 3.1.

Habituation

The habituation items are given when the baby is in a sleep state. First a flashlight is shone on the baby's face for a couple of seconds, and the baby is observed for movements. The flashlight stimulus is presented for 10 trials or fewer, until the baby no longer startles or makes any

Table 3.1: *Items on the Brazelton Neonatal Behavioral Assessment Scale*

Habituation
Flashlight
Rattle

Bell
Pin prick

Orientation
Inanimate visual (ball)
Inanimate auditory (rattle)
Inanimate visual & auditory (rattle)

Animate visual (face)
Animate auditory (voice)
Animate visual & auditory (both)

Reflexes
Ankle clonus
Plantar grasp
Babinski
Passive movements (arms & legs)
Pull-to-sit
Standing
Walking
Placing

Incurvation
Crawling
Glabella
Rooting
Sucking
Nystagmus
Tonic neck deviation
Defensive movements
Tonic neck reflex
Moro reflex

movements. A similar series of 10 trials is performed using a rattle (a small plastic box of popcorn kernels) and a bell. The final habituation series is performed with a toothpick, which is poked into one of the newborn's heels to elicit a startle or a foot-withdrawal response. This, too, is repeated until the newborn stops moving. Typically, the newborn awakens following the toothpick trial and becomes alert, which is a good state for him to be in when the orientation items are used.

Orientation

The orienting items include an inanimate visual stimulus, that is, a red ball that is moved across the infant's field of vision from left to right, and then from up to down, and then around through a 180-degree arc, to see if the newborn will follow it. For the inanimate auditory stimulus, the bell or rattle is shaken on each side of the baby's head to see if the baby will turn to locate the sound. The animate face stimulus involves the examiner moving her face, just as the red ball was moved across the newborn's field of vision. Talking to the baby on each side of his face to see if he will turn in the direction of your voice is called the auditory animate stimulus. The face and voice stimulus is typically the most powerful of the stimuli, as the examiner animates her face and voice as she moves her face again from side to side, up and down, and around. This sequence is typically done on the examiner's or parent's lap with the infant in a face-to-face position, and with the infant's head supported in one hand.

Reflexes

The rest of the exam involves reflex items, again in a predetermined sequence. Starting with the infant in a supine position in the bassinet or crib, first the researcher tests the foot reflexes. The foot grasp, or plantar grasp, is elicited by placing a finger at the base of the newborn's toes, which results in the toes curving around the examiner's finger. The second foot reflex is called the Babinski, which is the spreading or fanning of the toes as the examiner scratches the outside of the sole of the foot from the little toe to the heel.

Some reflexes indicate neurological problems, which highlights the diagnostic value of this assessment. Dorsiflexion of the great toe and fanning of the remaining toes as early as the first month of life is an early diagnostic sign of spastic cerebral palsy (Zafeiriou et al., 1999). In this study, plantar responses were examined in 204 high-risk infants, of whom 58 developed cerebral palsy, 22 had developmental retardation without motor disturbance, and 124 were normal at a follow-up examination at 3 years of age. Twenty-one of the 49 infants with various types of spastic cerebral palsy demonstrated dorsiflexion of the great toe with fanning of the remaining toes as early as the first month of life.

The examiner then performs passive movements of the infant's lower and upper limbs. This involves grasping both the baby's arms and pushing them into flexion, and then extending or pulling them down straight alongside the baby's body, and observing how much the limbs snap back into flexion. The same is done with the legs. A weak reflex here would involve very little movement back into the flexed position, and a strong reflex would involve considerable resistance of the newborn to the extending of the arms and legs.

This is followed by the palmar grasp, which involves the examiner placing her index fingers on the palms of each of the newborn's hands and feeling the tightness of the newborn's grasp. Typically, the normal reflex is a grasp that is tight enough to pull the infant to a sitting position, which is the next part of the Brazelton assessment. As the baby is pulled to a sitting position, the examiner looks to see if the head flops backward or the newborn attempts to bring the head to an upright position.

The next maneuver is to hold the infant under the armpits and lift her into a standing position to elicit the placing reflex, which involves the infant placing her feet on a flat surface as she is lifted. The examiner then stands the infant on her feet and leans her slightly forward for the walking, or stepping, reflex. The newborn shows her walking reflex by placing one foot in front of the other. One group of investigators showed that practicing the walking (stepping) reflex led to earlier walking (Zelazo et al., 1972). Other researchers expressed concern, however, that practicing reflexes would interfere with other developing functions, such as language.

The newborn is then placed in a prone position and watched to see if he will make crawling movements (another reflex), or at least free his head and arms to a position where he can rest and breathe easily. The newborn is then tested for incurvation, which involves the examiner moving a finger down first the right and then the left side of the infant's spinal cord and noting whether the infant's buttocks move to the side of the spinal column that the finger is lightly stroking (as in a hula dance motion).

Then the infant is taken into a cradled position, and the glabella reflex is tested. This involves lightly tapping the forehead between the newborn's eyes to see if she blinks. Next, the rooting reflex is tested. The examiner touches the corner of the newborn's mouth to see if the infant turns reflexively in the direction of the examiner's finger, as if turning to suck on the finger. Placing a finger in the newborn's mouth will elicit the sucking reflex.

The newborn is then checked for nystagmus and tonic neck deviation. The examiner holds the infant in a face-to-face position, with her hands under the infant's armpits and gently swings the infant to the right and to the left. The infant is observed for head movements and eye movements which should occur in the direction in which the examiner is moving the infant.

The newborn is then laid on her back, and the tonic neck reflex is tested. The examiner moves the newborn's face to the right side, so the right side is against the bed clothing, and the newborn typically assumes the fencing position with the left arm coming up close to the head, and the right arm extended out from the body.

The next is the defensive movement reflex. For this reflex, the examiner applies a piece of the newborn's bed sheet or towel across the top half of the infant's face, not including the nose, but covering the top half of the face. The newborn will typically make movements including arching the back, turning the head, and sometimes swiping at the cloth in an attempt to remove it. This is considered an important reflex for the prevention of sudden infant death syndrome.

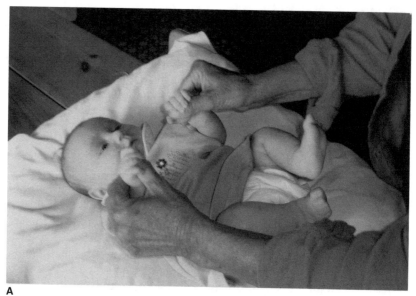

A

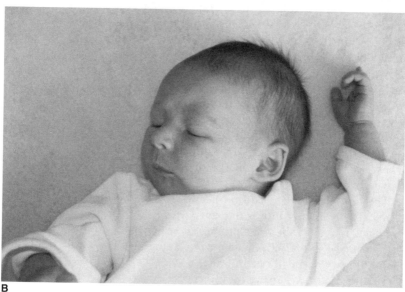

B

Figures 3.9a and b *Reflexes tested on Brazelton including Palmar Grasp/ Pull-to-sitting by Sarah (a) and Tonic Neck Reflex (fencing position) by Jes (b)*

Finally, the supposedly most aversive reflex maneuver is the Moro reflex. The examiner is holding the infant slightly off the surface of the bed, supporting the head with one hand and the back with the other. The hand supporting the head drops, and the infant's head falls about an inch. As the head drops, the arms stretch out and then come together as if to grab onto the examiner; this is called the monkey reflex, as it is the equivalent of a monkey's action when losing the front surface of the mother. The monkey grabs onto the chest region of the mother so as not to fall.

Many of these reflexes are active at birth, but disappear within the first few months. It is not clear why reflexes that are controlled by the midbrain develop, and then why they disappear. Some of them seem to have obvious adaptive value, such as the Moro reflex occurring if the infant begins to fall, so that the infant can still cling to the mother. The defensive reflex is also adaptive in enabling the infant to remove obstructing cloth. Reflex behaviors appear to be precursors of later voluntary behaviors, including the stepping and walking reflexes.

Organized behaviors

Throughout the Brazelton Neonatal Behavior Assessment Scale, the examiner is observing the infant for many behaviors that show organization and developing maturity. So, for example, the number of startles and the number of state changes are observed and recorded. The number of times the examiner needs to perform maneuvers such as holding and rocking to calm the infant and bring the infant to an alert state are also recorded.

The Brazelton Scale has been used in many studies to document the newborn's central nervous system integrity and response to social stimulation, and has been useful for differentiating the performance of infants with many different conditions, including preterm infants from full-term infants, and infants of depressed mothers from those of nondepressed mothers. The scale has also been very useful in predicting later development, such as the demonstration that optimal performance on the orienting items of the Brazelton is related to later social interaction behaviors of the infant, and motor performance predicts later motor skills.

The Brazelton has also been useful as a demonstration for parents so that they can understand their newborns' skills. We have adapted the Brazelton for use by parents in a scale called the Mother's Assessment of the Behavior of Her Infant (MABI) (Field et al., 1978). It is basically a demonstration of all the social items on the scale without the reflexes.

Summary

The perinatal period (from labor until the end of the neonatal period or the first month of life) is a brief, but very exciting period. The birth process is a time of real bonding for the parents, and the neonate is full of surprises, as can be seen in the next chapter on the senses. Parents worry about childbirth and about all the caregiving problems involving sleep disturbances and irritability. They also worry about the decisions that they make about how they are going to go through labor, how their baby is going to be delivered, whether they will breastfeed, and how and when their infants should go to sleep. Somehow these decisions appear to get made. The infant just goes on developing and becoming even more fascinating.

4

Being in Tune with the World (The Early Senses)

The Early Senses

The senses are presented here in the order of the earliest developing to the latest developing systems, starting with touch (and the related senses of temperature and pain), and moving to taste, smell, hearing, and visual senses (including perception of color, form, space, movement, and faces). Examples of the more complex intermodal perception (involving multiple senses at once) are also given. This chapter not only covers the most recent data on the different senses, but also provides many details on the research methods used to find out what infants perceive. The length of each section varies, as a reflection of the number of studies recently conducted on each sense. Many of the examples of research are taken from newborn studies to illustrate how skilled the infant is even from the first days of life.

Touch

The sense of touch is the first to develop in utero, and the most developed at birth. In evolution, virtually every animal's touch sense is the first to develop, so the newborn has already experienced significant amounts of tactile stimulation in utero. Fetal research has shown that as early as 3 months, the fetus will turn toward a tactile stimulus, much like a rooting reflex, and will respond to electrical stimuli and puffs of air that are even difficult for adults to discriminate (Humphrey, 1972; Jacklin et al., 1981). Despite these very sophisticated perceptual skills at as early as 3 months' gestation, the touch sense has been the most neglected.

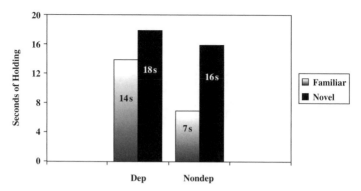

Figure 4.1 *Weight perception by infants of depressed and nondepressed mothers*

Although there is a term for touch perception, called haptic perception, very little research has been conducted in this area. Research by our group (Hernandez-Reif et al., 2000) suggests that touch discrimination by mouth and by hands occurs as early as the newborn period. Nipples with different textures (nubby versus smooth) can be discriminated by mouth and by hands. Using an habituation/recovery paradigm, the newborn showed haptic exploration by the mouth and by the hand, which gradually habituated. When the new texture was presented, there was a recovery response.

Haptic texture perception has also been investigated in 3-day-old infants using an habituation paradigm sequence with a smooth or granular object (Molina & Jouen, 2004). After holding the object, babies were given either the familiar or a new textured object. Two dependent measures were recorded: (1) holding time was used to assess habituation as well as reaction to novelty, and (2) hand pressure frequency exerted on the object was used to examine neonates' ability to adjust their manipulation to the texture of objects. Both measures revealed touch perception of the texture of objects.

Weight perception was also studied by our group (Hernandez-Reif et al., 2001). A light-weight (2 grams) or heavier-weight (8 grams) object (vial of cotton or pellets, respectively) was placed in the right hand of full-term newborns of depressed or nondepressed mothers. (See figure 4.1.)

After the infants habituated one weight by hand, they were tested with the opposite weight object. The infants of the depressed mothers did not respond to the novel weight, and only 15% of those infants showed hand movements that might have facilitated their perception of the object's weight (e.g., hand to mouth or face, turning/moving of the wrist or hand). In contrast, 78% of the infants of nondepressed mothers showed hand activity that might have facilitated weight perception, and as a group, they held the novel weight longer, suggesting that they had perceived the weight change.

Given the findings on newborn perception of weight, it was surprising to find that a French team was studying weight perception in much older (1-year-old) infants, although the authors not only showed the infants' weight perception, but they also demonstrated the infants' ability to adjust their hand manipulation of the weights (Molina & Jouen, 2002). Two dependent measures were recorded: (1) holding times in order to assess habituation as well as reaction to novelty; and (2) manual pressure exerted on the object, to investigate the infants' ability to adjust their manipulation to the object's weight. Both measures revealed infants' touch perception of weight.

Cross-modal or intersensory perception also occurs at the newborn period. Streri (2003) showed that newborns can visually recognize the shape of an object that they have previously manipulated with their right hand, out of sight. Newborns can extract shape information in a touch format and transform it into a visual format before they have had the opportunity to learn from the pairings of visual and touch experience. However, the same authors later showed (Streri & Gentaz, 2004) that this ability was absent when the left hand was involved.

Later, haptic habituation occurs for both hands (Lhote & Streri, 1998). Girls needed more time to habituate with their left hand than with their right hand, and they habituated more slowly than the boys did. Discrimination was also found for both hands and for both sexes. The infants' left hand retained better information on object shape than the right hand, and for both sexes.

Temperature

A related sense is the sense of temperature. Here virtually no research has been conducted with the newborn until recently, by our lab (Hernandez-Reif et al., 2003; 2004). In our study on temperature perception by mouth, we gave neonates of depressed and nondepressed mothers cold and warm nipples on alternating trials (Hernandez-Reif et al., 2004). Neonates of depressed mothers sucked twice as long as neonates of

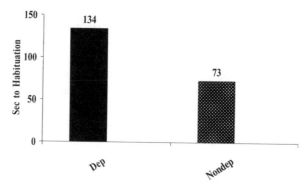

Figure 4.2 *Temperature perception by infants of depressed and nondepressed mothers*

nondepressed mothers, suggesting arousal, dysregulation, overactivity, or greater pleasure-seeking behavior in the newborns of depressed mothers. Although the newborns did not show a preference for cold or warm nipples, a temperature order effect revealed that neonates who received the cold nipple on the first trial, sucked significantly more on trials 2 through 8 than those who received the warm nipple on the first trial, suggesting that an initially cold nipple might elicit greater sucking.

In the study on temperature perception by hand, we gave newborns of depressed and nondepressed mothers cold or warm temperature tubes (vials containing cold or warm water) to hold in their hands (Hernandez-Reif et al., 2003). Both groups of infants habituated the warm and cold tubes, as indicated by a decrease in holding, and they showed dishabituation, as indexed by an increase in holding the new temperature tube. However, the newborns of depressed mothers (a) required twice as long to habituate; (b) showed a sensitization effect, meaning an increase in responding (holding the tube) from the second to the third trial of habituation; and (c) passively handled (not actively explored) the tube with their hand. (See figure 4.2.)

Pain

Still a third type of touch sense is the sense of pain. Most painful stimuli presented to the skin elicit a stress response as early as the newborn period (Diego et al., 2006). In an immune study, pain, as measured by the Premature Infant Pain Profile, was inversely related to immune cells, meaning fewer immune cells in those with greater pain (Rasmussen, 2001). Cortisol was also elevated and negatively related to immune cells, meaning fewer immune cells in infants with higher cortisol levels.

Gender differences have been observed in the pain response. In a study on cry sounds and cry faces in response to pain, gender differences were noted. Female infants cried louder than males, and their cries were higher pitched than those of males (Fuller, 2001). No gender differences were observed for facial expressions.

Pain has been measured by facial expressions and by physiological measures such as heart rate and transcutaneous oxygen tension (Diego et al., 2006; Fazzi et al., 1996). In this study, the painful stimuli included a routine blood test which elicited both facial grimacing and decreases in transcutaneous oxygen tension. In another heelstick procedure, facial expressions, behavioral states, and fussing were recorded (Wolf, 1996). Here, a developmental age difference was noted, with younger infants displaying fewer of these responses, and spending more time sleeping. Going into deep sleep following pain (for example, after a circumcision) is called the conservation withdrawal response, meaning that the infant withdraws into deep sleep to conserve energy. Stronger behavioral responses were accompanied by stronger heart rate responses to the heel-stick stimulus. Stronger behavioral and heart rate responses are, in turn, related to motor development in later infancy (Grunau et al., 2006).

Pain interventions

Touch can alleviate pain: for example, when the newborn sucks or stimulates the intraoral cavity, or is massaged. One of the theories for the effectiveness of touch alleviating pain is that tactile receptors are longer and more myelinated (more insulated), and they therefore can transmit a signal to the brain faster than pain receptors can. Pain receptors are shorter and less myelinated. The first received tactile message then "closes the gate" (a biochemical/electrical phenomenon), so the subsequently arriving pain message is not received. The adult analog is rubbing a bumped "crazy bone." This is called the "gate theory."

An illustration of the reduction in pain by sucking comes from a study in which we gave pacifiers to preemies during heelsticks (Field & Goldson, 1992). Nonnutritive sucking has also been used to alleviate pain during circumcisions (South et al., 2005). Other interventions to reduce pain have included the use of aromas such as milk and lavender (Kawakami et al., 1997). In the aroma study, newborns' responses to heelsticks were assessed using behavioral and physiological measures. The infants were randomly assigned to a lavender group, a milk group, or the control group. The control group showed a greater cortisol response than the two groups receiving the milk and the lavender. A familiar aroma during heelsticks also results in less crying and grimacing during the procedure (Goubet et al., 2003). Infants presented with an unfamiliar aroma or with no aroma during the heelstick had a significant increase in crying and grimacing.

Sucrose is another pain-alleviating substance. In a series of studies conducted by Elliott Blass and his colleagues, sucrose has been an effective pain-reducing substance, as judged by reduced crying in newborns following a heelstick (Blass, 1999; Blass & Shah, 1995). Sucrose has been compared to other substances such as water, and has been noted to be the most effective pain-reducer. Blass and his colleagues suggest that the sucrose releases endogenous endorphins (pain-relieving chemicals in the brain), and that seems to be independent of the dose of sucrose or the concentration.

In a study from our lab, infants who received water showed increased relative right frontal EEG activation from baseline to the postheelstick phase, a pattern that typifies negative affect (Fernandez et al., 2003). The EEG of infants in the sucrose group did not change. Heart rate increased rapidly in both groups during the heelstick phase. However, after the heelstick, the heart rate of infants who received sucrose returned to baseline, whereas the heart rate of infants who tasted water remained elevated.

Sucrose has also helped premature infants experience less pain during an eye exam (Gal et al., 2005). Examinations for eye problems related to prematurity are painful for the neonate. The use of a topical (surface) anesthetic for the eye examinations is routine in some neonatal intensive care units, but does not completely suppress painful responses. Sweet solutions were shown to reduce procedural pain in newborns. The addition of sucrose to topical anesthetic improved procedural pain control during the eye examination. Neonates were randomly assigned to receive treatment with either topical anesthetic plus sucrose, or topical anesthetic plus water (placebo) prior to the eye examination. In a subsequent eye examination, each baby received the alternate treatment. Pain was measured using the Premature Infant Pain Profile scoring system, which uses both physical and physiological measures of pain. The scores were recorded 1 and 5 minutes before and after the eye examination, and during initial placement of the eye speculum by two study nurses. The solution with sucrose was the most effective at alleviating pain.

When pacifiers and sucrose or dextrose were combined (Akma et al., 2002), sucrose followed by a pacifier resulted in lower pain scores and shorter crying time than dextrose when combined with a pacifier. Animal studies suggest that sucrose may involve opioids (naturally occurring substances in the bloodstream which have effects similar to those of opium), while rhythmic oral movements, as with a pacifier, increase the release of serotonin, which is involved in the blocking of painful stimuli (Lowkowski et al., 2003).

Positive effects also occurred following sucrose combined with holding. Crying, facial activity, heart rate, and vagal tone were measured before and after heelsticks for infants, who received water or sucrose with holding versus without holding (Gormally et al., 2001). Crying was reduced by sucrose and holding, and the interventions combined additively. The interventions interacted to reduce heart rate and lower vagal tone during the procedure.

The mother's heartbeat has also been used to reduce pain, as measured by a reduction in cortisol (Kurihara et al., 1996). In this study, the mother's heartbeat was compared to a Japanese drum. Cortisol decreased only during the mother's heartbeat. In another study by the same group, white noise and recorded heartbeat (not maternal heartbeat) sounds were presented to two different groups who were compared to a control group following heelstick stress. Both the heartbeat sounds and the white noise were presented at 85 decibels (i.e. at fairly loud volume). The control group showed more reactive behavioral responses and higher cortisol levels than the other groups. Thus, sounds, odors, and touch can alleviate pain as measured by cortisol, heart rate, and behavioral responses.

These interventions are critical inasmuch as repeated pain stimuli have been associated with long-term effects. The higher number of previous invasive procedures experienced since birth has been associated with dampened facial and heart rate reactions to a finger lance, and structural and functional changes in the brain and spinal cord occur with repeated painful experiences (Puchalski & Hummel, 2002). In addition, greater neonatal procedure pain exposure has been related to lower cortisol responses to stress and to lower facial (but not autonomic) reactivity to pain (Grunau et al., 2005).

Taste

The sense of taste is also well developed in the newborn, perhaps because of the significant experience with taste in utero. The amniotic fluid contains all the different tastes, including sweet, sour, salty, and bitter, and thus would provide the newborn with significant prenatal experience.

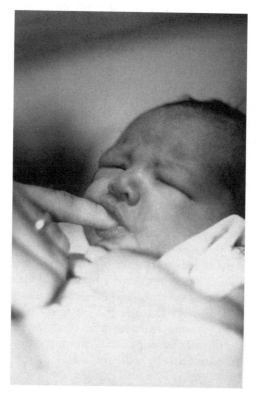

Figure 4.3 *Newborn tasting a bitter finger*

In several studies, newborns have been noted to make distinct facial expressions when they tasted the different sweet, sour, salty, and bitter solutions. The expressions are typically very similar to those of adults tasting the same solutions (Ganchrow et al., 1983). A smile occurs in response to sweet substances, puckered lips to sour, and disgust expressions to bitter. The newborn also shows preference for sweet solutions by sucking more rigorously (Crook, 1978). These facial expressions in response to these different tastes were replicated in a study by Rosenstein and Oster (1997). The authors coded newborn infants' facial responses to four tastes including sugar (sweet), citric acid (sour), sodium chloride (salt), and quinine (bitter). Their findings showed that newborns could distinguish the different tastes, which they interpreted as being an innate not a learned discrimination. (See figure 4.3.)

Steiner (one of the leading researchers on taste in newborns) and his colleagues (Steiner et al., 2001) have suggested that the taste of sugar elicits positive facial expressions in humans as well as other primates, whereas quinine elicits negative expressions. Expressions of human infants and great apes were more similar to each other than those of monkeys which was not surprising given that apes and humans are closer in evolution.

Smell

In a discussion of the underlying physiology of taste and smell, Bartoshuk and Beauchamp (1994) suggested that the acceptance of sweet, and the rejection of bitter, taste appear to be hardwired in the newborn, whereas emotional response to aromas depends much more on experience. With this hardwired versus experience interpretation, it would seem that these authors may have overlooked the fact that the newborns also had significant taste experience with the amniotic fluid in utero. This experience may simply result in the perception of taste stimuli before the perception of aromas.

Amniotic fluid also has odors that can be affected by the mother's diet (Menella et al., 1995). Despite unusual odors of the amniotic fluid, newborns can detect and prefer the amniotic fluid. They showed this when amniotic fluid was presented on one of the mother's breasts versus the other breast without the amniotic fluid (Barendi et al., 1997). Investigators had previously reported the newborns' ability to discriminate the breast pad of their mother from that of a stranger, and the odor of the milk from the mother's breast versus the milk from the breast of a stranger (Menella & Beauchamp, 1993). The research group at the Chemical Senses Center in Philadelphia (Menella, Beauchamp, & colleagues) has conducted many studies on both taste and smell by young infants. For example, in one of their studies, they presented infants different-scented toys. The infants showed a greater amount of time looking at the vanilla-scented toy versus an alcohol-scented or unscented toy.

In one of our studies, lavender was added to the bath oil for newborns (Field et al., 2001). The newborns who received the lavender, versus those who did not, spent more time in deep sleep and less time fussing, and their cortisol levels decreased following the exposure to the aroma. In a second study, we presented lavender and rosemary aromas to newborns on a cloth in a habituation paradigm (Fernandez et al., 2001). The newborns showed their discrimination of the two aromas, lavender and rosemary, by their different EEG responses to the different aromas. Like adults, they showed more relaxed, presleep-like EEG patterns during lavender than they did following rosemary, to which they showed more alerting EEG patterns.

In another study on EEG responses to aromas (Olko & Turkewitz, 2001), when positive smells were presented to the left hemisphere, neonates made significantly more head-turns toward the smell. This raises the possibility that approach behaviors may develop earlier than withdrawal behaviors. We demonstrated the EEG equivalent of approach behavior (shift to left frontal EEG) when we presented lavender to a predominantly right frontal EEG group of newborns (a slightly distressed group) (Sanders et al., 2002). The right frontal EEG group exhibited significant shifting to left frontal EEG activation, suggesting a positive approach response.

Aromas have also been used to reduce pain. For example, infants who smelled a familiar odor (their mother's milk or vanilla) cried and grimaced significantly less during the recovery phase compared with the heelstick phase (Rattaz et al., 2005). Infants who smelled their mother's milk exhibited significantly less agitation during the heelstick.

Sound, Voices, and Speech

Sound studies have been conducted as early as the fetal stage. At 36 to 39 weeks' gestation, the fetus discriminates tones on the musical scale (Lecanuet et al., 2000). In many studies (see Kisilevsky & Muir, 1991) fetal heart rate acceleration and fetal movement responses to hearing stimuli (recorded from ultrasound) declined over repeated trials and showed recovery to a subsequent new stimulus (a "vibroacoustic" stimulus). Also, recovery of the heart rate acceleration response (dishabituation) was observed on the first novel sound trial. Before and after birth, the magnitude of responses elicited by noise and vibration was significantly greater than that elicited by tones.

A number of studies have recently focused on newborn perception of different sounds. In one study, newborns were noted to differentiate various simultaneous streams of sound (Winkler et al., 2003). In another study, event-related potentials were recorded to frequently occurring (standard) sounds and to rarely occurring (deviant) sounds in a series (Ruusuvirta et al., 2003). Responses to deviants differed from those to standard sound, despite the fact that only the combination of sound frequency and intensity could be used as a cue for discriminating between these sound types.

In a study by the same group, sleeping newborns were presented a repeated tone carrying six common and six rare combinations of frequency, intensity, and duration (Ruusuvirta et al., 2004). Event-related potentials recorded from the infant's scalp were found to shift in amplitude toward positive polarity in response to rare combinations. Event-related potentials have been measured in newborns in response to duration changes in complex, harmonic tones known to elicit prominent mismatch negativity (MMN) response in adults (Cheour et al., 2002). Duration changes elicited prominent MMN responses in the newborns.

Speech sounds

The literature also features newborn responses to more complex stimuli like speech stimuli. Magnetic brain responses to speech sounds were measured in neonates (Kujala et al., 2004). The stimulation consisted of a frequent vowel sound with a steady pitch contour, which was occasionally replaced by a vowel with a steady pitch, or a vowel with a rising pitch, manifesting a change of intonation. The magnetic MMN response was obtained to the speech sound-quality change in all infants and to the intonation change in six infants.

The salience of speech stimuli is highlighted by "interaction synchrony" studies. Neonates and adults have been videotaped during interactions that show synchronous movements during speech and nonspeech (Austin & Peery, 1983). Although synchrony occurred during speech as well as nonspeech, it occurred more often during periods of speech. The duration of adults' movement was significantly shorter during speech and longer during nonspeech.

Discrimination of syllables has also been noted in newborns. The newborns demonstrated that they could discriminate syllables by, again, altering their sucking patterns (Moon & Fifer, 1990). The stimuli were two different syllables, and the reinforcers were a recording of the mother's adult-directed speech as well as quiet periods. During the final 6 minutes of the 18-minute session, 16 of the 20 infants showed bursts of sucking more frequently during the syllable that signaled the mother's voice, as opposed to the quiet period.

The Moon and Fifer (1990) study is probably one of the more sophisticated approaches to assessing speech discrimination. It followed a long history of research on different sucking models, starting with Soviet Union research documenting the Bronshtein Effect. This effect suggests that sucking could be increased or decreased by auditory stimulation (Moon & Fifer, 1990). Rachel Keene (1964) replicated the Soviet findings on sucking.

A number of studies using acoustic stimuli and various kinds of reinforcers for varying burst–pause sucking patterns were then conducted (Lipsitt, 1964; Sameroff, 1967). Syllable discrimination was studied using a sucking habituation procedure (Butterfield & Cairns, 1974). Operant learning paradigms were very effective with newborns (Cairns & Butterfield, 1975). In this paradigm, sucking after different syllables which would produce different types of music with voices either alone or with instrumental background music was more effective than instruments alone in affecting the duration of sucking (Cairns & Butterfield, 1975).

In a similar study on discrimination of consonant–vowel syllables, hearing event-related potential (ERPs) were recorded from various scalp regions of newborns in response to a series of nine consonant–vowel syllables. The ERPs recorded at birth predicted the verbal performance of these same children 5 years later (Molfese, 1997).

Different languages

Following on the syllable discrimination research (Moon & Fifer, 1990), researchers in Paris used a sucking procedure to test whether French newborns could discriminate lists of bisyllabic from trisyllabic Japanese words (Bertoncini et al., 1995). They documented that neonates could discriminate bisyllabic from trisyllabic words, and suggested that syllables are particularly salient units during the initial stages of speech processing. This processing was apparently independent of the language being heard by the neonate, in this case Japanese being heard by French newborns. In an infant-controlled habituation paradigm using, again, a sucking procedure, newborns were noted to discriminate lexical and grammatical words (Shi, 1999).

Despite infants' ability to discriminate bisyllabic and trisyllabic words in a foreign language, they appear to prefer their native language. This was demonstrated in a study (Moon et al., 1993) in which newborns whose mothers were speakers of Spanish or English were tested on audio recordings of female strangers speaking either Spanish or English. Infant sucking was used to control the language being presented. The infants sucked longer for their own native language than for the foreign language.

Even expressions of emotion are most preferred in the newborn's native language or the language the newborn was exposed to in utero (Mastropieri, 1996). This was shown by recording responses to different verbal emotions (happy, sad, angry, and neutral). Increased eye-opening was noted during happy speech as compared to the other emotional expressions. Infants born to Spanish-speaking mothers showed more eye-opening in response to happy vocal expressions in Spanish, and newborns of English-speaking mothers showed more eye-opening to the happy expressions in English.

Preference for the mother's voice

Starting in the early 1980s, a number of studies were conducted that demonstrated the newborns' preference for their mothers' voice. In a classic study already mentioned, newborns were presented with audiotapes of their mothers and other mothers reading the same Dr. Seuss story (DeCasper & Fifer, 1980). By varying the interval between bursts of sucking on a pacifier, an infant could trigger one or the other audiotape. In one group, the newborns were to shorten the intervals, and in the other group, the newborns were to lengthen them to produce their mother's voice. The newborns were able to produce their mother's voice by varying their sucking behavior, showing that they preferred her voice. This preference probably relates to fetal experience with the mother's voice. To demonstrate the effect of experience with the mother's voice prenatally, one group of pregnant women were asked to read the Dr. Seuss story *The Cat in the Hat* and another group to read a version in which the words "cat" and "hat" were replaced by "dog" and "fog" (DeCasper & Spence, 1986). The newborns showed a preference for the version of the story read to them in utero by again sucking on the pacifier either more or less vigorously.

In another study, newborns were noted to, again, prefer their mother's voice over unfamiliar voices, when presented voice samples in a nonnutritive sucking task. However, they did not prefer their mothers' whispered voices (Spence & Freeman, 1996). The newborns were noted to discriminate unfamiliar whispered voices, but those were not reinforcing for the newborns.

That newborns prefer their mother's voice is perhaps not surprising, since the mother's voice is reported to be the most intense acoustic signal that has been measured in the prenatal environment. The newborn and the fetus both show heart rate deceleration in response to speech sounds (Fifer & Moon, 1994). However, this appears to be affected by gestational age, as shown by event-related potentials collected while infants listened to the mother's voice alternating with a stranger's voice (deRegnier et al., 2002). The age of the child correlated with the development of recognition memory for the mother's voice.

Similarly, ERPs were recorded at term postmenstrual age in preterm infants born at less than 32 weeks' gestation (Therien et al., 2004).

Because infants must be able to detect and discriminate sounds before recognizing them, two approaches were used to assess these functions. The first evaluated the detection and discrimination of speech sounds. The second tested recognition of the mother's voice compared with a stranger's. Different patterns of speech sound discrimination were noted in preterm infants compared with term infants. Maternal voice recognition did not occur in the preterm infants.

To investigate the neurophysiological mechanism related to the infant's preference for the mother's voice versus another voice, auditory event-related potentials (ERPs) were recorded in response to the mother's voice and a voice of an unfamiliar female at the age of 4 months (Purhonen et al., 2004). Stimuli were presented in intermittent and alternating trains of four identical stimuli (mother's voice or an unfamiliar voice). A negative "shift" occurred in response to the mother's voice after a fraction of a second. This suggested that the infants paid more attention to their mothers' voice compared to unfamiliar voices.

Vision

Although newborns have very sophisticated visual perception skills, many mothers are still surprised to see their newborns following the red ball or tracking the human face on the Brazelton Neonatal Behavior Assessment. Because of their surprise, one of the increasingly popular newborn procedures is performing the Brazelton Scale in front of the mother so she can appreciate her newborn's perceptual skills. The visual perception skills reviewed here include perception of color, form, space, movement, and faces. These would seem to be less developed because of lack of in utero experience, but even visual perception is well developed in the newborn.

Color discrimination

Newborns have shown color preferences by their visual fixations. They can discriminate red, green, yellow, and blue, although they look longer at blue and green objects than red ones of equivalent brightness, suggesting that they may be more sensitive to short-wavelength stimuli (Adams et al., 1986: Jones-Molfese, 1977). Studies using the habituation–recovery approach are less definitive with regard to color perception. In one study using a habituation–recovery approach with procedures to minimize brightness cues, newborns discriminated a red from a green stimulus, but failed to discriminate either of these from a yellow stimulus (Adams & Courage, 1995).

The newborns were then habituated to white squares of varying luminance, and tested for recovery of habituation to colored stimuli (Adams, 1995). The newborns discriminated yellow-green from white, but not blue-green or purple from white. These, however, were small stimuli, suggesting that the color discriminations may depend on a larger stimulus. Adams and his colleagues went on to assess the amount of purity or intensity needed for the discrimination of color stimuli to occur (Adams & Courage, 1998). The newborns were habituated to large white lights of varying luminance, and then they were tested for recovery of habituation to green, yellow, or red lights that varied in the level of their purity. The newborns discriminated the colored lights from the white lights, but only when the purity values exceeded those used with adults (Adams & Courage, 1998).

Stimulus configurations have also been used in which sharp edges were eliminated from color fields to test color discrimination by 4-month-old infants (Thomasson et al., 2000). The three edges used were black borders, a dark surround, or blurred edges around the color test field. In each case, red, green, and violet test fields were used. Although performance decreased when sharp chromatic edges were eliminated, the data suggested that young infants could make the color discriminations.

Infants respond categorically to color. But the nature of infants' categorical responses to color is not clear. To assess this question, two stimuli from the same color category were used with 4-month-old infants (Franklin et al., 2005). The infants fixated the target color when the background color was from the same category. But, like adults, infants were faster at fixating the target when the background color was from a different category.

Form discrimination

Discrimination of form has been studied by using two-line angles (Quinn et al., 2001). After habituation to a simple two-line angle, the newborns were then given a stimulus with a change of orientation but not a change in angle. The newborns were then familiarized either to an acute or to an obtuse angle, and they showed a visual preference for a different angle. Newborns have also shown discrimination of two-dimensional drawings of a triangle, cross, circle, and square (Slater et al., 1983).

Discrimination of movement or stimulus rotation has also been shown (Laplante et al., 1996). In an habituation–recovery procedure in which newborns were able to control the number of trials required to reach an habituation criterion, the newborns were habituated to a black and white Maltese cross rotating in either a clockwise or counter-clockwise direction. Following habituation, half the newborns were presented a Maltese cross rotating in the opposite direction (rotation change), and half were presented a Maltese cross rotating in the same direction (rotation the same). The newborns in the rotation change condition displayed a recovery of their visual fixations during three test trials given after the habituation trials.

Newborns' sensitivity to "optic flow" has also been assessed (Jouen et al., 2000), by placing the newborns inside a dark room and presenting a 10-second moving light pattern at seven different velocities. The newborn reacted with backward leaning of the head in ways that were related to the optic flow velocity.

Face perception

The face is visually very complex stimulus. It has fixed features (the mouth is always below the nose and the nose under the eyes). It has many contrasts (hair against face, eyes against forehead and cheeks). It is three-dimensional, and is always changing as facial expressions change and talking occurs and eyes are dancing.

Mother's face

Face perception has been the most popular area of research of the vision sense, and preference for the mother's face (Bushnell, 2001; 2003) requires very little exposure. Newborns show a preference for their mother's face versus that of a female stranger at 78 hours (Pascalis et al., 1995), at 49 hours (Bushnell et al., 1999), and, in our study, they showed that preference even as early as 45 hours (Field et al., 1984). (See figure 4.4.) In these studies, newborns showed a preference for their mother's face by looking longer at her face or by sucking harder for her face. They only appear to learn her face if they also hear her voice (Sai, 2005).

Gaze patterns of 6- to 26-week-old infants viewing a video of their mother's face showed greater gaze at the mouth and eye regions, even at the youngest age (Hunnius & Geuze, 2004). The newborn's ability to recognize a learned face was tested in still another model using three transformations; (1) a photo negative transformation, (2) a size change, and (3) rotation in the third dimension (Walton et al., 1997). The newborns were able to make all three discriminations.

Female versus male faces

Looking at face perception in general, investigators had used visual preference procedures to examine gender categorization of female versus male faces by 3- to 4-month-old infants (Quinn et al., 2002). Infants

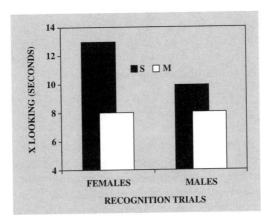

Figure 4.4 *Recognition of stranger's vs. mother's face by female and male newborns*

familiarized with male faces preferred a female face over a novel male face, but infants familiarized with female faces divided their attention to a male face and novel female face. Infants reared with male primary caregivers showed a preference for males. Infants reared with female primary caregivers displayed recognition memory for individual females, but not males.

Female and male faces were discriminated by 8-month-old infants, but not by 6-month-old infants (Yamaguchi & Masami, 2000). Six-month-old infants who were habituated to the female face looked consistently longer at the novel male face in test trials, but they did not look longer at novel female faces.

Faces of different races

Caucasian infants were habituated to a single face (Sangrigoli & De Schonen, 2004). Recognition was assessed by a novelty preference paradigm. The infants' recognition performance was better for Caucasian than for Asian faces. The results suggest that face processing in 3-month-olds may be race-experience dependent.

Silhouettes

Several investigators have examined the perception of specific properties of faces by infants. In an attempt to understand whether young infants can perceive faces from silhouettes alone, the familiarization–novelty preference procedure was used with 3- to 4-month-old infants who were presented silhouettes of cats and dogs (Quinn et al., 2001). The general shape or external contour of the head was enough for these young infants to form representations of cats and dogs.

Inversion effects

One of the most popular questions in face perception research involves the inversion effect. Do infants perceive the face when it is inverted? The face inversion effect was studied using a habituation procedure followed by a novelty preference test (Chiata et al., 2004). When infants were habituated to a face shown in a variety of poses and required to recognize a new pose of the same face, infants' recognition was greater for upright than for inverted faces.

Processing the face as a whole or as a collection of independent features was studied in 6-month-old infants exposed to two female faces and then tested on a familiar face, a switched face (consisting of all familiar features but a new combination of those features), and a novel face. In the upright condition, infants looked longer at the switched face than at the familiar face, whereas in the inverted condition, infants did not.

Event-related potentials have also been recorded to novel and familiar upright and inverted faces in 6-month-old infants (Webb & Nelson, 2001). Greater negativity responses were demonstrated for familiar faces and for upright faces.

Internal features

Internal features have also been the focus of face perception studies. In a study on internal features, 2- to 5-month-old infants were presented with adult females dressed in white laboratory coats until habituation occurred (Blass & Camp, 2004). The adult then left the room, and, one minute later, either she or an identically dressed woman entered the room. Looking time increased when the new adult with the same outfit entered the room. The infants used internal face features alone to see the differences in these two adults. Looking times increased when the adult entered the room even when the outer features of hair, ears, and neck were masked in the second, identically dressed adult. In another study, newborns discriminated face-like stimuli relying on their internal features (Turati & Simion, 2002). Although newborns used information about internal facial features in attractiveness preferences, when they were presented with facial stimuli, dynamic or static, they were able to attend to both internal and external facial features.

Still another set of studies focused on the internal features including different arrangements, and omitting features of the face. Using a head-turning procedure, newborns tracked moving stimuli containing face-like features and stimuli containing two eyes rather than a blank face (Easterbrook et al., 1999). When the stimulus contained a linear arrangement of facial features, one eye or one mouth, it was tracked less far. The newborns also turned their heads farther to a face compared to two eyes (Easterbrook et al., 1999).

Preferences were tested for faces with the eyes open and the same face with the eyes closed. The neonates spent more time looking at photographs with the eyes open than photographs with the eyes closed (Batki et al., 2000).

Spatial distances have also been altered by lengthening and shortening faces (Thompson et al., 2001). In a visual preference test, two versions of the same female face were presented, one lengthened or shortened, and one unmodified. Infants looked longer at the unmodified faces.

Attractive faces

The dimension of attractiveness has been studied by many researchers. Newborns and young infants spent more time looking at attractive faces when those were shown with unattractive faces. In this paradigm, each pair of faces has identical internal features (and different external features) or identical external features (and different internal features) (Slater et al., 2000). In the latter condition, infants looked longer at the attractive faces.

Another study on attractiveness familiarized infants with unattractive female faces (Ramsey et al., 2004), and familiarized another group of infants with attractive female faces. They then tested both groups of infants on novel faces from the familiar or novel attractiveness category. Results showed that 6-month-old infants categorized attractive and unattractive female faces into two different groups of faces.

Face–voice combinations

By 3 months, infants have learned which of several familiar voices goes with which face (Slater et al., 2003). In a face–voice procedure, 2- to 6-month-old infants were habituated to the faces and voices of two same-gender adults speaking, and then they received test trials where the faces and voices were synchronized yet mismatched (Bahrick et al., 2005). Four- and 6-month-olds, but not 2-month-olds, detected the change in face–voice pairing. Only the 6-month-olds showed matching and memory for the face–voice relations.

The ability of 3-month-old infants to learn the association between voices and faces was investigated by familiarizing each infant with two alternating stimuli presented on a video (Brookes et al., 2001). Each stimulus was a voice–face combination. On the postfamiliarization test trials of familiar and novel voice–face combinations, greater attention was paid to the novel combination.

Neural bases of face processing

A variety of tests have been used to understand face perception in infants. A group of French investigators (Tzourio-Mazoyer et al., 2002) studied the neural bases of face processing by mapping the brain activity of 2-month-old alert infants (with positron emission tomography as described in chapter 1) while the infants looked at unknown women's faces. The authors observed the activity of different cortical areas in the brain that largely overlapped the adult face-processing area of the brain.

Face processing is mediated largely by neural networks in the right hemisphere of the brain. When visually normal individuals were compared to patients who had received visual input from only one hemisphere during infancy, the data showed that early deprivation of visual input to the right (as opposed to the left) hemisphere severely impaired the development of face processing (Le Grand et al., 2003).

Cross-modal Integration

The use of several different models and several different modes of stimulation has highlighted the amazing perceptual skills of the newborn. As the field grows older, there seems to be more focus on even more sophisticated perceptual skills involving cross-modal integration, or the use of some or all of the senses at once. In this process newborns seem to have an innate ability to transfer information across tactile and visual and across visual and hearing modalities. Information from one modality that has been linked with information from another modality has been called intersensory redundancy and is thought to facilitate infants' learning (Bahrick, 2004).

In a study on intermodal integration, newborns were given an object to touch (either a small cylinder or a prism) by placing it in one hand (Streri & Gentaz, 2004). The newborns were prevented from seeing the object, and then on test trials they were shown pictures of the two objects side by side. On these trials they looked longer at the novel object that they had not previously touched, suggesting that they visually recognized what they had previously touched.

Using an auditory and visual stimulus paradigm, newborns were familiarized with toy–song pairs during an infant-controlled habituation procedure (Morrongiello et al., 1998). The newborns were then given a test to determine whether they had learned these sight–sound pairings. The results supported the conclusion that infants just a few hours old can learn sight–sound pairings. Even when the sound toys were moved to a new location, the newborns recognized that the sound was a characteristic of that toy.

The newborn's ability to learn visual–auditory associations was also investigated by familiarizing 2-day-old infants with two alternating visual stimuli (differing in color and orientation), each accompanied by its own sound (Slater et al., 1997). During the posthabituation trials, the newborn's attention recovered to a new visual–auditory stimulus. These examples are perhaps not surprising, inasmuch as most of the stimulation experienced by newborns is multimodal, or involves more than one sense.

In another study, the same research team familiarized 2-day-olds to two different, simple visual stimuli (a red vertical line and a green diagonal line) where each was accompanied by its own sound (Slater et al., 1999). In one condition, the sound was presented during the visual stimulus, irrespective of whether the baby looked at the visual stimulus or not. In the second condition, the sound was presented only when the baby looked at the visual stimulus (it turned off automatically when the newborn looked away, and turned on when she looked again). In this instance, each sound–sight pair was synchronized so that the baby either had both together or none at all. The newborns only learned the sight–sound combinations when the on/off presentation was synchronized.

Numerosity

It is not clear where the perception of number should be placed in this chapter in terms of the senses, but the newborn appears to show some perception of quantity. The concept of numerosity appears to be innate, inasmuch as infants, even in the first week of life, seem to discriminate visual information on the basis of numerosity (Butterworth, 2005). This skill becomes more sophisticated, of course, with development. Two experiments investigated numerosity discrimination in 6-month-old infants, comparing their performance on both large numbers (4 versus 8 elements) and small numbers (2 versus 4 elements) (Xu, 2003). For some unknown reason, the infants succeeded in discriminating 4 from 8 elements, but they failed to discriminate 2 from 4 elements. Although later math skills have been attributed to males, research on cognitive development suggests that males and females have similar abilities, leading them to develop equal talent in math and science.

Memory

Given the impressive perceptual skills of newborns, the question arises as to how much of what they perceive can they also remember. Recognition memory for visual stimuli is present even at birth (LaPlante, 1997). In the study described above, half the newborns were habituated to a stationary Maltese cross and half to a rotating Maltese cross. Following habituation and a delay period, the "habituated" Maltese cross was re-presented for three trials. The Maltese cross was then modified by the direction of rotation being reversed, and by the cross going from being stationary to rotating. These newborns retained that visual information for at least 2 minutes. Following the longer delay intervals, the first test trial appeared to "prime the newborn's long-term memory," so that the newborn successfully matched the habituated Maltese cross on the subsequent trials.

Postconceptional age and postnatal experience appear to affect neonatal recognition memory. Postconceptional age has been correlated with recognition memory for the mother's voice, for example, and postnatal experience has affected latency measures (deRegnier et al., 2002).

Social Perception

Perceiving stimulation using several different senses and with different senses at the same time is critically important to being in the social world. Some examples of the newborn's social perception are their ability to imitate and their empathetic responses to other newborns' cries.

Imitation

Imitation of facial expressions/actions by the newborn suggests that the newborn can match what it sees on someone else's face with some inborn knowledge of its own face to be able to use this match to make the expression (happy, sad, surprised) and action (tongue protrusion, mouth opening). Some suggest that this skill is innate and a form of social interaction (Metzoff, 2004).

Although the newborn's imitation abilities have been the source of continuing debate in the literature, dozens of studies have provided a database on the neonate's ability to imitate (see Heimann, 1999, and Maratos, 1998, for reviews). Two popular imitation paradigms are those of Meltzoff and Moore (1984), using mouth opening and tongue protrusions (infants sticking out their tongues), and Field et al. (1986), using happy, sad, and surprised facial expressions. (See figures 4.5A and 4.5B.)

Some have suggested that imitative behaviors are merely reflexive. For example, in a replication of the Meltzoff and Moore paradigm (Courturier, 1996), tongue protrusions and mouth openings were modeled for newborns; the newborns were also exposed to alternate trials of a passive face. The infants showed greater alertness during the modeled faces than the passive faces. In the tongue-protrusion condition, infants produced higher rates of tongue protrusion than mouth openings, but only in the modeled face, not the passive face trials. But in the mouth-opening condition, the rate of mouth opening was not greater than the rate of tongue protrusion, either during the modeled face or the passive face. The author interpreted these results as an "immediate stimulus-matching reflexive response that is restricted to tongue protrusions."

Empathy

Empathy is another impressive skill of the newborn. Infants as young as 18 hours old show distressed cries in response to another newborn's cry (Sagi & Hoffman, 1976), but less so to the sound of their own cry (Martin & Clark, 1982). In a more recent study, facial expressions and nonnutritive sucking rates were used to assess the newborns' discrimination of their own cry from other newborns' cry sounds (Dondi et al., 1999). The newborns were presented with either their own cry or the cry of another infant when they were awake. The newborns showed more distressed facial expressions and for a longer duration during the cry of another infant. In addition, their sucking decreased during the

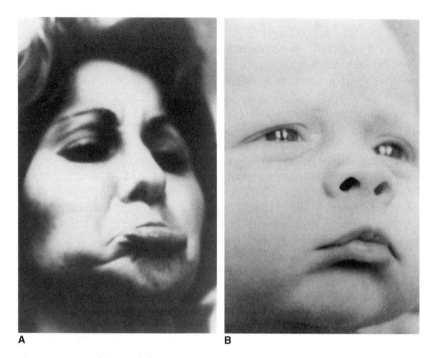

A   **B**

Figures 4.5a and b   *Sad face (a) imitated by newborn (b)*

other infant's cry. A similar result was shown in a second experiment during which the same conditions were presented, but during sleep. Although the responses were delayed and less intense during sleep, the newborns discriminated their own cry from that of another newborn. The greater distress response to the other newborn's cry was interpreted as an empathy response. We were unable to show that response in infants of depressed mothers (Field et al., 2006).

In a similar study, newborns were presented another newborn's distressed cry to both ears to determine if the distressed cry response was related to one or the other side of the brain in the newborn (Ragan, 1996). A highly significant effect was found for frequency, response duration, and latency to respond. Seventy-seven percent of the infants responded to the right-ear presentation of the other infant's distressed cry. Female infants also showed a significantly greater response to the right-ear presentation of the other infant's distressed cry. Thus, it appears that the ear response to distressed cries is specifically located in the right ear as early as the newborn period, and, again, was interpreted by the authors as an empathy response (Ragan, 1996).

Summary

In summary, these are some of the amazing perceptual skills of infants and some of the interesting paradigms for studying what infants cannot tell us verbally. As our technology has developed, we have been able to use more sophisticated measures (such as cortisol, EEG, and ERP). However, even the simplest measures, such as looking, sucking, and facial expressions, often converge with the more complex measures to yield the same results.

Although the different experimental models are rarely compared in the same study, as could be seen for the various methods of stimulating the infant, many of the different models were used by different investigators to yield very similar results. For example, in the face discrimination studies, at least eight different paradigms were used to assess the infant's preference for different faces. Other paradigms that have been most recently developed – including, for example, functional MRI – might tell us more about the underlying brain activity associated with these perceptional abilities. However, until these technologies are non-invasive and less expensive, the field will likely continue to use the approaches described here. They are simply tools for knowing what infants feel, smell, taste, hear, and see.

5

Body Talk with Parents and Others (Social Development)

Parent–infant interactions are the playground for infants learning social communication skills, including being responsive to each other and taking turns in conversation. Usually parents place themselves in a face-to-face position for interactions, and they simplify their behavior, as in "baby talk," or "motherese," exaggerating their facial expressions, and imitating their infant's behavior. The parents' and infants' behaviors become synchronous and attuned to each other. These dynamics can be interrupted if the infant interacts with a stranger, if the mother becomes still-face (has no facial expression), or if the mother or father is depressed. Interventions with interaction coaching can be helpful. The latest research on these topics is briefly reviewed in this chapter.

Face-to-Face Interactions

Mother–infant face-to-face interactions have typically been studied between 3 and 5 months when infants are most interested in their mother's face. Prior to that, mother–infant pairs are filmed during feeding interactions, which are not often studied, perhaps because many feeding interactions are breastfeedings, and are often considered relatively private interactions. After 5 or 6 months, infants are less interested in sitting face-to-face with adults and they are more interested in exploring objects (with their newfound fine motor skills), as well as the larger world, as they learn to crawl around.

Coding interactions

Mother–infant interactions are typically videotaped at home or in a lab, and then coded, using a rating scale or a time-sample coding of behavior, which involves checking off a list of behaviors every time-sample unit, for example, every 10 seconds. More elaborate, micro-analytic, continuous coding systems have also been developed for use with laptop computers.

Time-sampling and continuous coding systems have been compared for their reliability (Bornstein, 2002). Frequencies based on time-sampling and continuous coding were evaluated in this comparison. Time-sampling and continuous coding revealed different frequencies of infants' and mothers' behaviors across individuals and across cultural groups. However, the time-sampling adequately preserved the relative ranking of infant and mother behaviors among individuals and between cultural groups. The author concluded that if research is concerned with the relative standing of individuals and/or groups on frequency of infant or maternal behavior, then time-sampling and continuous coding yield comparable results.

Models for Mutually Responsive and Synchronous Interactions

Different models have been developed by different researchers to describe optimal mother–infant interactions. These include the mutual regulation model (Tronick, 1990) and the psychobiological attunement model (Field, 1985). In these models, mothers and infants are seen to be mutually responsive to each other and to achieve synchronous (i.e., matching) states, both behaviorally and physiologically. An example of studies demonstrating this phenomenon explored mutual regulation during the natural interactions of mothers and their 4-month-old infants (Van Egeren, et al., 2001). Close analysis of a wide range of behaviors and analysis of contingencies indicated that both mothers and infants communicated primarily through vocal signals and responses, although mother touching and infant looking also elicited responses. Mutual responsiveness between partners occurred mostly when the same behavior was observed for the mother and infant, for example mother and infant smiling. Interaction context consistently influenced mutual responsiveness. For example, less mutual responsiveness occurred when the infant was exploring or being held.

In another study on infants and mothers observed weekly in face-to-face interactions from 4 to 24 weeks, infants produced more speech-like sounds when their mothers were smiling, when they were looking at their mothers' faces and when the infants themselves were smiling (Hui-Chin et al., 2001). Infant speech-like sounds occurred most frequently during Duchenne smiling (cheek-raised smiling), which is thought to be more emotionally positive than non-Duchenne smiling (smiling without cheek-raise). And the infants produced more speech-like sounds following their smiling and gazing at mother, and after their mothers smiled.

Using the same sample of data, three patterns of mother–infant communication were classified including a symmetrical pattern (mutual engagement by mother and infant), an asymmetrical pattern (mother active while infant inactive), and a unilateral pattern (mother active while infant disengaged) (Hui-Chin, 2002). Two types of infant nondistress vocalizations were categorized including speech-like and nonspeech-like vocalizations. The rates of speech-like and nonspeech-like vocalizations were associated with symmetrical interactions and they were not associated with unilateral interactions. Speech-like vocalizations were more likely to occur during symmetrical mother–infant interactions.

Several robot studies have attempted to further explore the dynamics of early interactions. In a study between a robot and a human caregiver, the robot used expressive displays to modulate the interaction intensity, similar to the feedback from the infant to the parent during their early interactions (Breazeal & Scassellati, 2000).

Interaction Behavior and Heart Rate

The relationship between behavior and heart rate was also studied during the same mother–infant interaction study (Hui-Chin, 2002). A 4-minute baseline EKG was collected from the infant, and the subsequent 15-minute mother–infant interaction was videotaped and coded for patterns ranging from symmetrical patterns to disruptive patterns. Infant vagal tone was associated with more symmetrical patterns.

A relationship between social stimulation and increased heart rate has been interpreted as increased arousal (Field, 1985). Infants are noted to look away when aroused. In a dissertation study, 2-month-old infants participated in a social interaction, while their heart rate, movement, and gaze direction were recorded (Huntington, 2001). Five minutes of uninterrupted interaction was followed by two 10-second periods of interruptions where the adult looked down and away from the infant. Both movement and heart rate tended to decrease over the course of the first 5 seconds. Before the end of the interaction, the infants' activity and heart rate tended to increase and continued to do so immediately after the interaction ended. These results suggest that increased motor activity may play a role in shifting the infant's attention toward or away from the adult. When the interruptions occurred, the infants responded with decreased activity, increased heart rate, and increased gaze. After the end of the interruptions, both activity and gaze increased, and heart rate decreased, suggesting that the interruptions were arousing for the infant. Activity and heart rate were related, with activity consistently leading heart rate.

Interactions and Later Development

Many studies have reported relationships between early interactions and later cognitive development. For example, in a study conducted at 6 months, mothers and infants were observed during an interaction which was coded for degree of reciprocity and engagement, and at 12 months, infant cognitive skills were assessed (Poehlmann & Fiese, 2001). Responsive and engaging interactions at 6 months significantly predicted higher cognitive scores at 12 months.

Because the mothers' behaviors may impact their infants' social, cognitive, and language development, researchers have explored predictors of maternal play. In a longitudinal study, mother–infant pairs were followed from age 5 to 20 months to determine how infants contribute to their mother–infant interactions (Dixon & Smith, 2003). The habituation rates of 5-month-olds and difficult temperament of 13- to 20-month-old infants were found to predict maternal play quality at 20 months. These data support the possibility that mothers adjust some of their interaction behavior to accommodate their infant's cognitive abilities and temperament.

Still-face Interactions

The still-face interaction, during which the mother is asked to remain "still-faced" and quiet, is known to be disturbing to infants based on their behavioral and physiological responses (see Adamson & Frick, 2003, for a recent review). In a recent study, mothers and 3-month-old infants were observed during still-face interactions (Moore & Calkins, 2004). The mothers' and infants' matching behavior states were coded, and infants' heart rate and vagal tone were recorded. Infants who showed the greatest increases in negative affect and heart rate and decreases in vagal tone during the still-face showed less positive affect, lower vagal tone, and less behavior state matching during the spontaneous and reunion (after the still-face) interaction periods. (See figure 5.1.)

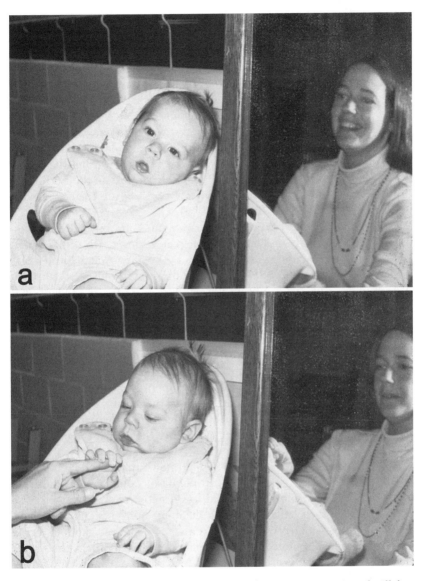

Figure 5.1 *Spontaneous face-to-face mother–infant interaction (a); and still-face interaction (b)*

Other individual differences have been noted during still-face interactions, including heart rate differences (Haley & Stansbury, 2003). In this study, heart rate was monitored in 5- and 6-month-old infants during a modified still-face procedure. Infants of more responsive parents showed greater regulation of heart rate and negative affect during the procedure than infants of less responsive parents.

In a variant of the still-face procedure, infants' and mothers' gaze was monitored during three segments of face-to-face interaction, including a live interaction segment alternated with a video replay of the previous segment (Nadel et al., 1999). The mother's behavior during the replay was, of course, not related to the infant's behavior. As in the traditional still-face, the infants showed negative emotions during these disturbed interactions (Stormark & Braarud, 2003).

In another variant of the still-face paradigm, 3-, 6-, and 9-month-old infants interacted face-to-face with a female stranger, who interrupted the ongoing interaction with 30 seconds of happy and neutral faces (Striano & Liszkowski, 2004). The 3- and 6-month-olds showed negative responses, but the 9-month-olds showed no response, suggesting a developmental transition by the end of the first year.

In still another variant of the still-face paradigm, 4-month-old infants either saw and heard their mother, only saw their mother, or only heard their mother interacting with them (Striano & Bertin, 2004). Only those infants who observed their mother's face become still showed a negative response. These findings provide further support that it is the mother's still-face not her silence that contributes to the still-face effect. And 6-month-old infants showed less negative affect when the parent gazed at the infant versus when the parent gazed above the infant (Delgado et al., 2002).

We conducted a similar study with depressed mothers and their infants (Field et al., 2005). As compared to infants of nondepressed mothers, infants of depressed mothers showed less negative change (less increase in frowning) in their behavior during the noncontingent replay segment. This finding was interpreted as the infants of depressed mothers being more accustomed to noncontingent behavior in their mothers, thus experiencing less violation of expectancy in this situation. In a comparison between depressed infants seeing their mothers' still-face versus their mothers moving behind a screen (still-face versus separation), no differences were noted in their behavior (Field et al., 2006).

The negative effects of the still-face experience can be long-lasting. Twenty-month-olds who had participated in a still-face procedure at 5 months, looked away from the face of the person who had shown the still face significantly more than the faces of two other novel persons

(Bornstein et al., 2004). Toddlers who had interacted with a stranger in the still-face condition just once when they were infants apparently retained a memory of that experience into toddlerhood.

Infants At Risk for Disturbed Interactions

A number of different groups of infants and parents are at risk for difficult or disturbed interactions because of responsivity problems in the infants and/or parents. Some of these, including preterm infants and depressed mothers, have been the focus of many interaction studies. Twins might be considered at risk because of the mother's necessary division of time for their interactions. One study on twin–mother interactions, however, suggests that mothers tended to treat both infants similarly regardless of infant behavior (DiLalla & Bishop, 1996). When the twins were 7 and 9 months of age, mothers spent 2.5 minutes alone with each infant. Mothers tended to treat both children similarly, regardless of their being identical or non-identical, suggesting that maternal characteristics drove the mother–infant interactions. Even though identical twins were more similar on some measures than fraternal twins, mothers tended to treat both types of twins comparably regardless of infant characteristics or behaviors.

Short Maternity Leave

Mothers who are noted to be at risk because they had shorter leaves from their jobs compared with mothers who had longer leaves were observed to express less positive affect, sensitivity, and responsiveness during interactions with their infants in at least one study (Clark et al., 1997). The aim of this study was to assess the association between the length of maternity leave and the quality of mother–infant interactions. Employed mothers of 4-month-old infants were interviewed and videotaped in their homes during feeding time. Shorter length of leave had more negative effects on the behavior of the mothers during their interactions with their infants.

Preterm infants

For preterm infants, early interaction disturbances have been reported by many. In one study the preverbal behaviors of preterm and full-term infants were compared at age 4 and 7 months (Brown & Ruder, 1995).

Six randomly selected minutes of each dyad were analyzed for occurrences of preverbal behaviors including facial expressions, gestures, looking behaviors, touching, and vocalizations. Preterm infants showed fewer gestures and vocalizations, and less eye contact and touching. Mothers of preterm infants showed more gestures and fewer vocalizations during mother–infant interactions. Preterm infants of "controlling" mothers have worse personal–social development and hearing–speech development than infants of "cooperative" mothers (Forcada-Guex et al., 2006).

Preterm infants with BPD

Infants at even greater risk are preterm infants with bronchopulmonary dysplasia (lung disease) (Jarvis et al., 1989). In this study, these more serious lung-disease infant–mother pairs had less optimal interactions than respiratory distress syndrome pairs or healthy preterm infant–mother pairs. Mother–infant interactions were coded from videotapes of teaching sessions at 4 and 8 months (corrected for prematurity). These results demonstrated the importance of severity of illness, not only for health status, but also for mother–infant interactions.

Mothers who score high on the Minnesota Multiphasic Personality Inventory (MMPI)

Those mothers who score high on this inventory on Hysteria, Paranoia, and Ego Control tend to have less favorable interactions (Kaeller & Roe, 1990). This study assessed 3-month-old infants and their mothers. Mothers and a female researcher took turns talking to the baby for 3 minutes, and infants' vocal responses were recorded. Mother–infant behaviors were recorded for 30 minutes following the 3-minute interactions. High MMPI scores on Hysteria, Paranoia, and Ego Control were associated with less favorable mother–infant interactions, and high scores on the Femininity and Ego Control scales were related to infants' low vocal response scores.

Depressed Mothers and Infants

For the last few decades, researchers have been studying the interactions of depressed mothers and their infants. The mother's flat expressions, limited intonation, and unstimulating behavior, and the infant's limited interest and responsiveness make their interactions difficult. Unfortunately, the incidence of maternal postpartum depression is increasing. In primarily white middle-income populations, approximately 15% of mothers experience depression (Chaudron et al., 2005). Among Hispanic mothers, 23% reported high levels of depressive symptoms. Only half the women experiencing these symptoms had identified themselves as needing help with depression. In one survey, US-born black women had an odds of depression that were 2.9 times greater than African-born women and 2.5 times greater than Caribbean-born women (Miranda et al., 2005).

Cross-cultural differences exist not only for the incidence of depression, but for the symptoms of depression. In one study, relative to Caucasian Americans, African Americans reported less pessimism, dissatisfaction, self-blame, and suicidal feeling, and a greater sense of punishment and weight change (Ayalon & Young, 2003). Self-dislike was a stronger manifestation of depression in Caucasian Americans, and sleep disturbance, loss of appetite, and loss of libido were stronger symptoms of depression in African Americans. Group differences were not accounted for by marital status, age, or education.

Sleep disturbances are the most common symptom for depressed mothers, a symptom that affects interactions with their infants (Thase, 2000). Sleep disturbances are important because the same neurotransmitters that affect mood, interest, and energy also affect sleep. Sleep disturbances may be responsive to treatment with some antidepressants, and they may be worsened during treatment with other antidepressants. In a study by our group, sleep disturbances in postpartum depressed women were related to low levels of serotonin (Field et al., 2006).

Excessive sleeping has also been reported by depressed mothers (Wolfson et al., 2003). In this study, mothers who developed symptoms at 2 to 4 weeks (the most common time for postpartum symptoms), reported more total sleep time at the end of pregnancy in comparison to those mothers who reported fewer depressive symptoms. Although 2 to 4 weeks is the must common time for postpartum depression, some experience depression during pregnancy (as was already discussed in chapter 3), and that would affect their first interactions with their newborn, as well as contribute to dysregulation in their newborn.

Bonding with the infant is a serious problem for depressed mothers. On a new, simple, eight-item self-rated mother-to-infant bonding questionnaire designed to assess the feelings of a mother toward her new baby (Taylor et al., 2005), there was a strong correlation between the bonding scores at 3 days and at 12 weeks. Those with high depression scores at 3 days had worse bonding scores in the first few weeks.

Early breastfeeding is also negatively affected by maternal depression (Field et al., 2004), with fewer depressed mothers breastfeeding, and those who do having problems or stopping breastfeeding earlier. It turns out that breastfeeding might at least help their infants experience less physiological disorganization. In a recent study, already described, depressed mothers who had stable breastfeeding patterns were less likely to have infants with highly reactive temperaments (Jones et al., 2004). In addition, their infants did not show the negative EEG patterns typically noted for infants of depressed mothers.

Breast milk is affected by the depression and by the related fatigue and stress factors, even though breastfeeding may be therapeutic for both the depressed mother and her infant. A recent study on breastfeeding explored relationships between fatigue, depression, stress, and infection in the postpartum period (Groer et al., 2005). A sample of breastfeeding mothers were seen at 4 to 6 weeks postpartum, and they completed fatigue, mood, and stress scales as well as a maternal and infant infection checklist. Morning blood and milk samples were collected. Fatigue was correlated with symptoms of infection in both mothers and babies and with stress and depression. The data suggested that fatigue, stress, depression, and infection were related in postpartum mothers, and that these relationships extended to serum hormone levels in their breast milk.

Neonatal behaviors are affected by maternal depression if the mother's depression is chronic. The disorganization we had observed in newborns of depressed mothers including less optimal performance on the Brazelton Neonatal Behavior Assessment, greater right frontal EEG asymmetry and reduced vagal tone (Jones et al., 2004), may contribute to the disturbed sleep, colic, and difficult temperament reported later (Dennis & Ross, 2005). In a study on Barbadian mothers and their infants, for example, maternal depressive symptoms were associated with difficult temperament including decreased infant adaptability, reduced approach, negative mood, and an increased sensory threshold (Galler et al., 2003). Infants of depressed and anxious mothers were also more resistant to change and preferred constancy.

Difficult temperament and colic, which often appear around 3 to 6 months, might be expected to negatively affect mother–infant interactions. In a study on colic, moderate to severe depressive symptoms were reported by 45% of the mothers of infants with colic (Maxted et al., 2005). More severe depressive symptoms in the mothers were related to fussy/difficult infant temperament.

Depressed mothers are less sensitive

The depressed mother's contribution to the newborn's problems are that depressed mothers are less sensitive to newborn cues and less responsive.

In a study in which depressed women rated tape recordings of a newborn infant's hunger cry (Schuetze & Zeskind, 2001), the cries were rated on four perceptual items (e.g., arousing/not arousing), and the depressed women also completed six caregiving items (e.g., cuddling during feeding). Depressed women had more difficulty discriminating the different types of infant cries, the cries were less likely to elicit caregiving, and the depressed women were less responsive to the highest pitched cries.

Infant-directed speech is also affected by maternal depression. Depressed mothers, for example, make longer statements or show a longer mean length of utterance (MLU) and less simplified or less infant-directed (ID) speech or baby talk. In a study on MLU, mothers reporting depressed mood were matched with nondepressed mothers on age of baby, sex of baby, educational status of mother, and parity (number of pregnancies) (Reissland et al., 2003). The mothers were video- and audiotaped in their homes while reading a book to their infants. Nondepressed mothers had a shorter MLU for younger babies in comparison with older babies, while depressed mothers showed no difference on their MLU. Depressed mothers spoke with a lower pitch and less modulation in their pitch, in comparison with nondepressed mothers. Depressed mothers used less exaggerated speech rhythms than is typical of ID speech.

In a study on 4-month-old infants, infants of nondepressed mothers readily learned that their mothers' speech signaled a face, whereas the infants of depressed mothers failed to learn that their mothers' speech signaled a face (Kaplan et al., 2002). Infants of depressed mothers did, however, show strong learning in response to speech produced by an unfamiliar, nondepressed mother. These outcomes indicate that the reduced perceptual salience of depressed mothers' infant-directed speech could lead to deficient learning.

In one of our studies (Field et al., 2005), behavioral responses were assessed in 3- to 6-month-old infants of depressed mothers placed face-to-face in front of a mirror versus in front of their mother. The infants showed more positive behavior (smiling) with their mother versus the mirror, but they also showed more negative behavior (gaze aversion, distress brow, and crying) toward their mothers versus the mirror. Infants of depressed mothers showed less gaze aversion with their mothers, perhaps because their mothers were less interactive. When in front of the mirror, the infants of depressed mothers vocalized more and gaze averted less than the infants of nondepressed mothers, suggesting that the mirror was particularly effective in eliciting vocalizations in infants of depressed mothers.

Depressed Mother–Infant Interactions and Later Development

Even interactions later in infancy (15–18 months) have been notably affected by maternal depression (Edhborg et al., 2001). Toddlers of mothers with high depression scores showed fewer attention skills in a free-play situation, and they were more likely to be classified as having an insecure attachment to their mothers.

Later developmental consequences of having a depressed mother include having elevated cortisol and lower performance on IQ scales as a preschooler. Stressed children with elevated cortisol had a history of high maternal cortisol exposure in infancy (Essex et al., 2002). Maternal depression beginning in infancy was the most potent predictor of children's cortisol. Preschoolers with high levels of cortisol exhibited greater mental health symptoms in first grade. In an older sample, maternal depression during the child's first 2 years of life was the best predictor of elevations in stress (cortisol) at age 7 years (Ashman et al., 2002). This is perhaps not surprising, inasmuch as research suggests that disruptions in early caregiving can have long-term effects on the body's stress system, the hypothalamic–pituitary–adrenal (HPA) axis, which mediates the cortisol response.

Children of depressed mothers are also at increased risk for developing internalizing problems and cognitive deficits in part because of impaired mother–infant interactions at 6 months postpartum (Milgron et al., 2004). Children's IQ scores were lower at 42 months of age. These effects were explained by lower maternal responsiveness at 6 months. Similarly, difficult temperament was apparent in the infants of depressed mothers. Male infants (compared to females) of depressed mothers were disproportionately vulnerable to impaired cognitive abilities.

Withdrawn and Intrusive Depressed Mothers

Depressed mothers have different interaction styles, and notably are withdrawn or intrusive (Field et al., 2006). In one of our studies, we compared intrusive and withdrawn mothers' ratings of their own interaction styles with their infants (aged 3 to 6 months), and the behaviors of videotaped models of intrusive and withdrawn mothers (Jones et al., 2001). Withdrawn mothers rated themselves as less withdrawn than the model withdrawn mother. Intrusive mothers viewed themselves as more intrusive than the model intrusive mother. Both groups viewed their own infants as more outgoing than the infants of the model intrusive and withdrawn mothers. The withdrawn mothers reported feeling more distressed when they observed an infant (of an intrusive or withdrawn mother) crying, suggesting that they felt more empathy toward the crying infant than the intrusive mothers.

Another study reported associations between maternal intrusive behavior and toddler inhibition, and nonsocial behaviors at age 4 suggesting that intrusive maternal behavior is damaging (Rubin et al., 2002). In contrast, when 1-year-old infants of intrusive and withdrawn depressed mothers were compared by our group, infants of intrusive mothers were noted to be more exploratory and perform better on mental development assessments (Hart et al., 1998).

Not all depressed mothers have intrusive or withdrawn interaction styles. Many have "good" interaction styles. In one of our studies comparing these different-style mothers (Field et al., 2003), all depressed groups scored higher on depression and anxiety scales and had similar elevated stress hormones including cortisol, norepinephrine, and epinephrine during pregnancy. The depressed mothers and their newborns also had greater relative right frontal EEG activation. Despite these group similarities, the infants of the "good interaction" mothers did not show high amounts of indeterminate sleep, and they received better scores on the Brazelton Scale. The more organized behaviors of the newborns may have contributed to the better interaction ratings of the "good interaction" depressed mothers.

Depressed Mothers with Comorbid Diagnoses

Depressed mothers with comorbid diagnoses (additional mood disorders that occur simultaneously like anxiety) have been noted to have difficult interactions. For example, in one study, maternal depression predicted less optimal mother–infant interactions and insecure infant attachment. However, this "depression effect" was accounted for by mothers with comorbid anxiety (Carter et al., 2001). The comorbid depressive symptoms were associated with later behavior problems and lower competencies for boys, and the quality of early interactions predicted behavior problems in the girls.

In a study we conducted, depression in mothers was comorbid with anxiety and anger. In this study (Field et al., 2004), depressed mothers with high and low anxiety, and depressed mothers with high and low anger, were compared on their spontaneous interactions with their 3-month-old infants. The high- versus low-anxiety mothers spent less time smiling, showing exaggerated faces, gameplaying, and imitating, and

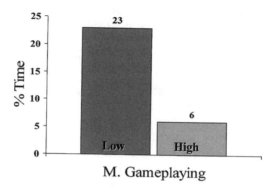

Figure 5.2 *High-anxiety mother gameplaying with infant*

more time moving their infant's limbs, but equivalent amounts of time speaking and touching. The infants of high- versus low-anxiety mothers spent less time smiling and more time showing distress brow and crying, but spent equivalent amounts of time showing other behaviors (speaking, motor activity, gaze aversion, and imitation). The high-anger versus low-anger mothers differed in the same ways that the high-anxiety mothers differed from the low-anxiety mothers. However, the infants of high- versus low-anger mothers differed on all behaviors (less time spent smiling, speaking, and showing motor activity and imitation, and more time spent showing distress brow, gaze aversion, and crying), suggesting that the comorbidity of depression and anger in the mother had the worst effects. (See figures 5.2 and 5.3.)

Mothers with panic disorder also experience interaction problems. In one study (Warren et al., 2003), panic disorder mothers displayed less sensitivity toward their infants, and they reported having parenting problems concerning infant sleep and discipline. Infants with panic disorder mothers, in turn, had higher cortisol levels and more disturbed sleep.

Intervention Studies

The increasing number of interaction disturbance studies have highlighted the need for early interventions. Several have been tried including "infant psychotherapy" and interaction coaching, various alternative

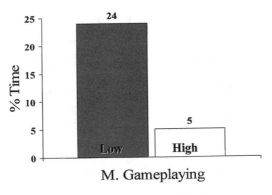

Figure 5.3 *High-anger mother gameplaying with infant*

therapies like massage and music, and even the natural therapy of having a nondepressed father around. In an "infant psychotherapy" study, mothers and infants participating in two infant–mother psychotherapeutic interventions were followed 6 months after treatment ended (Cohen et al., 2002). One treatment was an infant-led psychotherapy called "Watch, Wait, and Wonder" that was focused on the interaction behaviors of the infant. The other was a more traditional mother–infant psychodynamic psychotherapy focused more on the mother's feelings about mothering. Positive effects were observed from the beginning to the end of treatment in both groups, including infant symptoms and parenting stress. Mother–infant interactions were also improved at a 6-month follow-up session. Decreased maternal depression, gains in infant cognitive development and emotion regulation, and improved infant–mother attachment security were observed only in the "Watch, Wait, and Wonder" group.

Interaction coaching is a set of techniques that has been used to improve mother–infant interactions, first with preterm and postterm infants (Field, 1977) and more recently with depressed mothers and their infants (Field et al., 2004). Examples of the interaction coaching techniques are giving the mothers an instruction to "imitate" their infants, which is intended to slow down mothers who are overstimulating, or asking the mothers to "keep their infant's attention," which is intended to increase the mother's stimulation. Imitation has been successfully used with intrusive mothers, and attention-getting has been effective with withdrawn mothers in a study by our group (Malphurs et al., 1996).

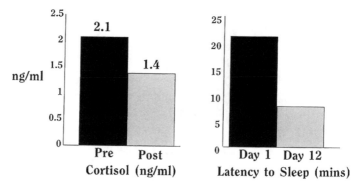

Figure 5.4 *Lower cortisol and shorter latency to sleep by infants of depressed mothers receiving massage from their mothers*

Another technique is second-by-second interaction coaching by a bug-in-the-ear speaker, with the coach giving immediate feedback and suggestions to the mother on modifying her behavior.

In a recent review on interventions for depressed mothers, nine studies that met study criteria were examined (Dennis et al., 2004). The interventions studied included antidepressant medication, estrogen therapy, critically timed sleep deprivation, and bright light therapy. All of these were noted to be effective. Massage therapy has also been effective. Touch is one of the most neglected forms of stimulation during mother–infant interactions. In a dissertation on touch (Stepakoff, 2000), depressed mothers engaged in less affectionate touch, and more object-mediated touch, than nondepressed mothers.

We conducted a study having depressed mothers massage their infants (Field et al., 1992). This intervention resulted in lower depression and cortisol levels in the mothers, and better sleep, less irritability, and lower cortisol levels in the infants. (See figure 5.4.) In another study, we explored the music effects on EEG in intrusive and withdrawn depressed mothers with depressive symptoms (Tornek et al., 2003). Rock music was more effective than classical music in moving the EEG in a positive direction (i.e., toward left frontal EEG activation).

In still another study, we targeted adolescent mothers with depressive symptoms for early intervention (Field et al., 2000). A "dysregulation" profile was noted in the infants of depressed mothers, including lower

Brazelton scores, more indeterminate sleep, and elevated norepinephrine, epinephrine, and dopamine levels at the neonatal period, and greater right frontal EEG activation, lower vagal tone, and negative interactions at the 3- and 6-month periods. A group of maternal variables from the neonatal and 3-month assessments accounted for 51% of the variance in the mothers' continuing depressive symptoms. These variables included greater right frontal EEG activation, lower vagal tone, and less positive interactions at 3 months, and elevated norepinephrine, serotonin, and cortisol levels at the neonatal stage.

In the second part of that study, a similar sample of mothers with and without depressive symptoms was recruited and followed to 3 months. Those symptomatic mothers who had values above (or below) the median (the middle of the curve on the predictor variables identified in the first part of the study) were then randomly assigned to an intervention or a control group at 3 months. These groups were then compared with each other, as well as with the group without depressive symptoms, at 6 and 12 months. The intervention, conducted from 3 to 6 months, consisted of free daycare for the infants and a rehab program (social, educational, and vocational) plus mood instructions and massage therapy. Mother–infant interactions significantly improved, and the mothers' biochemical values and vagal tone normalized. Their infants also showed more positive interactions, better growth, fewer pediatric complications and normalized biochemical values, and by 12 months, their mental and motor scores were better than those of the infants in the control group.

Fathers

One of the best therapies may be the presence of a nondepressed father. In one of our studies, fathers were able to compensate for the negative effects of depressed mothers on early interactions (Hossain et al., 1994). The infants' interaction behaviors improved with their nondepressed fathers. In a Swedish study (Edhborg et al., 2003), infants of depressed mothers showed less persistence in play with and less joy in reunion after separation from their mothers than infants of nondepressed mothers. In contrast, most fathers in the families where the mothers were depressed seemed to have joyful relationships with their infants and secure attachments 15–18 months postpartum, as if the father "compensated" for the mothers' depressive symptoms.

Another study investigated whether father involvement in infancy may reduce or exacerbate the effects of maternal depression on infants' behavior problems (Mezulis et al., 2004). Father involvement was associated with lower internalizing behaviors.

Unfortunately, many fathers are also depressed. In an Australian study, for example, 20% of mothers and 12% of fathers were significantly distressed at mid-pregnancy (Morse et al., 2000). In a Norwegian study, psychological distress was reported by 37% of the mothers and 13% of the fathers a few days after childbirth (Skari et al., 2002). Severe intrusive stress symptoms were reported by 9% and 2% of mothers and fathers, respectively. In an American study (Goodman, 2004), the incidence of paternal depression ranged from 1% to 26% in community samples, and from 24% to 50% among partners experiencing postpartum depression.

When both parents were affected, their offspring had the highest risk of major depression, anxiety disorder, and alcohol dependence, and the earliest age of onset for major depression (Foley et al., 2001). The highest risk of conduct disorder and drug dependence occurred in the groups where only the father was affected and where only the mother was affected, respectively. Mother's Major Depression Disorder (MDD) was a stronger predictor of Major Depression Disorder in male compared to female offspring. Father's Major Depression Disorder was a stronger predictor of MDD in female compared to male offspring.

In a Finnish study (Mantymaa et al., 2003), the father's psychiatric problems predicted high internalizing and externalizing problems in the children such as depression and behavior problems, and the mother's psychiatric problems before pregnancy predicted high externalizing (behavior problem) scores in the child at 2 years. Mother's hostility and/or intrusiveness during early mother–infant interactions predicted high externalizing scores. In one study (Marmorstein et al., 2004), depressed mothers tended to partner with antisocial fathers. Depression in mothers and antisocial behavior in fathers were both significantly and independently associated with offspring depression and conduct disorder. In other studies, paternal depression at 1 month postpartum was significantly related to internalizing and externalizing psychopathology in the offspring at 2 to 3 years (Klein et al., 2005; Ramchandi et al., 2005). Finally, when maternal and paternal depression were combined, they had an additive effect on externalizing disorders in adolescents (Foley et al., 2001). Thus, paternal depression during infancy appears to exacerbate the effect of maternal depression. However, this effect may be limited to depressed fathers spending moderate to high amounts of time caring for their infants (Harjan, 1992).

Fathers have been relatively ignored in the early development of infants. Even at birth, they hold a special relationship with their infants. An Australian research group found that the earlier fathers held their babies, the

A   **B**

Figures 5.5a and b *Different carrying styles of fathers of different cultures: (a) Romania, (b) Africa (photo by Regina Yando)*

sooner they reported feelings of warmth and love for them (Sullivan, 1999). In a dissertation study on fathers' touching behavior, fathers touched the infant's back, torso, shoulder, and face most frequently (Goebel, 2002). Patting, contact without movement, and lifting were the fathers' most common tactile actions. Approximately half of fathers' touch was of moderate intensity, while an equal percentage of strong and light intensity touch was used. Only 10% of fathers' touch was nurturing, involving kissing, hugging, or caressing the infant. These findings suggest that fathers have different patterns of touch than those of mothers.

To determine the responsiveness of new fathers and nonfathers toward infant cues, a group of Canadian researchers exposed fathers and nonfathers to infant cries and to non-cry sounds. They measured emotional response, heart rate, and saliva testosterone (male hormone) and cortisol as well as plasma prolactin (female hormone) responses prior to and after the cry presentations (Fleming et al., 2002). They found that fathers hearing the cry stimuli felt more sympathetic and more alert compared to groups who did not hear the cries or to nonfathers who heard the cries. Fathers and nonfathers with lower testosterone levels had higher

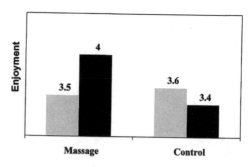

Figure 5.6 *Increased enjoyment observed in fathers after massaging their infants*

sympathy and/or need to respond to the infant cries than fathers with higher testosterone levels. Fathers with higher, as opposed to lower, prolactin levels were also more alert and more positive in response to the cries. Fathers hearing the cry stimuli showed a greater percentage increase in testosterone than fathers not hearing the cry. Experienced fathers hearing the cries showed a greater percentage increase in prolactin levels. These results indicated that, as with a number of other species, human fathers are more responsive to infant cues than are non-fathers, and fathers' responses to infant cues are related to both hormones and to caregiving experience.

In one of our studies (Cullen et al., 2002), we examined the effects of fathers giving their infants massage. Infants were given massages by their fathers for 15 minutes prior to their daily bedtime for 1 month. By the end of the study, the fathers who massaged their infants were more expressive and showed more enjoyment and more warmth during play interactions with their infants. Although the massage-group fathers did not change in their overall caregiving time, the control-group fathers spent significantly less time caregiving by the end of the study. (See figure 5.6.)

Summary

These, then, are some of the infants' early social experiences with their parents. At around 3 to 6 months, face-to-face interactions with parents are critical for infants learning communication skills such as turn-taking in conversations. Disruptions of the interactions, such as when the mother is asked to remain still-face, lead to negative behavior and stressful physiological responses in the infant. If the mother or father are chronically "still-faced," as in maternal or paternal depression, serious cognitive and behavior problems may occur. Among those who have naturally disturbed interactions are high-risk infants such as preterm infants and high-risk parents such as depressed mothers. Fortunately, researchers are exploring interventions that can alleviate the effects of disturbed interactions. Interaction coaching and alternative therapies like music and massage have been effective, along with natural therapies like having a nondepressed father around when the mother is depressed. What becomes clearer with increasing research in the dance of early interactions is that "it takes two to tango:" both the parent and the infant.

6

Being Emotional
and Temperamental
(Emotional and Personality
Development)

Emotional development covers a broad range of phenomena including, for this chapter, *perceiving emotional expressions, displaying emotional expressions, empathy, imitation,* and *temperament.* These are present from birth, as in neonatal imitation and empathetic responses by newborns to the cries of other newborns. Some are born "poker-faced" (unexpressive), and others, at the extreme opposite, can be described as "wearing their heart on their sleeve" (very expressive). The different facets of emotional and personality development are interrelated, and develop together over infancy.

Discrimination of Faces and Emotional Expressions

Mothers' and strangers' faces can be discriminated from birth, as was noted in chapter 4 above (Field, 1984; Hernandez et al., 2004). However, apparently the different facial expressions (happy, sad, and angry) are not differentiated by the infant except in the mother's face. In a study on 3-month-old infants' ability to discriminate different faces, infants alternately viewed their mother and father and an unfamiliar face of a woman and man portraying expressions in an intermodal preference task (Montague & Walker-Andrews, 2002). The infants looked differently at their mothers' expressions, but did not differentiate their fathers' or unfamiliar adult facial expressions.

EEG responses to mothers' and strangers' faces

In one of our studies (Diego et al., 2004), EEG (brain waves) was recorded in response to mothers' and strangers' mock facial expressions (happy, surprised, and sad) during a peek-a-boo game for 3- to 6-month-old infants of depressed and nondepressed mothers. The infants of depressed mothers exhibited less positive and more negative emotion, and were less likely to look at the facial expressions displayed by both their mother and a stranger. The infants of depressed mothers also showed greater relative right frontal EEG asymmetry (the depressed withdrawal EEG pattern) than the infants of nondepressed mothers throughout the different expressions of the mothers and strangers. Finally, the infants of depressed mothers showed higher stress hormone (cortisol) levels after the session. Both groups of infants showed significantly greater right frontal EEG activation during their mothers' and stranger's sad versus happy expressions. In addition, infants showed greater right frontal EEG asymmetry during the stranger's surprised versus happy expression.

A similar study was conducted by our group with infants of depressed intrusive and withdrawn mothers (Diego et al., 2002). When intrusive and withdrawn mothers with depressive symptoms modeled happy, surprised, and sad expressions, their 3-month-old infants did not show different responses to these expressions or show EEG changes. When a stranger modeled these expressions, the infants of intrusive versus withdrawn mothers looked more at the surprised and sad expressions and showed greater relative right EEG activation. These findings suggest that the infants of intrusive mothers with depressive symptoms showed more differential responding to the facial expressions than the infants of withdrawn mothers. Increased cortisol levels suggested that they were also more stressed by the facial expression sessions.

Making faces

Seven facial expressions are universal, including *happy*, *sad*, *surprised*, *angry*, *afraid*, *interested*, and *disgusted*. The necessary musculature for these expressions first appears at 3 months' gestation (Humphreys, 1972). Neonates clearly can smile, frown, and look surprised, based on the neonatal imitation of facial expressions shown by our group (Field et al., 1985).

Smiling is one of the first expressions to occur. Parents often think that newborns are showing "gas" smiles, although these are probably facial-expression-like grimaces that are merely triggered by changes in arousal. The smile becomes more reliable around 2 or 3 months.

"Duchenne" and non-Duchenne type smiles have received the lion's share of attention lately. The Duchenne smile is a full smile that is sometimes called a "felt" smile. It includes the bilateral raising of the lip corners and the raising of the cheeks. It is called the Duchenne smile after the nineteenth-century French anatomist, who defined the expression as pure joy (Carvajal & Iglesias, 2001). The literature generally suggests that the Duchenne smile emerges in the first or the second month of life. In a recent videotaped collection of preterm infant faces, however, a sophisticated coding system called baby FACS revealed that the Duchenne smile occurred even as early as the newborn period, with a similar intensity and duration as that of older infants and adults (Dondi et al., 2004).

In a study in which infants were observed weekly from 1 to 6 months of age, smiling without cheek raising or mouth opening occurred more often than periods without smiling, both when the mothers were smiling and when the infants were looking directly at the mothers' faces (Messinger et al., 2001). Duchenne smiling occurred more often than non-Duchenne smiling when the mothers were smiling. Open-mouth (play) smiling occurred more often when the infants were looking directly at their mother's faces. Duchenne smiles and play smiles occurred together when the mothers were smiling and when infants were looking at their mothers' faces.

Smiling soon leads to laughter, at around 6 months. These expressions are assumed to reflect feelings of pleasure and joy. Laughter sometimes increases the infant's arousal level to such a degree that mothers are seen to lessen their stimulation to calm them down.

Crying also occurs from birth. Typically, crying increases until about 2 months, and then gradually decreases. Crying has been known to occur approximately 2 to 3 hours per day during the first few months, with crying peaking typically in the evening hours (Fabes & Martin, 2000). Cry sounds can communicate different conditions, including a hunger cry, a pain cry, or an anger cry. Crying is generally interpreted as infant distress or anger. Key sources of frustration can lead to infant anger, including any kind of restraint of their movements, taking away toys, and general frustration or instances where they are thwarted in doing something they want to do.

The emotions of anxiety and fear typically emerge later in the first year at around 9 months. Infants show these emotions when their parents are leaving (as in separation anxiety) or when they are being approached by a stranger (stranger anxiety). These emotions not only appear on the face, but are often accompanied by crying and clinging to the parent. Separation and stranger anxiety tend to occur more in infants who are carried by their mothers and do not have daycare experiences. Both of these anxieties appear to decrease in the middle of the second year.

Other emotional expressions such as fear appear slightly later. In a Hungarian study, infant girls showed fear expressions earlier than boys

(3 versus 4 weeks) (Nagy et al., 2001). Facial expressions are also discriminated earlier by girls (Field, 1985).

Anger has been demonstrated as early as 4 to 5 months during frustration situations (Sullivan & Lewis, 2003), but it is usually studied at later ages. Anger faces seem to differ across individual infants, rather than being universal like the smile. Anger is sometimes accompanied by elevated stress hormone (cortisol). For example, when 15-month-old infants were confronted with a stranger and with a frightening robot, higher cortisol levels occurred in more anger-prone infants (van Bakel & Riksen-Walraven, 2004).

Shame, guilt, pride, and jealousy are nonbasic emotions that do not emerge until the second year of life (Draghi-Lorenz et al., 2001). Shame, guilt, and pride have received very little attention, but several studies have been conducted on jealousy. Jealousy may occur earlier than previously thought (Hart et al., 1998). In this paradigm, infants are seated next to their mother, who is given a book to read or a doll to hold. Twelve-month-old infants typically respond to their mothers holding a doll (but not the book) with rage and attempts to physically remove the doll. More recently, Hart has shown this jealousy reaction even as young as 6 months.

Emotion regulation

Emotion regulation is the ability of infants to control their emotional reactions (see Fox, 1994. for a review). This ability is considered critical for infants to interact with their world. Although parents provide significant amounts of control in the early months, infants also have their own self-regulatory behaviors, such as sucking on their hands, rocking, and other self-soothing behaviors.

Empathy

Empathy may be considered an emotional state. Although many would claim that empathy develops much later, a rudimentary form of empathy occurs in the newborn. In many studies on newborn cry sounds, the newborns have shown differential distress responses to their own and other newborns' cry sounds. They show more facial distress at the sounds of other newborn cries than their own (Dondi et al., 1999). We have preliminary findings that this is less true of infants of depressed mothers (Field et al., 2006).

Figure 6.1 *Newborn Tory imitating my surprise expression on our sailboat*

Imitation

Newborns have shown imitation of facial actions such as tongue protrusion and mouth widening (Meltzoff & Moore, 1977) and imitation of facial expressions such as happy, sad, and surprised faces (Field et al., 1982). (See figure 6.1.) These findings have been replicated by many others, suggesting that neonatal imitation is a robust phenomenon. Newer studies, using slightly different stimuli and paradigms, confirm this skill in newborns. For example, in a study on auditory–oral (hearing and speaking) matching behavior, newborn infants were presented with the consonant sound /m/ and the vowel sound /a/ – an early form of vocal imitation (Chen et al., 2004). Auditory–oral matching behavior by the infant was defined as showing the mouth movement appropriate for producing the model sound just heard (mouth opening for /a/ and mouth pursing for /m/). Infants showed significantly more mouth opening after /a/ models than after /m/ models, and more mouth pursing after /m/ models than after /a/ models.

In another study, newborns spontaneously produced previously imitated gestures while waiting for the experimenters' response (Nagy & Molnar, 2003). Imitation of gestures was accompanied by heart rate increases, while the initiation of gestures by the infant was accompanied by heart rate decelerations (usually accompanying attentiveness). The heart rate direction differences suggest that infants are not only capable of imitating, but they also know the difference between imitating and being imitated.

Another variation is presenting visual–auditory incongruities for imitation, in this case, speech without sound (as in mime), or sound heard without lips moving (as in ventriloquism) (Lebib & Baundonniere, 2000). Three-month-old infants were more imitative when the visual and acoustical stimuli were presented together. The mime was more disturbing for the infants than the ventriloquist.

Imitation occurs naturally during mother–infant interactions. Infants from Greece and Scotland were observed interacting with their mothers and fathers at home every 2 weeks, from the second to the sixth month of life (Kokkinaki, 2003). Direct matching of expressions preceded, accompanied, and followed imitation. This coordination was the same in Greece and Scotland, and for parents and infants of both sexes.

Giving mothers an instruction to imitate their infants has been very effective at slowing them down (being less overstimulating) and making them more contingently responsive during early interactions with their infants (Field, 1977; Malphurs et al., 1996). Affect attunement and imitation were compared cross-culturally in mother–infant pairs from Sweden and the former Yugoslavia during the first year of life (Jonsson et al., 2001). Imitation and age were inversely related (i.e., the greater the age, the less the imitations), but affect attunement was positively related to age. Affect attunement was noted as early as 2 or 3 months. By 6 months, affect attunement occurred more frequently than imitation. The amounts of imitation and affect attunement were similar cross-culturally and across gender. The authors concluded that imitation is the most important process during the earliest months, but that affect attunement occurs earlier than previously thought.

Various facilitators of imitation have been studied, for example, praise and face-to-face live models versus TV models. Modeling and praise effects on infant imitation were studied (Poulson et al., 2002) using a motor-with-toy, a motor-without-toy, and vocal responses. The percentage of maternal models that were matched by the infant within 6 seconds increased following the model-and-praise treatment condition.

In a TV study, an adult modeled a series of actions with novel objects, and the infant's imitation of those actions was assessed either immediately or after a 24-hour delay (Hayne et al., 2003). Some infants watched the demonstration live, while others watched the same demonstration on a prerecorded videotape. Both 24- and 30-month-old infants imitated the actions modeled on TV. Their imitations were better when they watched the live demonstration.

Imitation has been a controversial issue for many years, and in many research studies. Several investigators have now documented the emergence of imitation very soon after birth. At least one investigator continues to fail to reproduce the results of these studies. For example, in a recent study using peer and adult video models for infant imitation, no effects of modeling were seen at 13 or 23 weeks of age (Abravanel & DeYong, 1997). This was not surprising inasmuch as we have reported that imitation decreases across early infancy and then reemerges later in infancy as deferred imitation (Field et al., 1986). In a study comparing peer and adult models, videotapes of a peer and an adult modeling tongue protrusions and mouth opening/closing were shown to infants at 13 and 23 weeks, and no imitation of the peer occurred at either age (Abravanel & DeYong, 1997). The only imitation observed was imitation by 12-week-old infants of tongue protrusions modeled by the adult.

Several theories have been advanced about the mechanisms involved in infant imitation. According to Meltzoff, one of the leading imitation researchers (Meltzoff & Decety, 2003),

> both developmental and neurophysiological research suggest a common coding between perceived and generated actions. Mechanisms involved in infant imitation provide the foundation for understanding that others are "like me" and underlie the development of theory of mind and empathy for others. Imitation recruits not only shared neural representations between the self and the other, but also cortical regions in the parietal cortex that are crucial for distinguishing between the perspective of self and other.

Greater similarity between identical versus non-identical twins on neonatal imitation

To determine the degree to which differences at birth are inherited in neonatal abilities to imitate facial expressions, identical and non-identical twins were given the face discrimination–imitation procedure in which a model presented a series of happy, sad, and surprised facial expressions and the infants' looking and facial expressions were coded (Field, 1989). For the database in general, the analyses revealed more matching within the identical pairs than within the

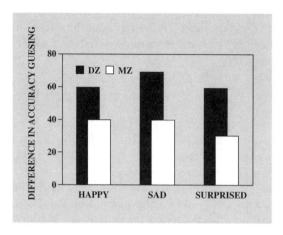

Figure 6.2 *Newborn twin imitations of facial expressions with identical (MZ) twin imitations being more similar than those of fraternal (DZ) twins*

non-identical twin pairs. The difference scores for looking between individual infants within twin pairs were greater for the non-identical twins than for the identical twins. Similarly, on a 5-point expressivity rating, a greater difference was observed in expressivity between infants belonging to the non-identical versus the identical twin pairs. There was a similarly greater discordance between the non-identical twins for the measure of accuracy with which the model's facial expressions could be guessed by looking at the expression on the neonate's face. This was suggested by differences in the percentage of discordance between infants within twin pairs on whether or not their expressions were accurately guessed. These data suggest that individual differences in imitative behavior at birth are innate or inherited. (See figure 6.2.)

Temperament

A considerable body of research has accumulated on infant temperament. This literature has focused on genetic and environmental determinants of temperament, on the use of temperament as a predictor for later development, on the physiological measures of temperament, and on temperament factors that place infants at risk.

Temperamental characteristics such as activity level, shyness, inhibition, and difficult temperament are commonly thought to be inborn traits. In one of our earliest studies, we noted that newborns could be placed along the same continuum as described for adult temperament by Eysenck (Field, 1982). This continuum was called internalizer–externalizer or introverted–extroverted. Some newborns were noted to be poker-faced, but at the same time physiologically reactive. Those newborns were labeled internalizers. At the other extreme were externalizers who "wore their heart on their sleeve" but were physiologically nonreactive. Those in the middle we called generalizers. Generalizers tended to be both facially expressive and physiologically reactive. The distributions for infants and adults are similar: approximately 20% internalizers, 60% generalizers, and 20% externalizers. This system has not been used in the literature. Rather, the literature on temperament has focused primarily on behavioral inhibition.

The measurement of temperament is typically done by parent ratings on the Infant Temperament Questionnaire (Carey & McDevitt, 1978). Because parents' perceptions often differ from those of teachers or independent observers, researchers have developed laboratory temperament observations (Goldsmith & Rothbart, 1991). In both the parent report and laboratory assessments, the temperament dimensions have included (1) activity level (which involves inactive versus active motor behavior); (2) rhythmicity (regularity of schedule, predictability of behavior); (3) approach or withdrawal (the initial response to a new stimulus); (4) adaptability (response to change and routines); (5) sensory threshold (level of stimulation required to evoke a response); (6) intensity of response (energy level of response); (7) quality of mood (degree of happy versus unhappy behavior); (8) distractibility (the extent to which extraneous stimulation interferes with ongoing behavior); and (9) persistence and attention span (length of time activities are pursued despite interruptions). These dimensions are summarized by three types of infants, including the easy infant, the difficult infant, and the slow-to-warm-up infant.

Parent and observer disagreement on ratings

Common criticisms of these parent-report temperament studies is that they are based on subjective ratings. Temperament studies may be biased, as parents have often disagreed with observers on their temperament ratings. A recent study, for example, compared ratings by mothers of their own children's behavior and ratings by trained observers (Seifer et al., 2003). Very little agreement occurred between the mothers and observers.

One of the problems may be the complexity of the temperament questionnaire being used. A new measure of infant temperament, the

Pictorial Assessment of Temperament (PAT), is a 10-item measure of "difficult" temperament that is quick and easy to use and avoids some of the problems of paper-and-pencil measures of temperament (e.g., complexity of response choices, dependence on respondent's educational level and verbal skills) (Clarke-Stewart et al., 2000).

Twins and the genetics model of temperament

Genetics research has used the twin model to assess the similarities in temperament between identical versus nonidentical twins. In a large sample study, genetic and environmental underpinnings of individual differences in temperament were explored with 3- to 16-month-old infant twins and their parents (Goldsmith et al., 1999). Mothers completed the Infant Behavior Questionnaire (IBQ), and a subsample of 9-month-old twins participated in a behavioral assessment of temperament in the laboratory as well. For the "Smiling and Laughter" and "Duration of Orienting" dimensions, both genetic and shared environmental effects were noted. Shared environmental effects accounted for co-twin similarity on the "Soothability Scale," and, genetic effects accounted for co-twin similarity on the "Distress to Limitations," "Distress to Novelty," and "Activity Level" scales. With a subsample, the authors combined the mother's report, the father's report, and the lab measures of stranger distress and found that genetic influences were most important for these measures.

In a study conducted by Saudino and Eaton (1991), an attempt was made to measure the heritability of infant temperament based on the motor activity levels of twins. Temperament researchers generally assume genetic contributions to behavioral differences, but empirical support is based largely on parent ratings of twins. These subjective ratings may be biased by parental exaggeration of non-identical twin differences or of identical twin similarities. An objective assessment of the genetic hypothesis was made on motor activity level. The activity level of infant twin pairs was measured both by parent ratings and by motion recorders over a 2-day period. Data from the motion recorders showed evidence of genetic influences based on the greater relationship between the activity levels of the twins in identical pairs versus those in non-identical pairs. The parent ratings were also more similar, for identical versus non-identical twins. The motion recorder results confirmed a genetic contribution to temperament differences in infancy.

Parental factors

Studies on parental factors that predicted infant temperament suggest some relationship between parent characteristics and infant temperament. For example, a study by Pedersen et al. (1996) showed that mothers who rated infant cry recordings as more annoying during their pregnancies described their infants (3-month-olds) as more fussy/difficult and unpredictable. The pregnant women were monitored for their cardiac responses, and for their ratings of how annoying they found the recordings of unfamiliar infants' cries. Women, who had increased heart rate to the cries, described their postnatal marital relationships more negatively.

Father characteristics

Fathers' characteristics have also been related to infant temperament. For example, in a study on fathers' and mothers' expressivity, fathers' but not mothers' negative expressivity was associated with the infant's expression of anger and distress, but in a negative direction (Stifter & Grant, 1993). That is, fathers who showed more negative expressivity had infants who showed less anger and distress when frustrated. In this study, frustration was created by having 1-month-old infants and mothers play with a toy after which the mothers were cued to remove the toy from the infants' reach but within their sight. After 2 minutes, the toy was returned to the infants. The degree to which infants were interested in the toy predicted the intensity with which they became angry when the toy was removed.

Predicting infant temperament from neonatal characteristics

Attempts have been made to predict infant temperament from newborn characteristics, including, for example, a study conducted on the relationship between behaviors on the Brazelton Neonatal Behavioral Assessment Scale and subsequent temperament ratings (Tirosh et al., 1992). The Brazelton Scale was given to full-term healthy neonates, and the Infant Behavior Questionnaire was given at 4 months. Neonatal assessment items from the clusters of orientation and motor maturity were correlated with the temperament factors "fussy–difficult" and "unpredictable." Items from the autonomic stability cluster correlated with the "unadaptable" temperament factor.

Predicting later development from infant temperament

Temperament has been followed longitudinally (Denham et al., 1995) across the period of 6 weeks through 30 months. The investigators explored developmental change and individual differences in anger, fear, interest, happiness, and soothability. Mothers of infants completed the Infant Behavior Questionnaire at various points over a period of 30 months. Increased ratings were noted for happiness, fear, and interest, and a decrease followed by an increase for anger. The "soothability" dimension did not change over time. Caregivers who perceived their infants to be positive at 4 months had infants who tended to be positive at 8 months. Negative emotionality at 8 months was followed by negative emotionality at 12 months. These findings suggest that parents may shape their infant's temperament according to their perceptions.

For another example, the relationship between infant temperament and fatness and activity patterns at 3 years was investigated (Wells et al., 1997). The measures included body composition, behavioral activity, and temperament at 12 weeks; and body composition, diet, and behavioral activity at 3 years. Easily soothable infants had leaner childhood skinfold thickness, and they were more active in childhood. Infants' distress was also related to childhood diet.

Temperament and physiological correlates

Relationships between infant temperament and physiological and biochemical variables have also been assessed, including relations between infant temperament and vagal tone, frontal EEG asymmetry, and cortisol. In a study on the relationship between infant temperament and vagal tone, 60 3-month-old infants participated in a laboratory study (Huffman et al., 1998). Temperament was evaluated via laboratory observations and maternal ratings. Vagal tone was collected during a resting baseline period and during the laboratory assessment of temperament. Infants with higher baseline vagal tone were rated in the laboratory as showing fewer negative behaviors and were less disrupted by the experimental procedure. Infants who showed lower vagal tone during the laboratory assessment were rated on maternal report temperament scales as having longer attention spans, and being more easily soothed.

In another study, the moderating roles of frontal EEG asymmetry and gender were explored with respect to temperament (Henderson et al., 2001). The relationships between maternal reports of negative reactivity at 9 months and maternal ratings and laboratory observations of social wariness and sociability at 4 years were examined, as well as the moderating roles of (1) frontal EEG asymmetry as assessed at 9 months of age and (2) the infant's gender. Negative reactivity predicted social wariness for infants with right frontal EEG asymmetry (the negative EEG behavioral withdrawal pattern), but not for those with left frontal EEG asymmetry (the positive EEG behavioral approach pattern) and for boys but not for girls. The only significant predictor of sociability was gender. Specifically, at 4 years girls were rated higher on sociability than boys.

Temperament and cortisol

The relationship between cortisol and temperament has also been studied (Gunnar et al., 1992). These authors examined behavioral and cortisol responses to separation among infants aged 8 to 20 months. A significant cortisol response to a 30-minute separation was noted when the substitute caregiver responded sensitively to infant distress, but was busy and relatively noninteractive. Altering the behavior of the substitute caregiver such that she was warm, responsive, and interactive throughout the separation produced a significant reduction in cortisol and negative affect. In the second study, the effects of group versus singleton care were examined using the less stressful mode of substitute caregivers. No differences were noted in distress or cortisol.

Infants (2 months old) with higher cortisol levels have required more time to calm after immunizations (Wilson et al., 2003). And high cortisol reactivity has been found in more anger-prone, 15-month-old infants (van Bakel & Riksen-Walraven, 2004) in response to a stranger and a frightening robot, and in infants with higher levels of cognitive development as assessed with the Bayley Scales of Infant Development.

Infants at risk for negative temperament

Temperament has been used to identify infants at risk for developmental delays. For example, prenatal and postnatal stress experiences have been related to more negative temperament (Personen et al., 2004). Infant temperament ratings were most negative by mothers with stress scores above the median at both the pre- and postnatal periods.

Excessive crying has been considered a condition that may predict greater developmental problems, for example, mother–infant interaction disturbances. Crying is also thought to derive from maternal risk conditions, including prenatal stress and anxiety and psychopathology. In one study, crying was measured in community and clinical samples (St. James & Halil, 1991). The clinical infants showed the same crying patterns as the general community infants, but were found to cry substantially more. Although mothers of firstborns were more likely to seek clinical referral, there were no birth-order differences in crying amounts.

In another community–clinical sample comparison, extreme crying was associated with prenatal stress, anxiety and maternal psychopathology (Papousek & von Hofacker, 1998). Infants between 1 and 6 months of age, who were referred to an intervention program because of persistent crying, were examined and compared to an age-matched community-based control sample with no current crying problem. Three groups, including referred extreme criers, referred moderate criers, and controls, were compared on psychological state and infant temperament, the quality of the mother–infant relationship, and intuitive parenting in mother–infant face-to-face interactions. In comparison with the general community samples of infants with persistent crying, the clinical sample had high levels of infant distress for long periods of time, with sleep–wake organization problems, neuromotor immaturity, and difficult temperament. Extreme crying was also associated with prenatal stress and anxiety, and partnership conflicts. Mothers in both referred groups scored similarly low on feelings of self-efficacy, and high on depression, anxiety, exhaustion, anger, adverse childhood memories, and marital distress. Mother–infant relationships were more often distressed or disturbed among referred dyads than among controls, and 40% as compared with 19% showed negative interaction patterns.

High-risk infants and temperament

Medical risks such as preterm birth have also been explored for their relationship to infant temperament (Langkamp et al., 1998). In one study, temperament of preterm infants was compared to that of healthy, term infants. The mothers completed the Early Infancy Temperament Questionnaire when the infants were 4 months corrected age (corrected for prematurity). Mothers rated preterm infants as having more negative mood, being less adaptable, and being more difficult.

Another risk group is infantile anorexia. In a study on infantile anorexia, toddlers with infantile anorexia, fussy eaters, and healthy eaters were compared (Chatoor et al., 2000). Mothers and toddlers were videotaped during a feeding session, and the toddlers were weighed and measured. The toddlers with infantile anorexia were noted as being more difficult, irregular, negative, and dependent.

Frustration and inhibition

Two temperament qualities that have been studied by many infant researchers are frustration and inhibition. In a study on frustration, infants were classified as easily frustrated and not easily frustrated, and then they were compared on emotion regulation, physiology, and temperament (Calkins et al., 2002). The male and female infants were equally likely to be classified as frustrated and not easily frustrated, although the male infants were less able to regulate physiologically. Easily frustrated infants were less attentive and more active. These infants were also rated by their parents as being more reactive physiologically and less able to regulate their emotional reactions.

In a study by one of the leading research teams on inhibition, 4-month-old temperament ratings were related to inhibition over the first 2 years of life and to behavioral reticence at age 4 years (Fox et al., 2001). Those infants who were continuously inhibited displayed right frontal EEG asymmetry as early as 9 months of age. The same researchers reported relationships between the physiology of behaviorally inhibited infants and the physiology of fear (Fox et al., 2005). And another group reported that inhibited toddlers had more intrusive mothers and showed nonsocial behavior at age 4 years (Rubin et al., 2002). In a German study, higher cortisol levels were reported for inhibited toddlers (Shieche & Spangler, 2005).

In a study showing relationships between early inhibition and later externalizing behavior problems, children and their mothers were observed at 2 years, and their social behaviors with unfamiliar peers were rated at 4 years (Burgess et al., 2003). At 4 years the low inhibited group had higher activity levels and displayed less reticence. Uninhibited temperament was related to a greater incidence of externalizing behavior problems. The same group also suggested that stable behavioral inhibition may be a risk factor for psychopathology, particularly anxiety disorders in older children (Fox et al., 2005).

Longitudinal studies suggest that infants with an inhibited temperament tend to develop into children who avoid people, objects, and situations, and uninhibited children approach novel people and situations. The behavioral and physiological features of these two temperament types are fairly stable from infancy into early adulthood. Even adults who had been classified as inhibited during the second year of life showed greater brain activity (based on magnetic resonance imaging) to novel versus familiar faces (Schwartz et al., 2003).

Social Referencing

Another emotional development that has received less attention in recent years is social referencing. In this paradigm, infants are observed looking at the mother during fearful situations like being at the edge of the "visual cliff," which is a stage that appears to have a drop-off, but only because of a visual illusion. By 1 year of age, infants typically look at their mothers when they reach the edge of the cliff. In a variation on that test, 12-month-olds on a visual cliff received positive facial-only, vocal-only, or both facial and vocal cues from their mothers. Infants' crossing times and looking at the mother were recorded (Vaish & Striano, 2004). Infants crossed the cliff faster when they were given facial/vocal and vocal versus facial cues, and they looked at their mothers more during the face/voice compared to the voice only condition. These findings suggest that vocal cues, even without a visual reference, are more potent than facial cues in guiding infants' behavior.

In another variation on the social-referencing test, 7- and 10-month-old infants were presented with a remote-controlled toy dog that barked at 30-second intervals as they faced an experimenter who either looked toward them or looked away from them (Striano & Rochat, 2000). Seven-month-old infants looked toward the experimenter more after the dog barked. The 10-month-old infants also looked more after the barking, but only when the experimenter was watching them. These results suggest that by 10 months, infants look at people in fearful situations, but only if they are being watched.

Summary

Emotional development is, thus, a multifaceted phenomenon of infants coming to recognize emotional expressions in mothers (and their fathers and strangers) and what they convey – as, for example, from feeling states like happiness during mother–infant interactions, to more complex "social-referencing" messages telling them not to cross the visual cliff. The infants' looking times and EEGs have been instrumental in measuring these discriminations.

How much neonatal imitation and empathy contributes to this process is unknown, but both the newborn's imitation and empathy appear to be hardwired skills that do not require much experience. Similarity in these skills among identical twins is evidence of genetic effects.

The development of emotional styles or temperament and their continuity suggests similar genetic underpinnings. The slight modification of temperament extremes (externalized or inhibited infants) by their parents suggests environmental influences as well. Frustrating situations like the jealousy paradigm, and risk conditions like prematurity or being born to a depressed mother, may further modify emotional development and temperamental style. Since we are often described by our personality style, being "poker-faced" or "wearing our heart on our sleeve," introverted or extroverted, early emotional development has significant repercussions for our social lives and commerce with the world.

7

Moving Around in the World/Moving the World (Motor and Cognitive Development)

Significant milestones occur for basic motor development across the first 2 years of life. According to the Denver and the Bayley Scales of Infant Development, the scales most frequently used for assessing motor development during infancy, those skills range from being able to hold the head erect at about 2 months to jumping off the floor at about 2 years.

Motor Control

Head control

During the Brazelton Neonatal Behavioral Assessment Scale, the newborn shows an ability to bring the head to a center position and hold it for a matter of seconds. At 2 months, head control can occur in a sitting position or from a position lying on the stomach.

Rolling over

Rolling over from the stomach to the back and from the back to the stomach occurs at around 3 months, and usually happens when the infant sees something interesting and tries to move his or her head to a better position. The moving head, then, causes the body to roll over. Usually, rolling from the stomach to the back occurs before the more difficult rolling from the back to the stomach, ranging between 3 and 5 months. This is a time when infants need a protective surface so as not to roll off from a high place.

Sitting without support

Sitting alone briefly without support happens sometime around 6 months, and coming to a sitting position from a standing or lying down position does not usually happen until a couple of months later. This is a critical motor milestone in that it allows infants to explore more by their hands and to have more control over reaching and grasping and other fine motor skills (discussed below).

Little is known about the development of postural adjustment during early infancy. In a Swedish study, postural adjustments during sitting were observed at 1 to 5 months of age (Hedberg et al., 2005). Electromyograms (EMGs, used to monitor muscle movements) were recorded for neck, trunk, and leg muscles while the infants experienced a series of horizontal forward and backward movements on the surface that supported them. Videos of the infants' motor behaviors suggested that the postural adjustments at all ages were direction-specific and showed large variations. Similar results have been reported in the Netherlands (Hadders-Algra, 2005).

Crawling

Crawling begins to appear around 7 months of age once the infant has been able to sit alone and can roll over. The infant usually moves forward by resting on the hands and knees and sliding the body forward or back-ward, sometimes drawing the legs under them. The drawn-up legs often help move the infant forward. This is also a critical milestone in that infants can now secure things for themselves. At this time, the parents need to be making a baby-safe environment. And more night wakings occur at his time (Scher & Cohen, 2005).

Although boys outshine girls in a range of motor skills, there are no reported gender differences in motor performance during infancy (Mondschein et al., 2000). Gender bias in mothers' expectations about their infants' motor development, however, does occur. Mothers of 11-month-old infants estimated their babies' crawling attempts, and their crawling down steep and shallow slopes (Mondshein et al., 2000). Mothers of girls underestimated their girls' performance, and mothers of boys overestimated their boys' performance. When the infants were tested on the same slope moments after mothers provided their ratings, girls and boys were identical on their motor performance.

Creeping

Creeping is often confused with crawling, but it more often occurs on the hands and feet than on the knees. Again, the motion is typically

Figure 7.1 *Will holding up head at 2 months*

forward, although going backwards can occur later, as muscle strength and coordination improve.

Standing

Standing up typically occurs first with infants pulling themselves up on furniture at around 9 months. This usually leads to walking by holding on to the furniture, and later standing alone at around 10 months of age.

Walking

Walking by holding on to furniture very quickly progresses to walking alone at approximately 12 months. Walking first occurs with the feet pointed outward, and often with the arms held up for balance. The infant makes foot-lifting movements with the legs far apart to maintain balance. Maybe this is the origin of the term "toddler." Lots of falls occur, and lots of cheering spurs the toddler on. More mature gait happens 4 months later (Hallemans et al., 2005).

The role of sensory information for postural control is important as infants develop walking at the end of the first year (Metcalfe & Clark, 2000). While standing quietly, either with hands free or while lightly touching a contact surface, the sway amplitude indicated that infants used light touch for reducing sway. While using the contact surface, movement patterns of the head and trunk were coordinated, as compared to the no-contact condition.

Finding goals is affected by crawling and walking (Clearfield, 2004). Novice and expert crawling and walking infants were observed finding a hidden goal in a large space. Infants were first tested with far-away goals. Infants with fewer than 6 weeks' experience either crawling or walking could not find the goal. Infants with more experience were more successful. Novice and expert crawlers and walkers were then tested with a nearby goal. Again, novice crawlers and walkers with fewer than 6 weeks' experience could not find the goal, whereas those with more experience could.

Running

Running happens almost by accident as the toddler moves quickly to get from point A to point B, usually from one parent's outstretched arms to the other parent's outstretched arms. Somewhere between 18 and 24 months, the toddler goes from very uncoordinated fast stepping movements to actually showing coordinated movements.

Climbing

Climbing up stairs, or walking up stairs, seems to depend a lot on having stairs and on encouragement from parents to use stairs. In our toddler nursery classroom, we had climbing structures, and toddlers typically negotiated those stairs by crawling up them, at around 15 months, and then by climbing on their feet, hanging on to the rail, at about 18 months.

Throwing a ball overhand

This milestone is also highly variable depending on whether parents are trying to develop young athletes or whether it is not in the parents' repertoire. But on average, most infants can throw a ball overhand somewhere between 18 and 24 months.

Figure 7.2   *Tory climbing stairs at 12 months*

Jumping

Jumping appears to depend on whether there are jumping-downstairs opportunities. Encouragement and help are also needed with that exercise.

Cross-cultural differences in motor skills

Cross-cultural differences have been noted in motor skills, suggesting a strong genetic component. Motor precocity has been described for some groups of African infants, and motor development delays have been noted in American Indian infants and infants of southeast Asian heritage (Aina & Morakinyo, 2005; Cintas, 1988). In some cases, variations from North American infant care practices are striking, as is the motor precocity described in some African infants. The developmental delays seen

141

in American Indian infants and infants of Oriental heritage suggest that the sequence and timing of motor development in infants and young children are not universal.

The motor development of Brazilian infants during the first year of life was compared with the widely used US Bayley Scales of Infant Development (1993) sample (Santos et al., 2001). The Brazilian infants' scores increased with age, with the greatest increase occurring over the first 8 months. As a general comparison, the Brazilian sample was similar to the US sample in the third, fourth and fifth months. The differences within these months occurred for sitting and grasping. These were interpreted as differences related to childrearing practices and the influence of biological maturation.

Dynamic systems

New technology has been developed for studying motor development including limb dynamics (Thelen et al., 1991). Thelen has described a research program studying the limb dynamics of human infants. Studying the limb dynamics of spontaneous kicking revealed the self-organizing qualities of the neuromotor system. A similar use of that system on the transition from spontaneous waving to reaching suggested that the infant had come to have intentions about what they were doing.

Thelen and her colleagues have also described motor skills as emerging in development as a dynamic process through repeated perception–action loops (Thelen, 1990). Knowledge of the external world is integrated with knowledge of self-movement, as the body moves through the world. This process leads to new movements as infants continually explore their body and space through movement. These new movements modify the infant's neuromuscular structures.

Changes in arm posture, and movement of the arms in relation to step width, have also been studied over time for 4- to 6-month-old infants who had just begun walking (Ledebt, 2000). Arm postures and movements were coded from video recordings, and step width was calculated from force platform data. Arms were held in fixed postures during the first 10 weeks. A decrease in these fixed postures was correlated with a decrease in step width. The emergence of arm movements occurred when balance control improved. The author suggested that arm postures fulfill the dual task of stabilizing the body in an upright posture, while moving it forward.

The age at which infants who used babywalkers reached locomotor developmental milestones was compared to those who did not (Garrett et al., 2002). A cross-sectional survey was conducted of normal, healthy infants attending daycare centers. Parents of infants completed surveys that recorded the age at which their child reached the developmental milestones of raising their head when prone, rolling over, sitting with support, sitting alone, crawling, standing with support, walking with support, standing alone, and walking alone. Infants who used babywalkers crawled, stood alone, and walked alone later. The amount of babywalker use and the extent of developmental delay were highly related.

Pointing

Infants point for various reasons. One reason is to share attention to events with adults. This has been called "declarative pointing" (Liszkowskl et al., 2004). In a recent study, an adult reacted to 1-year-old infants pointing in different ways, and infants' responses were observed. When the adult shared attention and interest, infants pointed more frequently and tended to prolong each point. When the adult did not look at the infants, the infants pointed less often. The authors suggested that 1-year-old infants point declaratively and understand that others can be interested in the object of their pointing.

Figure 7.3 *Tory declarative pointing at 12 months*

In another study on the effect of a parent's attention on the pointing of infants from 1 to 2 years of age, infants were presented an interesting sight on one or the other side of a room while the parent was either looking toward that side or not (Moore & D'Entremont, 2001). The 1-year-olds pointed more when the parent was looking at them, whether or not the parent had already seen the interesting sight. In contrast, the 2-year-olds pointed more, both when the parent had not seen the sight, and when she was no longer looking at the sight. These findings are consistent with the idea that when they first start to point, infants use that gesture to enhance the interaction rather than to redirect the attention of the partner. By 2 years of age, infants point to redirect the other person's attention to the interesting sight and to share that attention.

Infants also look at an adult pointing, although it is not clear that the infant understands the relation between the person who points and the object of pointing. An habituation paradigm was used to assess this understanding in 9- and 12-month-old infants (Woodward & Guajardo, 2002). Infants saw a person point to one of two toys, and then they saw events where the object or path of motion taken by the arm changed. Twelve-month-olds looked longer at the object than the person's motion, suggesting that they understood the relation between the person and the object. Nine-month-olds, on the other hand, looked equally long at the object and the arm motions. These findings suggest that between 9 and 12 months, infants come to understand pointing as a gesture that people use to turn the infant's attention toward something interesting.

An EEG study suggested that the processing of declarative pointing occurs following development of the frontal region of the brain (Henderson et al., 2002). The authors examined the relationships between electrical activity in the brain at 14 months, as measured by EEG, and declarative pointing at 18 months. EEGs were recorded using the Electrical Geodesics System's dense array sensor nets (a large net with many attached electrodes for recording brain waves). Analyses revealed significant correlations between power in the frontal region at 14 months and declarative pointing.

Fine Motor Skills

Until about 4 months of age objects are explored by mouth. Literally everything goes into the mouth, and, while there have been very few studies on exploration by mouth, there are many studies (already discussed in the chapter on the senses) indicating that the very young infant perceives different characteristics by mouth including shape, form,

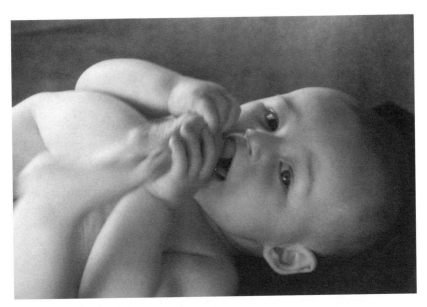

Figure 7.4 *Three-month-old Garrett exploring by mouth*

temperature, and texture. Exploration of objects by hand requires the development of reaching and grasping, and then manipulation by hand occurs at about 4 months of age. Pre-reaching movements occur as early as the newborn period. Swiping at objects, and reaching and grasping with the fist being open, and the infant carefully grasping the object, does not occur until about 4 months. This is commonly referred to as visually directed reaching inasmuch as vision and reaching and grasping are coordinated. Closer to a year, the infant shows the ability to grasp objects between the fingers and the thumb. By the time this stage occurs, infants can easily pick up cubes of food and cheerios, and just about any finger food in front of them.

Visually directed reaching

Four infants were followed from 3 weeks to 1 year to explore the development of successful reaching (Thelen & Spencer, 1998). This development followed a sequence: (1) the infants were able to control head movements several weeks before the onset of reaching; (2) controlling head and shoulder movements; and (3) visually directed reaching which appeared around 4 months.

Manipulating objects

As already mentioned, most objects initially go into the mouth and are explored by mouth. As they reach somewhere between 4 and 5 months, infants will explore objects in other ways including poking and banging and dropping the object. It is around this time that they begin to also show a hand preference for reaching the objects, and a hand preference for holding the objects.

Pre-reaching infants can manipulate objects earlier with "sticky mittens" (Needham et al., 2002). In the sticky mitten study, infants wore "sticky mittens" with palms that stuck to the edges of toys that allowed the infants to pick up the toys. After 10 to 14 10-minute play sessions, the experienced infants showed more object engagement and more sophisticated object exploration compared to their inexperienced peers.

Understanding relationships between objects

Understanding relationships between objects occurs at a very young age. A recent study, for example, investigated the ability of 5-month-olds to

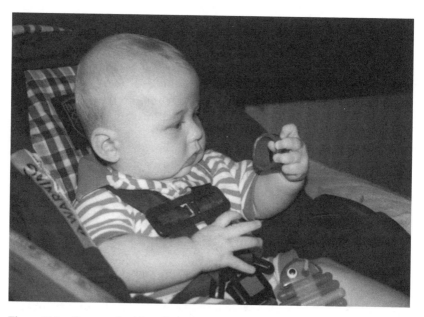

Figure 7.5 *Six-month-old Will exploring by hand*

integrate tactile and visual information, and use that information to interpret physical events. Infants held a ball that was either rigid or compressible (Shweinle & Wilcox, 2003). After holding the ball, the infants watched the ball move back and forth through a tunnel. The ball was either larger or smaller than the tunnel opening. When the ball was much larger than the tunnel opening, the infants correctly judged that the ball that was compressible could pass through the tunnel, but not the rigid ball. When the ball was much smaller than the tunnel opening, the infants correctly judged that both the compressible and the rigid balls could fit through the tunnel.

Inanimate objects and people

Infants' discrimination between inanimate objects and people was researched in 4-, 8-, and 10-month-old infants (Kosugi & Fujita, 2001). The authors compared infants' responses to object–object collision, a person pushing an object, object motion without a visible cause, and human action without a visible cause. The 8-month-old infants, but not the 4-month-old infants, realized that physical contact was necessary to move inanimate objects, but not to move people.

Another animate/inanimate study investigated whether 10-month-old infants expected people to talk to a human-like robot (Arita et al., 2005). Each infant observed a person and an interactive robot behaving like a human, a noninteractive robot remaining stationary, and a noninteractive robot behaving like a human. Then the infants were shown a second person talking to the robot and to the first person. The infants, who had previously observed the interactive robot, showed no preference for the person or the robot. Infants who had not seen the interactive robot looked longer at the second person talking to the robot, rather than the second person talking to the first person. The authors suggested that infants interpret the interactive robot as a person and the noninteractive robot as an object, implying that infants categorize interactive robots as a kind of human being.

In still another animate/inanimate contrast study, 9-month-old infants were shown a video of a series of stationary and moving objects (Pierroutsakos & Troseth, 2002). The infants hit at and attempted to grasp the items depicted on the screen. A decline in manual behaviors and an increase in pointing and vocalizing toward the video were found with 15- and 19-month-old infants. The authors suggested that infants need to learn that pictures are both objects and representations of something else.

Goal-Directed Actions

Goal-directed actions and understanding goal-directed actions appear to emerge around 9 months. In a study illustrating the understanding of goal-directed actions, a female adult handed infants toys (Behne et al., 2005). Sometimes the transaction failed, either because the adult teased the child with the toy, or played with the toy herself, or because she accidentally dropped the toy. Infants at 9, 12, and 18 months reacted with more impatience (e.g., reaching, looking away) when the adult was teasing the child than when she dropped it. Six-month-olds, in contrast, did not show this difference.

In a similar study from Germany, goal-directed actions were studied in the context of an imitation game (Carpenter et al., 2005). Twelve- and 18-month-old infants saw an adult do such things as make a toy mouse hop across a mat with sound effects. In one condition (House), the adult ended by placing the mouse in a toy house, whereas in the other condition (No House), there was no house present. Infants at both ages simply put the mouse in the house (ignoring the hopping motion and sound effects) in the House condition. The authors suggested that this happened because the infants interpreted the adult's action in terms of the final goal, and ignored the means to get there (the hopping). In contrast, infants copied the adult's action (both the hopping motion and the sound effects) when the house was not present, because the infants saw the action itself as the adult's only goal.

Goal-directed actions by 9-month-olds were also demonstrated in a study in which 9-, 14-, 19-, and 24-month-olds were encouraged to use tools to achieve a demonstrated goal (McCarty et al., 2001). Each tool was most efficiently used when held by the handle with the thumb toward the head of the tool. The tools were presented at midline and pointed toward the left and right on alternating trials. The infants, in order to grasp a tool in both directions, needed to plan their actions in advance. The tools included a spoon, hairbrush, toy hammer, and magnet. The goals were to feed one's self, feed another, brush one's hair, brush another's hair, hit pegs, and retrieve metal objects. The infants showed better gripping with the self-directed tools (i.e., hairbrush-to-self and spoon-to-self), suggesting that they could plan their actions better when they were directed toward the self than when they were directed toward an external goal.

Object Permanence

Object permanence also begins to emerge at around 9 months. The infant then knows that an object that is placed or moved behind a barrier still exists, and the infant will attempt to find it or reach for it. In an experiment of this kind, 9-month-old infants were presented the task of visually tracking and reaching for a rolling ball that disappeared and reappeared from behind a wall (Berthier et al., 2001). On some trials, the infant observed the experimenter place a barrier on the ball's track. The infant's looking for the ball was faster when the barrier was not present. Younger infants (4 months old) can perceive an object trajectory when the object is out of sight for a very brief time (Bremner et al., 2005), and perception of opposite moving dots occurs even earlier, at 3 months (Kanazawa et al., 2006).

Knowing that the mother is permanent happens earlier than knowing that objects are permanent. In a study comparing mother and object permanence, 7- to 14-month-old infants were tested on object and mother permanence using a delay period before the infants were allowed to search for the hidden objects (Slaughter & Boh, 2001). Infants searched for their mothers and a large toy, which were hidden under curtained tables. The delay period before each search was until the infants either failed to search or searched in the wrong location. Infants were able to tolerate longer delays before successfully searching for the mother than for the toy. These results support previous studies showing that mother permanence precedes object permanence in infants.

Gender Differences

As was noted earlier in chapter 4 on the senses, newborn boys looked longer at a mobile and girls looked longer at a face. A group from England documented a similar phenomenon on 1-year-olds (Lutchmaya & Baron-Cohen, 2001). The infants were presented with a video of cars moving, or a face moving, in a looking-preference test. The males watched the cars, and the females watched the faces. These data suggested that gender-stereotypic preference and knowledge of gender-stereotyped toys occur at an early age.

In a related study, 12-, 18-, and 24-month-old girls and boys were tested for their preference for photos of vehicles or dolls, and for whether they "matched" these two sets of stereotyped toys with the faces and voices of male and female children (Serbin et al., 2001). A preference for gender-stereotyped toys appeared by 18 months. Girls were able to associate the gender-stereotyped toys with girls' and boys' faces by 18 months, but the boys were not.

In a similar study by the same group from Canada, 18- and 24-month-old infants were shown identical pictures of masculine or feminine items (e.g., hammer, bear, dress, cat) on two computer screens with an accompanying gender-neutral prompt saying, "This is the one I like. Can you look at me?" (Eichstedt et al., 2002). Immediately following the pictures, two adult faces, one male and one female, appeared. By the middle of the second year, the infants related such items as fire hats, hammers, fir trees, and bears with males.

Learning

Many theories have been developed about how the infant learns, including Piagetian theory, classical conditioning, operant conditioning, imitation, and exploration.

Piagetian theory

Piaget was a Swiss psychologist who developed a theory on child development, based on extensive observations of his own children. In Piaget's theory there are mental schemas and motor schemas that are organized patterns of action or thought processes occurring by the process of adaptation. Adaptation, in turn, takes place through assimilation, which basically means "taking in the existing world," and accommodation, which basically means the infant alters her behavior to what is existing, based on experiences with the world. These two processes are complementary, and they are sometimes in balance and sometimes out of balance.

Piaget defined stages of infant development during what he called the sensorimotor period as follows: (1) exercising reflex schemas such as looking and crying and sucking; (2) primary circular reactions, where the reflexes now serve as a foundation for new patterns of behavior, and the behaviors are repeated in a circular fashion; (3) secondary circular reactions, in which the infant's repeat behaviors now involve objects outside their body. During this stage the infant begins to develop object permanence, for example; (4) coordination of secondary circular reactions, in which the schemas or behaviors the infant is developing can now be used to solve problems. At this stage, cause and effect relations develop; (5) tertiary circular reactions, which is a stage when infants seem to make things happen just to experiment. Now they realize that they can find an object that is hidden in several locations, and they can get a parent to retrieve an object that they have dropped from the high chair, they can take things apart, and they can put things into containers and dump them out; and (6) inventions of new means through mental combinations. Now infants can invent solutions and can hold things in their memory. They also have more flexibility in their actions. For example, at this time, deferred imitation occurs, and infants can imitate actions that they have seen happen previously.

Piaget has had a very powerful influence on the field of infancy and infant development, and his observations have created the foundation for much of the empirical research conducted. Many researchers have reported earlier occurrences of these developmental milestones, but there seems to be some validity in, at least, the sequence that Piaget has defined.

Classical conditioning

The example typically given for classical conditioning is Pavlov's experiment on dogs learning that food follows the sound of a bell, so they would salivating for food at the sound of a bell. Generally, infants learn a response to a stimulus, such as they learn to root when their cheek is stroked in a reflex way. If then the mother says "sweet baby" every time she stimulates the cheek next to the lips, the baby will soon turn to root at the sound of "sweet baby."

Operant conditioning

Operant conditioning usually entails a reinforcement following a spontaneous action by the infant. So the infant's sucking behavior leads to a reinforcer, such as the mother's voice. We have seen many examples of the operant conditioning paradigm throughout this book, such as the infant sucking harder in order to hear the mother's voice, or sucking less hard in order to hear the mother's voice. Habituation (as was discussed earlier), classical conditioning, and operant conditioning can occur as early as the newborn period.

Imitation

Generally, learning by imitation occurs by the infant copying the behavior or action modeled by a parent or other adults or siblings. Infants receive reinforcement for imitating others' behaviors. This process starts as early as the newborn period, when infants are seen to imitate facial expressions and facial actions (already described). Imitation then continues to occur very frequently during parent–infant interactions, when rounds of playing are a feature of reciprocal imitations. Much of learning about how objects work comes from mimicking actions demonstrated by parents, as a new toy, for example, is introduced.

Exploration

Another question is whether infants learn better from simply manipulating objects or observing them being manipulated. A group of French researchers investigated whether infants learn an action better from their own experience or by observing an adult performing the action (Provasi et al., 2001). Three different containers were presented to 9- and 12-month-old infants. On each container, a knob popped a lid which lifted a toy. In the observing condition, the infants were shown an adult demonstrating the turning of the knob, and then could play with it. In the other condition, the child could play with the closed container. The observers performed better than the doers.

Another study suggests that infants learn merely by exposure during passive exploration (Boller, 1997). This study assessed the effect of passively exposing infants to visual information in a sensory preconditioning test in five experiments with 6-month-olds. In the basic test, infants were simultaneously exposed to two stimuli, trained on one of them, and tested on the other. Infants learned an association between the two stimuli after preexposures of one hour per day for one week, but not after 2 minutes or one hour on a single occasion. When stimulus 1 was the focal cue, however, infants transferred responding to stimulus 2 after a single preexposure lasting only 2 minutes. These findings suggest that infants learn information about specific stimuli and the relationships between them simply as a result of passive observation.

Problems of learning

Several problems-of-learning studies have been reviewed by Pomerleau et al. (1992). The problems they noted included the brevity of the learning sessions, the choice of dependent measures, and the management of variability in performance. They suggested that the use of single-subject designs, and the use of variables encountered in infants' daily learning experiences may be the solution to some of the problems.

Bower (1989) has argued that since infants use logical-hypothesis testing to organize information they acquire, they are learning much like adults. Bower investigated the process by which infants acquire knowledge of themselves and of the world. Based on the findings of contemporary research, some of it his own, the author argued that even very young infants are more rational in their exploration of the world than they have been given credit for, and that they use logical-hypothesis testing to organize the information they incessantly seek to acquire. Bower showed how infant responses fit a model of exploration similar to that of adults. And he suggested that even their most irrational-seeming behavior stems from a rational base.

Motivating the infant is one of the challenges of learning researchers. Motivational factors are highlighted in a study showing that infants learn arbitrary pairings of different stimulus features such as different colors being paired with different tastes (sweet/tart foods) (Reardon & Bushnell, 1988). Seven-month-old infants were familiarized with sweet and tart foods fed them from distinctively colored cups. On a subsequent choice trial, the infants consistently selected the color that had been paired with sweetness. These results indicate that infants can readily learn at least certain arbitrary bimodal correspondences.

Parents' reinforcement can help the learning process. Performance on learning tasks has been linked to mothers' responsivity (Ayoun, 1998). In this study, the relationship between maternal responsiveness and infant cognition was examined during the search for hidden objects and the learning of a contingency rule. Mother–infant pairs were observed in a laboratory setting when the infants were 11 months old. The experimental session included three phases: a search for hidden objects, the learning of a contingency rule on a touch screen, and a mother–infant play session using a standardized toy. The results indicated a link between performances in the search and contingency task. Infants who succeeded in both tasks had mothers who displayed greater responsiveness.

Memory

Several memory studies have focused on the kinds of stimuli being remembered, the types of cues being provided, and the timing between the presentation of the initial stimulus and the representation to assess memory. Many of these studies were conducted on 3-month-old infants by Carolyn Rovee-Collier and her students, including Jeffrey Fagen. These studies addressed several aspects of memory, including the following findings: (1) new stimuli can impair the retention of old stimuli; (2) location cues can facilitate memory; (3) features of the objects are learned as cues, and (4) nonverbal reminders can serve as cues.

New stimuli impair memory

More specific details are the first to be forgotten and the last to be retrieved. In a study on using novel stimuli to facilitate retention, Rovee-Collier and her colleagues (Rovee-Collier et al., 1994) showed how what we remember about an event is selectively distorted by new information. This was studied in 3-month-old infants who learned to move a particular crib mobile by foot kicking. Infants who were passively exposed to a new mobile 1, 2, or 3 days later, subsequently treated the new mobile as if they had actually been trained with it. After the longest exposure delay, they no longer recognized the original mobile. After the longest delay, the new mobile could prime the forgotten memory, but the original mobile no longer could. These data suggest that what we remember about an event is distorted by what we encounter later.

New location of objects impairs memory

An old object is not remembered if it is placed in a new location (Hayne et al., 1991). These studies were designed to examine the role of place cues in memory retrieval during early infancy. Three-month infants were trained to move a mobile by kicking it. Two weeks later, if they were reminded about the mobile in a new place, they could not remember it. If the same procedure was used one day later, the infants did remember the mobile. These findings suggest that infants as young as 3 months store information about the place where an event occurs, and they suggest that the familiar context/location is important for remembering the event (kicking the mobile).

Too many details impair memory

In a study addressing the number of different details and its relation to infant memory (Bhatt & Rovee-Collier, 1997), figures were displayed on a mobile, and the figures were different colors. Three-month-old infants learned to activate a mobile comprised of either two or three kinds of blocks that differed in color, in the figures displayed on them, and in the figures' colors. Twenty-four hours later, the infants trained with two objects discriminated the combinations of features, but those trained with three objects did not. Infants trained with three objects discriminated novel features, but not the relations among them. The size of the memory load constrained the infants' long-term memory for relational information.

General features of objects are easily remembered

General features of objects are the last to be forgotten and the first to be remembered, while specific features are the first to be forgotten and the last to be remembered (Hayne & Rovee-Collier, 1995). Three-month-old infants were trained to kick their feet to produce movement of an overhead crib mobile, and they were tested 2 weeks later. Twenty-four hours prior to the test, the infants received a 30-minute reminder treatment. The results showed that only the moving, training mobile alleviated forgetting after the 2-week period. The global or general features were the last to be forgotten and the first to be remembered following the reminder treatment. The specific details were forgotten first and the last to be remembered.

Nonverbal reminders can help memory

Nonverbal reminders can maintain early memories (Rovee-Collier et al., 1999). In this study, a nonverbal reminder helped 2-month-old infants recover forgotten memory after 3 weeks. In the second study, 2-month-old infants received a reminder every 3 weeks through 6 months of age, and a final test was given at 7 months of age. Infants were able to remember 4 months later, and most remembered 5 months later if they were given nonverbal reminders. The authors suggested that their periodic reminders maintained early memories over significant periods of development. This finding challenged popular claims that preverbal human infants cannot maintain memories over the long term because of "neural immaturity or an inability to talk about them."

Novel stimuli

After a short delay, a novel stimulus is preferred. A series of experiments were conducted on timing or the interval between presentation of a novel stimulus and the presentation of the stimulus to assess memory. In one study (Bahrick & Pickens, 1995), recent exposure to a stimulus (a one-minute delay) resulted in a novel stimulus being preferred, while no preference occurred if the delay was 2 weeks (intermediate delay). Preference for the familiar stimulus actually occurred following a long or remote delay (one month). Memory for object motion in 3-month-old infants was investigated across retention intervals of 1 or 3 months in three studies using a novelty preference method. Following exposure to an object undergoing one of two types of motion, visual preferences for the novel motion were assessed after retention intervals of one minute, one day, and one month. Results of both studies indicated a significant preference for the novel motion at the one-minute delay, a significant preference for familiar motion at the one-month delay, and no preferences at the intermediate. In a third experiment, memory was assessed after a 3-month interval, and, again, preference was shown for the familiar.

Memory lasts for two weeks

In a similar study, infants remembered for 2 weeks, but not 3 weeks. In order to recover the memory, the object needed to be presented with the original cue and in the original context (Hartshorn & Rovee-Collier, 1997). In experiment 1, infants remembered a train they saw after 2 weeks, but not 3 weeks, the same as had been found using a mobile. In experiment 2, the infants were presented the train set in the original context (room in the home), and they remembered the train, but not if the train or the location of the train changed. Infants in the next experiment failed to recognize the original train in a new place, as before, but could remember a different train in the original place.

Cues can lengthen memory

Two weeks is typically given as a period of memory, although it can be lengthened by cues. For example, in a study by Rovee-Collier and her colleagues (Hill et al., 1988), 6-month-old infants exhibited virtually no forgetting for 2 weeks, but forgetting was complete by the third week. The forgetting observed after 3 weeks was alleviated when the infants were cued with the original training mobile. Six- to 7-month-old infants were trained in an operant conditioning procedure in which kicks were reinforced by movement of a mobile. Memory was assessed in a forgetting paradigm with either the training mobile or a different one serving as the memory cue. When the training and test mobiles were the same, subjects exhibited virtually no forgetting for 2 weeks, but forgetting was complete by week 3. When the training and test mobiles were different, the infant remembered when cued with the training mobile, but they forgot when a different mobile was the reminder.

Memory for different stimuli

Many different types of stimuli have been used in memory tasks, including, for example, color and shape, hue, olfactory stimuli, and music stimuli.

Music: Infants who were trained and tested on the same music showed a 5-day retention of that music (Wasserman, 2000). Infants who experienced different music during the memory test did not remember the music. Even after a one-day delay, a change in the music disrupted infant memory. In the first experiment, 3-month-old infants were trained for 2 days to move an overhead mobile in a crib with a distinctive bumper and background music. Memory was assessed either 1 or 5 days later with (a) the same bumper and music, (b) the same bumper but different music, (c) a different bumper but the same music, or (d) both a different bumper and different music. Infants who experienced a change in the bumper displayed perfect memory. Infants who experienced different music during the retention test showed impaired memory. Infants trained and tested with the same bumper and music showed a 5-day retention, whereas infants who experienced a change to either one or both did not.

In a Canadian study, long-term memory for music was assessed (Trainor et al., 2004). Using a head-turning preference procedure, the authors found that after a one-week exposure to an old English folk song, infants preferred to listen to a novel folk song, indicating that they remembered that familiar melody. However, if the tempo (25% faster or slower) or instrument timbre (harp versus piano) of the familiar melody was changed, infants showed no preference, indicating that they remembered the specific tempo and timbre of the melodies.

In still another study on music, infants remembered the familiar, but not the similar but new music (Saffran et al., 2000). Seven-month-old infants heard two Mozart sonata movements daily for 2 weeks. Two weeks later the infants were tested on passages of the familiarized music and passages taken from the similar, but new music. The infants retained the familiar music.

Color and Shape: Color and shape memory was investigated in 5-month-old infants (Catherwood, 1994). Infants were presented with 18 rapid (250 msec) exposures of a colored shape, followed a second later by a different colored shape. Infants remembered the color, but not the shape.

The same group also assessed memory for the hue of colors (Catherwood et al., 1990). Infants were familiarized with one hue, and then they were presented, either immediately or after a 5-minute delay, with two tests in which the familiar hue was paired with a new hue, either from the same color or from a different color. Infants in both delay groups showed a preference for the hue from the familiar color.

Olfactory Stimuli: In a study using olfactory stimuli, no retention was shown. During the memory test, the olfactory context was either the same odor, a different odor, or no odor. Memory retrieval was completely disrupted for infants tested in the presence of the different odor (Rubin et al., 1998). In this study, 3-month-old infants learned to kick an overhead mobile in the presence of an ambient odor. Memory was assessed 1, 3, or 5 days later. During the memory test, the odor was either the same or a different odor. After the 3- and 5-day intervals, all groups showed forgetting. These results were not consistent with the studies of 3-month-old infants trained and tested on visual or auditory stimuli. Although 3-month-old infants can discriminate different odors as early as birth, odors apparently are not as well remembered as other sensory modalities.

Memory is affected by mood state

Memory is affected by infant mood state. An example of the importance of state is provided by a study (Fleckenstein & Fagen, 1994) in which infants were frustrated by being shifted from a mobile containing 10 objects that they had learned to move, to a mobile containing two objects. The frustration led to crying in several infants. The criers, who did not receive the reminder treatment, displayed forgetting. The infants who received a memory test 7 days later with some reminder treatment (a moving mobile) 24 hours earlier remembered regardless of which mobile was used.

Visual recognition memory

Research has shown that visual recognition memory across changing contexts is dependent on the integrity of the hippocampus (the memory center in the brain) in human adults and in monkeys (Robinson & Pascalis, 2004). To assess this skill on infants, images were presented on a background of one color during familiarization, and on a different color background during the recognition test. The research showed that recognition memory was impaired by a change in context at 6 and 12 months of age, but was unaffected at 18 and 24 months of age. Another study examined processing speed, short-term memory, and attention, and their relation to visual recognition memory (Rose et al., 2003). Attention and processing speed, but not short-term memory, were related to visual recognition memory. Infants who showed better attention (shorter looks and more shifts) and faster processing had better recognition memory.

Visual recognition memory is considered one of the best predictors of cognitive outcomes in children who are at risk for developmental delays (Bendell-Estroff et al., 1989). This study assessed infants at risk for mental retardation on the Bayley Scales of Infant Development and a measure of visual recognition memory at 3 months corrected age. The Bayley Scales were administered again when the infants were one year. At age 3 months, the Bayley and the measure of Visual Recognition Memory were not significantly correlated. Both measures, however, were correlated with the Bayley administered at one year. Each measure at age 3 months was related to a different source of variance in the one-year measure. Results were consistent with the hypothesis that at age 3 months, the Visual Recognition Memory measure is a better early window into later cognitive development than the Bayley Scales.

Imitation facilitating memory

Imitation has also facilitated memory. In two experiments with 6-month-old infants, the question was addressed about whether associating an imitation task with a learning task would affect infants' memory for either task (Barr et al., 2001). Infants who imitated target actions that were modeled for one minute by a hand puppet remembered the actions for only one day. The authors hypothesized that if the infants associated the puppet imitation task with a longer-remembered learning task, then they might remember it longer too. Infants then learned to press a lever to activate a miniature train (a task 6-month-olds remember for 2 weeks), and they saw the target actions modeled immediately afterward. These infants successfully imitated for up to 2 weeks, but only if the train memory was retrieved first.

Deferred imitation

One of the most sophisticated forms of memory is referred to as deferred imitation (imitation of a model that is no longer present). A study conducted by Andy Meltzoff (1995) showed that 14- to 16-month-old infants had long-term memory when a nonverbal method requiring them to reenact a past event from memory (deferred imitation) was used. A delay of 2 months was used first and a delay of 4 months was used next. In one group, motor practice (immediate imitation) was allowed before the delay was imposed. In the second group, the infants were prevented from motor practice before the delay. Deferred imitation occurred for both groups at both delay intervals, and the infants retained and imitated multiple acts. These findings suggest that infants have a nonverbal memory system that supports the recall of past events across long-term delays.

Infants' memory abilities were also tested between the ages of 9 and 16 months using deferred imitation (Carver & Bauer, 2001). Infants'

A

B

Figures 7.6a and b *Deferred imitation of gardening by Grace (a) (photo by Sandy Conde), and "Granddadding" by Garrett (b)*

memory for events was tested after delays ranging from 1 to 6 months. At 9 months, infants were able to imitate after delays of as many as 4 weeks, but not over long delays. In contrast, one month later, 10-month-old infants could imitate over delays of up to 6 months.

The effects of imitation on immediate and delayed recognition and on long-term recall have also been investigated using event-related potentials (ERPs) (Lukowski et al., 2005). Infants who were allowed to imitate showed higher levels of recall after one month compared to infants who only watched the experimenter's demonstration.

Long-term recall emerges late in the first year (Bauer et al., 2003). ERPs were this time used in 9-month-olds as an index of deferred imitation. ERP measures of recognition memory one week after novel laboratory experiences predicted whether and how much infants recalled about the experiences one month later.

Summary

It is truly amazing that in the short space of 2 years, infants learn to hold their head up, roll over, sit up, crawl, stand, walk, run, climb, throw a ball, and jump with their bodies, as well as to imitate. Those who reach developmental milestones earlier have been noted to achieve a higher educational level as adults (Taanila et al., 2005), at least in Finland. Watching how things work, and then remembering how they work with their minds, they start exploring objects with their mouths and then with their hands. Simple aids like "sticky mittens" can help their manipulations. Alongside learning is memory, which can be helped by cues and nonverbal reminders or hindered by too many details, changing contexts, or long delays. And some stimuli seem easier to remember than others, for example music versus aromas. Missing from this literature is the joy that infants must feel as they develop these skills and master their environments.

8

Finally Using Words (Language Development)

In the chapter on the senses we already noted that language development begins with the fetus perceiving differences in the sound patterns that are made by his mother's voice – for example, reading Dr. Seuss nursery stories. The newborn then showed the ability to discriminate the mother's from the father's voice, to discriminate the mother's voice from the stranger's voice, and to discriminate the mother reading one Dr. Seuss story versus reading another Dr. Seuss story.

Parents provide simplified speech during the first several months. This is called "motherese," "fatherese," or "parentese." The simplified speech provides a foundation for infant speech perception and speech production. Many studies document infants' perception of various speech characteristics such as syllables and consonants throughout the first year. At around 9 months the infant understands a few words, and at around 15 months the infant can comprehend simple questions and follow simple directions. The first real indication of verbal comprehension is the response to verbal commands that occurs at around 9 or 10 months, and, by 1 year of age, the infant typically has a vocabulary of about 50 words. The discussion on speech perception is followed by a discussion on speech production, starting with crying and sound-making at birth and moving on to having a working vocabulary of some 100–200 words at 2 years.

Motherese

Motherese or infant-directed speech often contains a simplified, restricted vocabulary. Increased repetition and pauses tend to be limited to sentence boundaries. Infant-directed speech is usually produced with higher pitch, and greater pitch and volume variability as well as melodic contours. It is not clear which aspects of infant-directed speech or moth- erese are effective in enhancing interactions or infants' language learn- ing. Thus, several studies have been conducted to assess the different qualities of motherese, for example, the high pitch and the exaggerated pitch contours.

The high pitch of "baby talk" and exaggerated pitch contours exist across languages and cultures. In a French sample of 6- to 7-month-old infants, the exaggerated pitch contours of infant-directed speech aided infants' learning vowel sounds (Trainor-Laurel & Desjardins, 2002). But the high pitch of infant-directed speech did not assist in vowel acquisi- tion. The authors concluded that the high pitch must serve another func- tion, such as attracting infants' attention.

Using pitch and other speech measures, another group classified adult- directed (neutral affect) versus infant-directed (positive affect) speech correctly more than 80% of the time, and classified the affective message of infant-directed speech correctly nearly 70% of the time (Slaney & McRoberts, 2003). They confirmed that changes in pitch provide an important cue for affective messages. In addition, they found that timbre provides important information about the affective message. Mothers' speech was significantly easier to classify than fathers' speech, suggest- ing a difference between fathers and mothers in the acoustic information used to convey these messages.

Positive emotion may be the critical aspect of baby talk or motherese (Singh et al., 2002). This group presented both baby talk and adult- directed speech with high positive emotion to 6-month-old infants to assess this question. When emotion was held constant, the infants shared no preference. When adult-directed speech stimuli presented more posi- tive emotion than baby-talk stimuli, infants preferred the adult-directed speech. Higher and more variable pitch were not determining the infants' preferences in this case, even though those characteristics may influence the emotionality of the speech.

Similar conclusions were drawn by a Canadian group (Trainor et al., 2000). Many researchers had found that infant-directed (ID) speech has higher pitch, has more exaggerated pitch contours, has a larger pitch range, has a slower tempo, and is more rhythmic than typical adult- directed (AD) speech. The Canadian group showed that ID speech involves expression of emotion to infants, in comparison with the more inhibited expression of emotion in typical AD speech. When AD speech expresses emotion, the AD speech has the same acoustic features as ID speech. In this study, infant-directed speech samples expressing love–comfort, fear, and surprise were recorded. The emotions were equally discriminated in the ID and AD samples. Acoustic analysis showed few differences between the ID and AD samples, but robust differences across the emotion samples. They concluded that ID prosody itself is not special. What is special is the expression of emotion in infant-directed speech as compared to the more inhibited expression of emotion in typical adult speech.

As already mentioned, motherese is also *universal*. ID speech has been compared in a tonal (Thai) and nontonal (Australian English) language (Kitamure et al., 2002). In this research, speech was collected from mothers speaking to infants at birth, and at 3 to 12 months, and also to another adult. Despite variations in the pitch modifications by Thai and Australian English mothers, the infant-directed speech was more exaggerated than the adult-directed speech in both languages.

Motionese

Infant-directed actions have been noted to accompany motherese and have been labeled "motionese" (Brand et al., 2002). In this study, mothers demonstrated the properties of five novel objects either to their infant (age 6–8 months or 11–13 months) or to an adult. The demonstrations for the infants were higher in interactiveness, enthusiasm, physical closeness to partner, range of motion, repetitiveness, and simplicity, indicating that mothers modified their infant-directed actions in ways that would keep their infants' attention and emphasize the meaning of their actions. These findings suggest that "motherese" is broader in scope than previously recognized, including modifications to actions as well as language.

Fatherese

Fathers have also been noted to use infant-directed speech. The terms "fatherese" or "parentese" are used when references are made to both mothers and fathers. In a Japanese study, fathers' and mothers' infant-directed speech was similar (Niwano & Sugai, 2003). However, the infants tended to respond to their mothers with more vocalizations than to their fathers.

Childrenese

Children use infant-directed speech at about 4 years of age (Weppelman et al., 2003). The results from this study indicated that 4-year-old

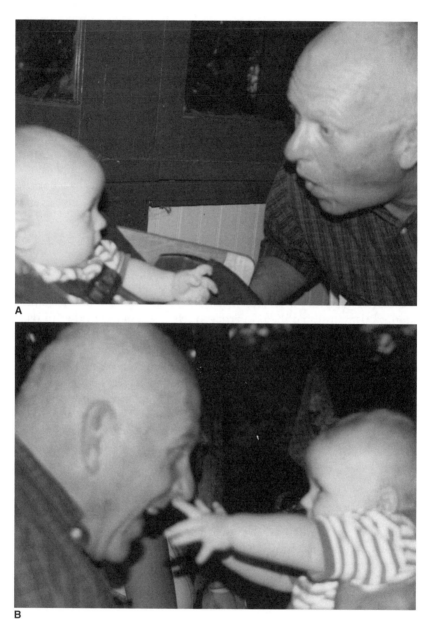

A

B

Figures 8.1a and b *"Grandfatherese" by Boppa for Will*

children modified some of the prosodic characteristics of speech when speaking to infants. In particular, they spoke more slowly when talking to infants than when speaking with adults. They also showed a trend for lowering the fundamental frequency of their speech, and they also seemed to alter their amplitude variability.

Grandmotherese

Finally, grandmothers use "grandmotherese," according to a British study (Shute & Wheldall, 2001). British grandmothers were audiotaped reading aloud to and conversing with their 1- to 3-year-old grandchildren and with an adult. Vocal pitch and rate of speech were extracted from the audiotapes by means of a vocal pitch coding system called the Visispeech Pitch Extraction System. Grandmothers showed raised pitch for both reading to and conversing with their grandchildren, with their modifications being greater for conversing versus reading. The time taken to read a story to the children was also significantly greater than the time taken to read to the adult. Both similarities and differences were noted between British "grandmotherese" speech and British "motherese" speech.

"Baby talk" to pets

People also talk "baby talk" to pets. A researcher actually compared talk to dogs with talk to infants (Mitchell, 2001). Talk to dogs and infants shared numerous features, including high pitch, a short average length of utterance, present-tense verbs, repetitiveness, and attention-getting words and sounds. Differences were also present. Talk to dogs included shorter sentences, more imperatives and exact repetitions, while talk to infants featured more questions and declaratives. Both forms involved trying to capture the listener's attention by focusing on an object or activity and by expressing friendliness and affection. They differed in that talk to infants was more likely to treat the other as a conversant and, especially, to tutor the other in naming objects.

People also seem to nurture pets and to ascribe intentional feelings to them as they do to infants. A similar study analyzed owner–pet interactions and how owners think about their pets' internal states (Fujisaki, 2002). The videos showed that owners' utterances were most frequently intended to attract the pets' attention, and, in many cases, they asked pets about their internal states or situations. When they talked about internal states, owners of both dogs and cats most frequently mentioned their pets' emotions. The characteristics of owner–pet interactions suggested that there may also be some similarities between adults' nurturance toward pets and toward preverbal human infants.

Singing to infants

Singing is another way mothers simplify their vocal behavior. In a study on singing, mothers sang more expressively in their infants' presence than otherwise (Milligan et al., 2003). Infants can recognize a melody when its pitch level is shifted upward or downward, provided the relations between tones are preserved (Trehub, 2001). They also recognize a tone sequence when the tempo is altered, so long as the relative durations remain unchanged. Melodic contour seems to be the most salient feature of melodies for infant listeners. Infants also show enhanced processing for scales with unequal steps and for metric rhythms.

Mothers sing regularly to their infants, doing so in a distinctive manner, characterized by higher pitch, slower tempo, and more emotional expressiveness. The pitch and tempo of mothers' songs are unusually stable over extended periods. Infants prefer the maternal singing style to the usual style of singing, and they are more attentive to maternal singing than to maternal speech. Maternal singing also has a moderating effect on infant arousal. The same research group also noted the relative stability of pitch, tempo, and rhythm in mothers' speech and singing (Bergeson & Trehub, 2002).

Infants prefer their mothers' singing versus their mothers' baby talk. Infants who were 6 months of age were presented with extended audiovisual episodes of their mothers' infant-directed speech or singing (Takayuki & Trehub, 2004). Visual fixations on the mother's image were longer for maternal singing than for maternal speech. Also the infants were less active, which may indicate greater attention during maternal singing than during maternal speech. The authors suggested that the repetitiveness of maternal singing may lead to more moderate arousal levels and therefore more attention.

Speech Perception

Brain regions for speech

French investigators have documented active brain regions that process speech early in infancy (Dahaene-Lambertz et al., 2002). Infants begin to learn their native language in the first months of life. To determine which brain region supports language processing at this young age, these researchers used functional magnetic resonance imaging to measure the brain activity evoked by normal and reversed speech in awake and sleeping 3-month-old infants. Left brain regions similar to those of adults were already active in infants. Additional activation in the right frontal region was seen only in awake infants processing normal speech. Thus, precursors of adult brain language areas are already active in infants, well before the onset of speech production.

Recognizing own name

For the next study, the title tells the whole story: "The Cocktail Party Effect in Infants Revisited: Listening to One's Name in Noise." The authors examined infants' abilities to recognize a familiar word (the infant's own name) in the context of noise. Infants were presented with repetitions of either their names or unfamiliar names in the presence of background babble. Five-month-old infants listened longer to their names when the target voice was 10 dB (but not 5 dB) more intense than the background noise. Nine-month-old infants also failed to identify their names at 5 dB, but 13-month-old infants succeeded.

As early as 6 months of age, infants can already recognize their own names, and they recognize adjoining, unfamiliar words from fluent speech (Bortfeld et al., 2005). The head-turning preference procedure was used to familiarize babies with short passages in which a novel word was preceded by a familiar or a novel name. The babies recognized the word that followed the familiar name, but not the word that followed the novel name.

Three experiments investigated 4-, 6-, and 8-month-old infants' perception of the audible, visible, and combined attributes of syllables (Lewkowicz, 2000). Infants in each experiment were habituated to a person mouthing and uttering a syllable, and then they were tested for detection of changes of either the audible, visible, or combined attributes of the syllable. When the attributes of the syllable were produced in an adult-directed manner, all three age groups detected all three types of changes. As early as 10 months electrophysiological data suggest that infants can recognize two-syllable words they have previously heard only in isolation when these words are now presented in continuous speech (Kooijman et al., 2005).

Categorizing rhymes

Categorizing syllables according to their ending sounds or rhymes were tested in 7- to 13-month-old infants (Hayes et al., 2000). Infants were conditioned to turn their head when one set of rhymes changed to another set of rhymes. Even the 7-month-old infants demonstrated an ability to categorize according to rhymes.

Face and voice synchrony

As early as 4 months infants can detect changes in face/voice pairings (Bahrick et al., 2005). Seven-month-old infants can also use synchronized visual–auditory stimulation to identify a speech passage even when a distractor speech passage is presented at equal loudness (Hollich et al., 2005). Infants succeeded in this task when a video of the talker's face was synchronized with the audio passage. Infants did not succeed in this task when an unsynchronized face and voice or static face was presented.

Vowel sounds

Six experiments tested young infants' sensitivity to vowel and gender information in dynamic faces and voices (Patterson & Werker, 2002). Infants were presented with side-by-side displays of two faces articulating the vowels /a/ or /i/ at the same time. The heard voice matched the gender of one face in some displays, while vowel and gender were placed in conflict in other displays. At 4 months, infants did not match face and voice on the basis of gender, but were able to ignore irrelevant gender information and match on the basis of the vowel sounds. The ability to match on the basis of gender was not evident until 8 months of age.

Two-syllable words

Infants begin to talk at about age one. The vocabulary they need to do so must be built on speech perception, and, of course, infants begin to recognize spoken words long before they talk. Most of the utterances infants hear are continuous, without pauses between words. Thus, developing a vocabulary requires them to break down continuous speech into individual words. Evidence from physiological measures has been presented that 10-month-old infants recognize two-syllable words they have previously heard only in isolation when these words are presented in continuous speech (Kooijman et al., 2005).

Native and nonnative language discrimination

A study from Spain analyzed language discrimination in 4-month-old bilingual infants who had been exposed to two Romance languages belonging to the same rhythmic category, Spanish and Catalan (Bosch & Sebastián-Galles, 2001). Using a familiarization-preference procedure, two groups of bilingual-to-be infants discriminated between these two familial languages. Thus, language discrimination does not appear to be delayed in bilinguals.

Another research team examined the electrophysiological responses of 7- and 11-month-old American infants to native and nonnative consonant contrasts (Rivera-Gaxiola et al., 2005). Analyses of the event-related potentials (ERPs) of the group data at 7 and at 11 months of age demonstrated that infants' discriminatory ERP responses to the nonnative contrasts were present at 7 months of age, but they disappeared by 11 months of age, consistent with the behavioral data reported in the literature. They also observed an increase in infant's responsiveness to native language consonant contrasts over time.

Early predictors of language development

EEG, joint attention, and parent report language measures were used in a longitudinal study of infants assessed at 14, 18, and 24 months of age (Mundy et al., 2003). Joint attention and EEG coherence at 14 months were related to language development at 24 months. EEG coherence and joint attention measures also predicted individual differences in language development. Infants' ability to follow the mother's focus of attention during everyday interactions also predicts word comprehension at the onset of vocabulary acquisition (Silvén, 2001). This relation existed as early as 3 months of age.

Speech Production

Crying

The earliest speech is heard at the newborn period in the form of crying and making sounds like hiccupping, burping, and sneezing. The cry is thought to develop into specific forms including a mad or angry cry, a pain cry, a hunger cry, or a fake cry (Wolff, 1969). Babies' cries can be easily distinguished by parents and other adults and children (Zeskind et al., 1984). Crying is generally thought to be an attention-getting mechanism, as it usually is conveying some discomfort on the part of the infant such as pain or hunger.

Cooing

Soon after birth, cooing sounds are heard. They are vowel-like crying and cooing sounds, which I have come to call "arias," because of their opera-like quality. In the second half of the first year, babbling occurs. This kind of speech involves both vowels and consonants, and typically in a repeated form like "ma ma ma" and "da da da." A relationship has been reported between the sounds that are frequently heard in babbling and the infant's first words (Bloom, 1998).

MAMA sounds

In a speech production study on very young infants, parents listened for "MAMA" sounds and noted the sounds that infants less than 6 months of age made, whether the sounds appeared to be directed to any person or persons, and whether they appeared to have a purpose (Goldman, 2001). The sound "MAMA" began at about 2 months, was usually part of a cry, and was always interpreted as a "wanting" sound. Most parents thought that the infant wanted some form of attention, but a minority thought it indicated hunger. Some infants uttering "MAMA" seemed satisfied if a caretaker approached and paid attention to them, while the others seemed satisfied if they were both paid attention to and picked up.

Babbling

Some have reported that babbling sounds are universal, so that the babbling of an American infant is like that of a Chinese infant (Oller & Eilers, 1982). A little later in the first year, babbling occurs (Oller et al., 1999). Babbling includes vowels and consonant sound combinations. The words "ma ma" and "da da" frequently emerge at this time. Shortly after, the first word appears at around 12 months.

Delayed babbling may be a predictor of neurodevelopmental disabilities including speech problems, language, and reading problems (Oller et al., 1998). By their tenth month of life, typically developing infants produce babbling, which includes the well-formed syllables required for meaningful speech. Research suggests that emerging speech or language-related disorders might be associated with a late onset of babbling. The onset of babbling was investigated in 1,536 high-risk infants at about 10 months (corrected age). Parental report by open-ended questionnaire was found to be an efficient method for ascertaining babbling status. Although delays were infrequent, they were often associated with genetic, neurological, anatomical, and/or physiological abnormalities. Over half the cases of delayed babbling were not, at the time they were discovered, associated with prior significant medical diagnoses.

First words

The first words that are heard from infants are usually nouns that refer to people or objects such as cat, dog, car, ball and birdie. A study on 50 words that infants use (Clark, 1995) suggested that the most common words were those for routines like night-night, people like mommy and daddy, household objects like cup and spoon, animals like dog and cat, and various activities like in and out and up and down. The use of a pitch pattern recognition system has revealed an accuracy of 92% in distinguishing the "communicative" from the "investigative" vocalizations of 10-month-old infants (Papaeliou & Trevarthen, 2006). Then, between about 1 year and 18 months, one-word phrases emerge, and, by 18 months, two-word phrases are heard. By 2 years of age, infants are producing three-word sentences. These are, of course, rough guidelines, as significant age variability has been noted for developmental milestones in speech perception and production.

Musical babbling

In one study, infants who received a weekly "musical education," from the sixth month of prenatal life onwards were able to sing in tune, and developed this skill earlier than usual (Tafuri & Vill, 2002). The amount and the quality of the vocalizations produced by the infants (2 to 8 months) in the educated group were greater than reported in previously published studies, and the analysis of the musical babbling revealed musical patterns.

Maternal Responsiveness Predicts Speech Production

Another study tested infants' ability to use social feedback for developing vocal behavior (Goldstein, 2002). Mothers and their 7- to 10-month-old infants were recorded as they played together. Mothers wore a wireless earphone in order to receive instructions from an experimenter.

The play sessions were divided into baseline recording (10 minutes), social response periods (10 minutes), and extinction periods (10 minutes). During the baseline and extinction periods, mothers were asked to play with their infants as if they were at home. During the social response period, half the mothers were asked to be contingently responsive (to respond to the infant's behavior immediately and with a similar behavior). During and after the social response period, infants whose mothers were contingently responsive used more syllables. The same investigators (Goldstein et al., 2003) showed that contingent, but not noncontingent, maternal behavior facilitated more complex and mature vocal behavior in 8-month-old infants' vocalizations. Babbling was sensitive to nonimitative social stimulation.

In a prospective longitudinal study maternal responsiveness, including descriptions, play, and imitations, were related to expressive language including first imitations, first words, 50 words in expressive language, combinatorial speech, and the use of language to talk about the past (Tamis-LeMonda et al., 2001). At 9 and 13 months, maternal responsiveness, vocalizations, and play were coded from videotaped interactions of mother–infant play. Information about their infant's development was obtained through biweekly interviews with mothers from 9 through 21 months. Maternal responsiveness at both ages predicted the timing of children's language milestones. Responsiveness at 13 months was a stronger predictor of the timing of language milestones than responsiveness at 9 months.

A dissertation examined mothers' utterances to 12-month-old infants, and their infants' vocalizations were recorded during 10 minutes of free play (Howell, 2001). Five maternal speech characteristics, a set of infant speech variables, and the amount and complexity of infant vocalizations were studied. The five maternal speech factors included (a) the number of utterances by mothers, (b) the number of different words used by mothers, (c) the mothers' use of contingent responses to infants' communications, (d) the mothers' time in joint attention with their infants, and (e) the mothers' affective speech to the infants. Mothers' total number of different words combined with the percentage of affective speech predicted the total number of infant vocalizations. Mothers' total number of utterances and percentage of utterances during joint attention predicted the infants' phonetic complexity.

Summary

Mothers and fathers play a significant role in their infants' language development. During the early months of perceiving speech, their "motherese" and "fatherese" simplify the language for early learning. The high pitch and exaggerated intonation are also found in mothers' singing, which infants love, and soon come to replicate in their own musical babbling. Maternal responsiveness continues to be instrumental in the infant's forming their first 50 words about people and objects, and their later language talking about the past. By the end of infancy, their some 200 words, their creative problem-solving, and their stubborn dispositions help them to navigate the way through their ever-growing worlds.

9

Taking Turns with Peers (More Social Development)

The Developing Self and Relationships with Others

The infant's self or personality develops in relationships with others, and relationships with others, in turn, depend on the infant developing a sense of self as being different from other people. Some refer to this as the Theory of Mind (Tomasello, 1995). The Theory of Mind is the point at which an infant realizes that other people have their own thoughts and feelings, which may differ from the infant's thoughts and feelings. The Theory of Mind is thought to develop somewhere between 1 and 2 years, around the time that social referencing occurs, which is the act of referring to other people for cues to guide the infant's behavior. It is also the time when self-recognition occurs and infants begin to use pronouns (you and I). Attachment is still another model that is used at this time to describe the infants' relationships with others, both parents and peers.

Social Referencing

The act of referring to other people for cues for the infant's behavior has generally been studied using the *visual cliff*. The infant is on the edge of what looks to be a cliff and is hesitant. First the infant looks at his mother's facial expressions to know whether to approach the cliff, the top of the cliff being a visual illusion. It has also been studied in the context of robots, and whether the infant should approach or not approach a robot.

Social-referencing studies have become increasingly creative. For example, in a recent study from France, 7- and 10-month-old infants were presented with a remote-controlled toy dog that intermittently barked at 30-second intervals, as the infants faced an experimenter, who either looked toward them or looked away from them (Striano & Rochat, 2000). Seven-month-old infants looked toward the experimenter more often after the dog barked, regardless of whether the experimenter looked at them or not. In contrast, 10-month-old infants looked more often after the barking, but only when the experimenter was looking at them.

Self-Recognition

Self-recognition has been studied in the context of the infants rubbing off a mark of rouge on their nose, when they see their nose in a mirror (Lewis & Crooks, 1978). Infants were assumed to have self-recognition if they touched the spot of rouge on their noses as opposed to trying to rub it off the mirror. This was thought to occur at around 18 to 24 months. We have noted self-recognition much earlier at 3 months based on the very different behaviors the infant shows when looking at a mirror image versus a same-age peer (Field et al., 1989). In this study, the infants showed more social behavior to the peers. These findings were later replicated in a similar paradigm with infants who had daily experience with a mirror. They were also able to discriminate self and mirror image of self as early as 3 months (Bahrick et al., 1996).

In an interesting variant of the self-recognition model, an Australian group investigated the association between infants' interest in their self-image and the onset of mirror self-recognition (Nielsen et al., 2002). A longitudinal study was conducted with infants who were seen at 3-month intervals from 9 to 24 months of age. At each session, the infants were given a preference test. In this test, they were presented with a video image of themselves alongside a video image of a same-aged peer in an unmarked and marked condition. From the 12-month session onwards, the infants were also given a version of the standard "mark test." The infants showed a preference for looking at images of themselves in both conditions. This result indicates that developing an interest in the self-image is an important component in the development of self-recognition.

Personal Pronoun Use and Pretend Play

In a study on the relation of self-recognition to personal pronoun use and pretend play, a longitudinal sample was seen around 15 to 21 months (Lewis & Ramsay, 2004). Self-recognition was related to personal pronoun use and pretend play, such that children showing self-recognition also used more personal pronouns, and they demonstrated more advanced pretend play (play that involves pretending to be someone else or something else, such as an animal, bus, or cartoon character). In another pretend play, longitudinal study, imitation, pretend play, and mirror self-recognition emerged between 18 and 21 months (Nielsen & Dissanayake, 2003).

Pretend Play

Pretend play, or the infant pretending to be someone else, is an index of the Theory of Mind. In the beginning stages, most pretend play involves self-care activities, such as combing one's hair with a doll brush or pretending to eat with play utensils. At a later stage, pretend play is directed toward dolls who are then fed and dressed. And even later, TV characters are assumed and exaggerated.

Autism

Infants with autism are not thought to have Theory of Mind (Nadel et al., 2005). They do not seem to show self-recognition, they do not show social referencing, and they rarely engage in pretend play. It is perhaps this lack of Theory of Mind that makes it difficult for them to relate to other people. Their interactions lack eye contact, they are not contingently responsive, and they are difficult to engage in infant games. They do, however, show increasing responsivity to people and awareness of others during imitation therapy sessions (sessions in which the adult imitates the child's behavior) and some semblance of imitation (See figure 9.1; Field et al., 2001; Nadel et al., 2005).

Another French group investigated the influence of developmental level on interaction and imitation in infants and young children with autism on the basis of family videos (Receveur et al., 2005). An evaluation of the videos of four different time periods (from 10 months to 4 years) showed that, at a very early age, infants later diagnosed as having autism showed different intensities of interaction and imitation deficits.

In a Canadian one-year follow-up study, the results indicated that by 12 months of age, siblings who were later diagnosed with autism may be distinguished from other siblings and low-risk controls on the basis of several characteristics (Zwaigenbaum et al., 2005). These included atypical eye contact, visual tracking, disengagement of visual attention, orienting to name, imitation, social smiling, reactivity, social interest, and

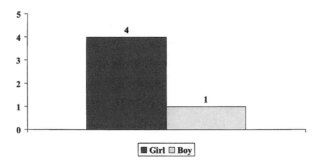

Figure 9.1 *Imitation by children with autism (average frequency for 10-minute sessions)*

emotion. Sensory-oriented behaviors also differentiated the siblings including prolonged latency to disengage visual attention, marked passivity, and decreased activity level at 6 months followed by extreme distress reactions, a tendency to fixate on particular objects in the environment, and decreased expression of positive affect by 12 months as well as delayed expressive and receptive language. Similar findings have been reported on an Italian sample in which 88% of the children with autism showed symptoms within the first year (Maestro et al., 2005).

Attachment

Attachment is another measure of the infant's relationships with others. The attachment or "strange situation" model was designed many years ago, and it has been the subject of hundreds of studies (Ainsworth et al., 1978). In this paradigm, infants 12 to 18 months of age are observed during eight different situations with the mother and stranger. The mother comes and goes, and the infant is left alone with the stranger. Two-thirds of the infants in the original study were considered to be securely attached, which is defined as the mother being used as a secure base as the infant explores the environment. Although these infants typically looked distressed when the mother left the room, they could usually be comforted when the mother returned. Two other groups were rated as insecurely attached. About 22% were said to be ambivalent or resistant in that they would run to their mothers when the mothers returned, but they showed some ambivalence by both clinging and showing resistance in their kicking and pushing away behaviors. The second group of infants, who were labeled insecurely attached, were described as avoidant, in that they totally avoided or ignored their mothers when their mothers returned. Finally, a group was labeled disorganized or disoriented, and their behaviors were extremely ambivalent in that they would turn and greet the parent, and then they would collapse to the floor (Main & Hesse, 1990).

Father attachment

Several investigators have addressed the issue of father attachment, while raising the question of whether infants are as "securely" attached to their fathers as to their mothers. In a meta-analysis (a large analysis of a number of studies), security of attachment to one parent was dependent upon security of attachment to the other parent (Fox et al., 1991). The meta-analysis comprised 11 studies that had examined the similarity of mother/father attachment to an infant. Security of attachment to one parent was dependent upon security of attachment to the other parent, and the type of insecurity (avoidant/resistant) to one parent was dependent upon the type of insecurity to the other. Among the possible explanations for this pattern of data are similar parenting styles and/or influence of infant temperament (possibly the tendency to cry upon separation) on classification of security/insecurity in the strange situation.

Fetal attachment

Although the previous meta-analysis suggested that fathers and mothers are equally attached during the infancy period, at least one study suggested that fathers report greater fetal attachment than mothers (White et al., 1999). This study examined the relationships among family dynamics, parental–fetal attachment, and infant temperament across the transition to parenthood. A sample of families in Helsingborg, Sweden, completed the Family Dynamics Measure and Maternal/Paternal Fetal Attachment Scale during the third trimester (last 3 months) of pregnancy. When the infants were 8 to 9 months old, mothers and fathers again completed the Family Dynamics Measure. The mothers completed the Revised Infant Temperament Questionnaire as well. Overall, the authors found small changes in family dynamics, with an increase in perceived role conflict and mutuality reported by mothers. Fathers reported greater fetal attachment than their partners. Greater paternal– and maternal–fetal attachment was related to more positive family dynamics, and maternal–fetal attachment was positively related to infant mood at 8 months.

Gorilla attachment

Gorillas demonstrate attachment behaviors during separation that are similar to those observed in human infants (Hoff et al., 1994). Three 27-month-old infant gorillas living with their mothers and a silverbacked male were separated to a cage for 24 weeks. The infants initially showed threat responses and increased movement, characteristic of the protest stage of depression in children. Within several days, these were replaced by the infants huddling together as well as self-holding and fetal positioning. Additionally, social and solitary play and object examination occurred at lower levels during the separation than in the preseparation condition. These changes were characteristic of the despair stage of separation. A substantial recovery of many infant nonsocial and social behaviors occurred in the later months of separation. Upon reunion, the infants did not immediately engage in attachment behaviors with their mothers for the first several days, indicating detachment. Following this, there was an increase in mother–infant attachment behaviors.

Biochemical assays of attachment

Several investigators have added biochemical assays to their measures of behavioral attachment. For example, in a study on the stress hormone cortisol and a measure of the strength of the immune system (immunoglobulin A) (Spangler & Shieche, 1994), securely attached infants had significantly lower cortisol levels and lower decreases in immunoglobulin (IgA). This study examined the effect of differing patterns of infant–mother attachment on adrenocortical and immunological function, and the usefulness of IgA and cortisol levels as indicators of stress in infants (cortisol would increase and IgA would decrease in stressed infants). Infants (age 12 months) were observed during the "strange situation." Securely attached infants had significantly lower cortisol levels compared with insecure infants after the strange situation. Changes in IgA levels revealed that secure babies had lower decreases in IgA secretion than all others. The results highlight the relationship between behavioral attachment patterns and activation of biochemical responses.

A similar study assessed the cortisol response to a separation during which the substitute caregiver was extremely sensitive (although she was busy and noninteractive) (Gunnar et al., 1992). By increasing the interactive behavior of the substitute caregiver, the researchers were able to reduce the cortisol levels and negative emotion. In this study, the social context of separation was manipulated with 9-month-old infants. The infants' cortisol was elevated after 30 minutes of separation during which the substitute caregiver responded sensitively to the infants' distress, but she became busy and relatively noninteractive when the infants were not distressed during the separation period. Asking the substitute caregiver to be warm, responsive, and interactive throughout the separation resulted in decreased cortisol and negative affect.

In a study by the same group of investigators, security of infant–mother attachment was assessed before childcare began and 3 months later. During the separation phase, cortisol increased over the first hour following the mothers' departures to levels that were 75 to 100% higher than those at home (Ahnert et al., 2004). Secure infants had lower cortisol levels during the adaptation phase, and they had higher fuss and cry levels during the separation phase.

Jealousy as another attachment paradigm

Jealousy is another paradigm that could be used to assess attachment with even younger infants. In this paradigm, we were able to show that young infants became more distressed when their mothers held a doll versus a book (Hart, Field et al., 1998). A more recent pilot study assessed whether jealousy could be documented in infants as young as 6 months of age. Six-month-old infants were seated next to their mothers, who alternately held a lifelike baby doll and a book. The infants fussed/cried more when the mothers were holding the doll, suggesting a form of jealousy as early as 6 months.

Attachment as a predictor of later development

Attachment theorists have long assumed a link between early attachment security and a variety of developmental outcomes. An analysis of 400 attachment studies published during the 1970s, 1980s, and 1990s (Cohen, 2000) suggested that attachment security did not predict social competence, behavior, or intelligence. The author pointed out weaknesses in attachment research including that there were very few predictive studies, rare replications using the same measures, and limited data reporting.

The first phase of this study involved computerized retrieval and subsequent categorization of over 400 attachment studies published between 1978 and 1998. The classification of those studies revealed that only 35 of them (less than 10%) investigated whether infant attachment security was actually associated with later outcomes.

The second phase involved supplementation of the phase 1 studies with 31 additional predictive attachment studies, published and unpublished, located through additional sources. All predictive studies were then analyzed and coded to determine whether they met the following criteria for inclusion in a meta-analysis: (1) use of the "strange situation" measure to assess attachment in mothers and their infants between 10 and 20 months of age; (2) investigation of the association between attachment and later (age 3 or above) outcomes in at least one of three domains: social competence, behavior, or intelligence; and (3) sufficient data reported to calculate or estimate effect sizes (level of statistical significance) by secure versus insecure attachment classifications, for pooling with the results of other predictive studies in the same domain. A total of 21 studies met all three inclusion criteria.

The third phase was the meta-analysis. Statistical testing revealed that attachment security did not predict social competence, behavior, or intelligence across studies and measures. Although some individual studies found that attachment helped to predict outcomes, the results were limited by the relatively small number of predictive studies reporting sufficient, comparable data.

Similarly, another large sample long-term follow-up study (Lewis et al., 2000) showed no continuity in attachment classification from infancy to late adolescence. Infants were seen in a modified strange situation at 12 months and given the Adult Attachment Interview at 18 years. In addition, data were collected on adolescent, mother, and teacher ratings of maladjustment at 13 and 18 years of age. The results indicated no continuity in attachment classification from one to 18 years of age, and no relation between infant attachment status and adolescent maladjustment.

Relationships between attachment and daycare

Relationships between attachment and daycare have been studied in the US, Australia, and Israel. In the US study, children at 6 years of age were first studied as 1-year-olds in order to determine differences in the developmental outcome of the offspring of employed as compared to "stay at home" mothers (Barglow et al., 1998). Peer competence was rated by laboratory play and psychological tests. Mothers' reports of children's behavior problems at age 6 were related to a higher number of maternal work hours during the infant's first year, but the children did better during overall play situations. Age 1 attachment ratings were a better predictor of free-play social competence than hours of maternal work.

In the Australian study (Harrison & Ungerer, 2002), mothers who expressed a greater commitment to work and less anxiety about using nonfamily childcare, and who returned to work earlier, were more likely to have secure infants. In the Israeli study, daycare increased the likelihood of infants developing insecure attachment to their mothers, as compared with infants who were either in maternal care, individual nonparental care with a relative, individual nonparental care with a paid caregiver, or family daycare (Sagi et al., 2002). Their results, however, suggested that it was the poor quality of center-care and the high infant–caregiver ratio that accounted for the increased level of attachment insecurity among center-care infants.

Daycare

The controversy regarding daycare effects on infants and young children (Belsky, 1990) began with a paper suggesting that extensive nonparental care initiated in the first year of life was associated with heightened risk of insecure infant–parent attachment relationships in infancy and elevated levels of noncompliance/disobedience and aggression in the toddler through the elementary school years. Belsky published another paper in the following year (Belsky & Braungart, 1991) suggesting that insecure–avoidant attachment of infants with extensive infant daycare histories could result from the children's routine separation experience. The daycare infants could be less stressed by, and more independent in, the strange situation than more traditionally reared infants because of their many experiences with separation.

This possibility was assessed in a later study in which daycare appeared to have a negative effect on secure children but had a positive influence on insecure children (Egeland & Hiester, 1995). The aim of this study was to explore the within-group effects of mother–infant attachment and daycare on children's social and emotional adaptation at 42 months and in early school years. For this high-risk sample, the effects of daycare depended on the quality of mother–infant attachment. For the secure group, children in daycare were more negative and avoidant at 42 months, and they were more externalizing and aggressive in kindergarten compared to the home-reared group. In contrast, daycare children who were insecurely attached were less withdrawn. Overall, daycare children were rated higher on externalizing behavior in kindergarten than home-reared children, but no differences were found in the later school years. The sequelae of attachment indicated that security of attachment during infancy differentially predicted later adaptation for daycare and home-reared children. Attachment was related to later adaptation for home-reared children, but it did not predict later adaptation for daycare children.

Positive effects of more time in daycare

Several studies have suggested positive effects of infant daycare, and particularly positive effects for those children who spent more time in daycare. In one study, 91% of infants who had been with their teacher for more than 1 year had secure attachments, as compared to 67% at the middle level of time and 50% at the lowest level of time (Raikes, 1993). The author investigated the role of time with a high-ability teacher on infant–teacher attachment in an infant care setting. Pairs involving infants aged 10–38 months were assessed. Relationships were classified as secure or insecure. An analysis that controlled the confounding effects of age of infant and age of entry into the center showed a significant effect for time with the teacher. Children who had more time with the teachers had more secure attachments.

Negative effects of part-time versus full-time daycare

In another study more negative attachment outcomes were associated with little or part-time daycare, rather than with full-time daycare (Roggman et al., 1994). The authors conducted four studies that showed that infants in daycare were at risk for insecure attachment. Data were analyzed using three types of attachment measures (secure, avoidant, resistant) and four breakdowns into full and part-time daycare groups (0, 4–5, and 37+ hrs/wk). The infants were aged 12–13 months. Contrary to the previous studies, no results from the present study were robust enough to emerge consistently, although there was a trend for more negative attachment outcomes to be associated with little or part-time daycare rather than with full-time daycare.

Positive effects of full-time daycare

In still another study, full-time, nonmaternal care was not associated with increased insecure attachment at age 1 year (Burchinal et al., 1992). The

Figures 9.2a and b *Peer affection in toddler (a) and preschool (b) daycare*

daycare attachment issue was examined with a longitudinal sample of infants whose parents all agreed to place their infant in a research daycare center by the age of 7 months. Daycare did not negatively change, and sometimes it enhanced the association between infant–mother attachment and the mother's involvement and warmth toward her infant during the first year of life.

Infant mental health professionals prefer home care

Despite these positive effects data, a survey of 402 members of an international organization of infant mental health professionals suggested that all forms of family care were endorsed over all forms of purchased care, and all forms of individual care were preferred to full-time daycare (Leach, 1997). Surprisingly lengthy periods of care by mothers were consistently endorsed, and all forms of family care were endorsed over all forms of purchased care. Although all forms of individual care were preferred to full-day group care for all age groups, half-day group care was preferred for infants up to the age of 2.

Quality of care versus experience

When quality of care is entered as a variable, it is a consistent predictor, whereas the amount of experience is not. In another large sample study, family income, family relations, temperament, and daycare quantity and quality were examined as predictors of toddlers' social interactions (Wolling & Feagans, 1995). The sample of children had been enrolled in either a high- or low-quality care center sometime during their first year. Although children enrolled in infant care during their first year have sometimes been noted to be aggressive with their peers and more noncompliant with adults, they have been characterized as more social with their peers as well. Findings revealed that quality of care was a compensatory factor in decreasing the social difficulties of temperamentally vulnerable children. Quality was a consistent predictor of children's nonsocial play and positive interaction with caregivers, whereas daycare experience was not. Family environment factors also impacted daycare social interactions.

High-quality laboratory school care

A series of studies have established positive effects for infants receiving high-quality, laboratory school care. For example, in one study, aggression and behavior problems were not associated with nonparental care

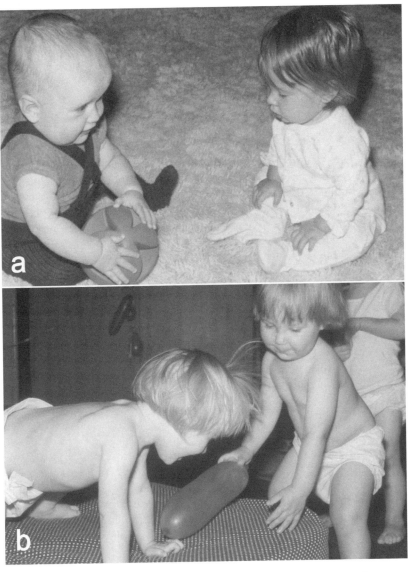

Figures 9.3a and b *Negotiating objects in infant (a) and toddler (b) daycare*

in the first 3 years, and higher levels of social competence were associated with group care experience (Balleyguier & Melhuish, 1996). This study was completed in France, where daycare is extensively used starting in early infancy. Children who had diverse daycare experience in the first 3 years of life were studied at 3–4 years of age when they were at nursery school.

Positive grade school outcomes following quality daycare

In one of our studies on quality daycare, the amount of time spent in full-time center-care was positively related to the number of friends and extracurricular activities of the children by grade school age, the parents' ratings of the children's emotional well-being, leadership, popularity, attractiveness, and assertiveness. These positive effects were negatively related to aggressivity (Field, 1991). This sample included grade school children who had received stable, full-time infant daycare and preschool daycare until they reached school age in the same high-quality daycare center. A second sample included sixth graders who had also received varying amounts (months) of stable full-time daycare, but this group attended a variety of quality daycare centers. In the second sample, teachers' ratings of their emotional well-being, attractiveness, and assertiveness were greater, they showed more physical affection during peer interactions, they were more often assigned to the gifted program, and they received higher math grades.

Cognitive gains

In a comprehensive review of the literature (Robert, 1996), daycare was related to greater performance on cognitive tasks and reduced crime and violence. Evidence also suggested that infant daycare was not associated with infectious disease. Data from observational studies on the effect of daycare injuries were also conflicting. Finally, studies in the US point to the positive effects of out-of-home daycare on maternal employment.

Infant–parent relationships

In another review, no harmful effects were found for infant–parent relationships (Lamb & Sternberg, 1990). The authors reviewed literature about the effects of alternative care on infants and toddlers and the types of settings used by parents in the US. They claimed that the data are limited because the association between daycare and attachment in infancy has only been examined using a single procedure, the strange situation, whose validity can be questioned. Another review of this kind suggested that the literature may be biased by the unavailability of unpublished data that often show no significant effects, highlighting the need for more studies (Roggman et al., 1994).

Externalizing behaviors

The definitive answers for daycare were to come from a study supported by the National Institute of Child Health and Human Development (NICHD) that involved many centers across the US. Its reports, however, have been somewhat inconsistent. In one of the first reports on long-term outcomes, they concluded that the more time children spent in any of a variety of nonmaternal care arrangements across the first 5 years of life, the more behavior problems and conflict they had with adults at that age and in kindergarten, as reported by mothers, caregivers, and teachers (NICHD Early Child Research Network, 2003). These effects remained, for the most part, even when quality, type, and instability of childcare were controlled for their potential confounding effects in the data analysis, and when maternal sensitivity and other family background factors were taken into account. Effects were modest and smaller than those of maternal sensitivity and family socioeconomic status, although they were greater than those of other features of childcare, maternal depression, and infant temperament. In contrast, another report from the same year suggested positive effects, including that early experience with higher quality childcare benefited children's engagement with their mothers through first grade when their mothers were depressed.

Higher language scores

Behavior problems were reported again in a publication the next year (NICHD Early Child Care Research Network, 2004), but this time they were qualified as not being in the clinical or at-risk range. At 54 months, children who experienced more center-care had somewhat higher behavior problem scores, as reported by caregivers, although these scores were not in a clinical or at-risk range. Center-care hours were also related to cognitive and language outcomes, with more hours in the infancy period associated with lower preacademic test scores and more hours in the toddler period with higher language scores.

Quality of care

Many other recent reports challenge the NICHD study findings. In a paper entitled "Child Care Quality Matters" (Love et al., 2003), three studies examined associations between early childcare and child outcomes among families different from those of the NICHD Early Child Care Research Network study. The results suggested that quality has an important influence on children's development and may be an important moderator of the amount of time in care.

High-quality care and fewer externalizing and internalizing problems

In another study, quality of care was also an important variable (Crockenberg & Leerskes, 2004). This study tested the effects of quality and type (center-based versus other) of nonparental care and infant temperament, on children's externalizing and internalizing behaviors at $2\frac{1}{2}$ years, controlling for childcare quality. Mothers rated depressive symptoms prenatally as well as infant temperament at 5 months, child-care quality and child behavior at $2\frac{1}{2}$ years. At 6 months, infants were videotaped for an activity response to novelty. Long hours in nonparental care were associated with: (1) more externalizing symptoms for children in center-care who had been identified as easily frustrated when they were infants; and (2) more internalizing symptoms for children who had been identified as both highly distressed and highly active in response to novelty as infants. Children in higher-quality childcare were less externalizing and internalizing than those in lower-quality childcare. Finally, in 2006 the NICHD Early Child Care Research Network reported that higher-quality care was related to advanced cognitive, language, and preacademic outcomes at every age, and better socioemotional and peer outcomes at some ages (NICHD Early Child Research Network, 2006).

Daycare center quality index

In a study on childcare in Greece, group size, adult–child ratio, caregiving style, and interactions between the caregivers and the infants were evaluated (Petrogiamnis, 2002). The infants were 18 months old, experiencing full-time daycare, had at least 6 months of out-of-home care, and were attending 25 daycare centers. The assessments included measures of cognitive, language, social, and emotional development. Interviews and observational techniques were used to assess the quality of the daycare environment and the interactions between caregivers and the infants. The course of development could be predicted by the overall daycare center quality index, as measured by the Infant/Toddler Environment Rating Scale.

More stimulating environment

The joint influence of childcare and infant attachment security was examined in the second year of life using six cognitive and language measures at 24, 30, and 36 months in a sample of low-income toddlers (Spieker et al., 2002). Center-care alleviated the adverse effects of insecure attachment on the cognitive and language development of low-income children by providing those children with a more stimulating environment than they would have experienced at home. Thus, this finding did not support the hypothesis that any type of out-of-home care would negatively impact secure children's language and cognitive development because of the time spent away from a secure mother–child relationship.

Less aggression in daycare children

A questionnaire study on several thousand Canadians reported more aggression in children receiving home care than group care (Borge et al., 2004). Aggression was more common in children with mothers' care than those attending group daycare. Taking social selection into account, physical aggression was significantly more common in children from high-risk families looked after by their own parents.

Specific aspects that determine quality of daycare

Given that infant daycare is likely here to stay, the more important questions to investigate are the specific aspects of daycare programs that determine quality. Among these are group size, same-age or mixed-age grouping, and staffing stability. Same- and mixed-age grouping was studied in the Netherlands (Pool et al., 2000). In this study, parent–child attachment relationships were assessed by means of a scale called the Attachment Q-Sort. Attachment security did not differ for children who had been in same-age or mixed-age grouping, or who had experienced a change of daycare center. In another study in the Netherlands, children showed more well-being in daycare when they had few parallel care arrangements, and when there was more daily stability in staffing patterns (De Schipper et al., 2002). Positive caregiving behavior was lower when staff turnover rate was higher. Children in more flexible childcare showed more noncompliance.

Cortisol as an index of daycare effects

Using the stress hormone cortisol as an index of daycare effects, several aspects of daycare were investigated (Legendre, 2003) in eight daycare centers. Infants' cortisol levels remained stable between 9:30 a.m. and 10:30 a.m. in the centers, whereas at home cortisol levels decreased at the same time of day. Infants' cortisol level changes differed across the eight centers, suggesting the influence of environmental factors. Cortisol level increases were related to large group size (more than 15 infants), age differences among infants (greater than 6 months), less available area per infant in the playrooms (less than 5 square meters), and large number of caregivers in the room (more than four adults).

In another study using cortisol as an index, at childcare, 35% of infants and 71% of toddlers showed increasing cortisol across the day. At home 71% of infants and 64% of toddlers showed decreasing cortisol (Watamura et al., 2003). Toddlers who played more with peers had lower cortisol levels. Children who showed more social fearfulness had higher afternoon cortisol levels and they experienced larger cortisol increases across the day at childcare.

Peer Interactions

Physical aggression

Temper tantrums, hitting, and biting occur relatively often in daycare settings, especially in the United States. In a study conducted by our group comparing behaviors in French and American preschools, significantly more physical aggression was noted in the American preschools (Field, 2001). In the same study, significantly more physically affectionate behavior was noted between French adults and children and between children and their peers in the same preschool settings, suggesting a relationship between physical affection and the lack of physical aggression.

Touching also decreases across the preschool period. In several studies we have noted the progressive decrease in touching behaviors including hugging, stroking, and kissing across the infancy to toddler to preschool period (Cigales et al., 1996; Field et al., 1994). We have also attempted to increase the amount of physically affectionate behavior by showing the teachers, who were afraid of being accused of touching children in the wrong places, the socially acceptable places they could touch children, such as their heads, backs, and shoulders. Although there was an increase in teachers' touching children following that intervention, the rates of touching were still extremely low. It is not surprising, in this light, that infant nursery teachers often complain of temper tantrums, hitting, and biting.

Peer attachment behavior in infants

Despite these negative behaviors, peer interactions feature positive behavior. Infants start at a very early age to socialize with their peers, including looking and smiling at them more often, and reaching out to them more often than they do when seated in front of a peer versus a mirror (Field, 1990). They also show turn-taking behavior and imitative behavior during the first year with their peers. Their attachments to each other, in fact, become so strong that when one infant of a close pair of infants is transferred from the infant to the toddler nursery classroom, the infant left behind typically experiences symptoms of depression including difficulty sleeping, changes in eating and toileting patterns, and negative affect (Field et al., 1984). They experience similar symptoms when they are separated from their mothers for a period of time, either when the mother is at the hospital having another child or when the mother is at a conference (Field & Reite, 1984). Infants who remain in their daycare programs versus those who experience a change such as a substitute caregiver have less severe separation symptoms. (See figure 9.4.)

Context effects on peer interactions

Being in a familiar setting not only seems to reduce separation problems but also seems to facilitate peer interactions. When we compared peers interacting in their own homes versus someone else's home they showed better interactions with their peers in their own homes. They also had better interactions when they were in larger spaces, spaces that were divided, and when there was a greater availability of toys (Field, 1990). The fewer the adults, the less negative behavior. In a parents' cooperative nursery, we noted that when mothers were out of the room conducting observations for the study, their infants were more interactive, and they showed less negative affect when their mothers were out of the room (Field, 1979). Mothers had more difficulty letting their infants just play with peers, and they also had more difficulty leaving their infants at nursery school than fathers (Field et al., 1984). In this study, we noted that mothers lingered and spent significant time reassuring their infants, which tended to elicit protest behavior on the part of the infant. Fathers,

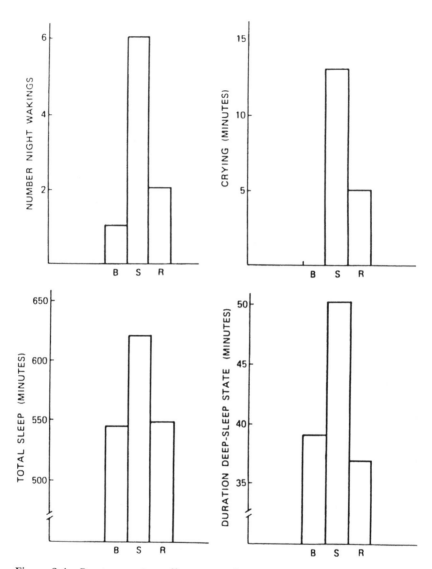

Figure 9.4 *Peer separation effects on night wakings, crying, total sleep, and duration of deep sleep, before separations (B), during separations (S), and during reunions (R)*

in contrast were more casual about their leave-takings, and their infants became more readily involved in play with their peers.

Summary

Social development has so many facets dealing with the self and with others. For the self, there is self-recognition, theory of mind, and pretend play, and for others, there is social referencing, imitation, and attachment. Many findings in the literature suggest the resilience of the infant. Hundreds of earlier studies on attachment using the strange situation had concluded that attachment to the mother was paramount. But those findings are now being challenged by father-, teacher-, and peer-attachment data. Many researchers had predicted undesirable outcomes for infants in daycare, but now many studies suggest the benefits of early group care for infants, especially in high-quality daycare centers. Surprisingly, infants become so attached to their peers that they show depression symptoms when they are separated from them. Since infants move on to spend the bulk of their lives with peers, these early experiences with peers are unquestionably valuable. As cross-cultural studies suggest, when infants' interactions with adults and peers are affectionate, they are less aggressive. Infants seem to thrive when they are not afraid, and when their social partners are responsive and affectionate. The nurturance received as an infant undoubtedly turns into the nurturance the child gives later as a parent.

Appendix: My Diary on Tory's First Year

Tory's First Month

Unreal
Cuddly, but fragile
Roots, but difficulty breastfeeding (getting suction)
Loves daddy's mustache
Bruised heels and partially closed left eye
Looks like a little adult with her big mop of hair
Certainly a Martini with the dark eyes and hair of her grandpa
Looks in the direction of sound
Looks alertly at faces
Weak passive movements and snapback
Complete floppiness on pull-to-sit
Tiny and floppy
A real kicker
Smiles and smiles and smiles in her sleep
Developing a repertoire of funny faces
Strains during her bowel movements
Has no schedule
Up most of the night
Makes panting sounds
Squeals in her sleep
Alert at night
Begging to focus on our faces
Stops crying in anticipation of being picked up
No longer cries on the changing table
Likes sucking on a pacifier, Bach, and lying in sunny spots
Slept through a restaurant meal and an 8-hour car trip

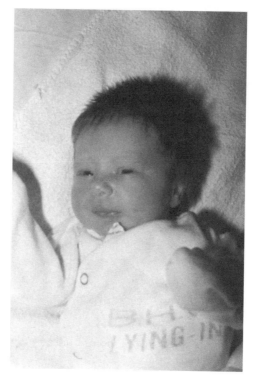

Figure A1 *Just born – first month*

An almost voluntary smile
Opened eyes wide on a DC elevator ride
No longer a tiny little baby
First smile

Tory's Second Month

First time on boat, first trip to a bar
Makes a lot of messes, constant diaper changing
Lunges head toward breast when hungry
Hangs onto clothing
More organized
Quiets to her musical Winnie-the-Pooh

200

Discomfited by lack of support in bath and hammock
Hates her bath – screams for the duration
Weak on pull-to-sit, standing and crawling reflexes
Good performance on orientation items
Cuddly and consolable
Up all day looking at environs
Loves to be in motion: hammock or snugli
Arches backward
Both a 1-month and a 2-month-old
First real vocalization
Eyes open and sucking in her sleep
Head lag still
Half smiles in response to tickling
Widened eyes to imitations of her vocalizations
Cries evolve into "Hi" sounds
Upchucked for first time
Looking at fist; accidentally noticing it as she swipes at things
Staring at objects or into space

Figure A2 *Imitating surprise with Mom – second month*

Standing on lap
Looking straight through us
Eyes darting and widening from highway light to highway light
First meeting with her babysitter, Darlene
Startle to bump on head
Broke into wide grin being passed to Grandpa Field
Fusses a lot at sunset even when feeding
Standing and walking more strongly and stronger pull-to-sit
Stares at her musical mobile and tracks the animals as they move around
Still sleeps in her bassinet in our room
Seems contented lying on the floor in sunny spots
Sleeps in old-fashioned cradle in living room during naptime
Arches her back and leans way back wanting to be upside-down
Grandma Martini found the perfect way to pacify Tory – laying her
   across your knee and rock a little bit
Tory is still without a schedule
The smiles in her sleep often look like they were meant for just you

Tory's Third Month

Crying real tears
Smiling more and more
Vocalizing to kitchen cabinet door
Focuses on objects and people
Played first real game with daddy pulling pacifier out of her mouth and
   Tory grinning each time
Swiping at photos on wall next to changing table
Good head control in sitting and standing position
Arching back and leaning over side of lap upside-down
Stares fixedly at objects, particularly yellow ones, a couple feet away
Screams with clenched fists for dinner
Enjoys water teether
Delightful vocalizations
Repeats sounds of her own as we imitate them
Reflexes beginning to disappear – Moro weaker, TNR almost gone
Good tracking, though she stops to talk a little
Looks less like a baby
Being on her tummy on your knee consoles her
Loved bath for first time
Series of sounds – speech sounds
Up all day wanting to talk and play (another growth spurt?)

No reaction to pat-a-cake
Less flatulence and less fussiness
Most vocal early – very early – in the morning
Emits oooh, aah, and hi sounds
Repeats imitations of her vocalizations
Midline hand play
Seems to notice her hands and then looks directly at her fist
Moves about crib – we find her 90° from her put-to-bed starting
    position
Beginning to sleep most of the night
Gaaah is favorite sound
Smiling a great deal
Looking people straight in the eye and staring
Reasonable facsimile of Barry's words "Daddy" – "Mommy" – same
    pitch and rhythm
Laughed at squeaky cow
Gah, buh, dah sounds
Inserts fist and sucks on it
Smiles at grandma and loves being with her
Clutches overhanging mobiles and playpen netting
Moves around playpen by pushing feet
Bath is now her favorite sport
Less eye contact in breast then bottlefeeding since angle is wrong
Feels our tension or so it seems
Thursdays are her best days (no wonder, says our astrologist friend, she
    was born on a Thursday)
Slept 9 hours straight for the first time
Grabs rings of playpen gym
Up the entire day
Yanking at bunny mobile
So many growth spurts, so many things to say about the third month
Attends to motion (gurgling liquid of hourglass and nodding head of
    animated dog)
Sustains attention for 15–20 minutes
Alternating days of sleep and wakefulness
Grasps her bunnies, watches them move and then looks at her hand
Distinguishes daddy and mommy from others
First real food (oatmeal) grimaces and spits it out
Clutching everything in sight
Violent reaction to shot – we walked her and we walked her some more
Most loquacious and sociable at breakfast
Talks too much while eating her cereal – trying to do two things at once

Figure A3 *Starting to roll – third month*

Imitations of her elicit her smiles
Sleeping 9 hours per night, a 2-hour nap in the a.m. and p.m.
Refuses to be held by others when upset, will go to mommy or daddy
Doctor says we should no longer correct for prematurity, she has
   "caught-up," clever little girl that she is

End of Tory's Fourth Month

12 pounds 5 ounces heavy and 60 centimeters long
Talked on telephone for first time – eyes darted back and forth as she
   listened
Dinner time is a very social hour
Recognizes strange environs
Loves little children

Rolls over by extending her arm to the side
Difficulty lifting head in a prone position
Kicks bunnies with feet and spins teething jack with hands
  simultaneously
Has distance vision since she follows my movements around the kitchen
  from her position in the dining room
Enjoys watching us do housework
Fussy after long trips
Has mastered eating cereal
Crying ceases when she hears me climbing stairs
Predictable schedule – 9 hours at night, 2 hour naps
Looks much older than a baby
Oriental looking – very dark
Furrows her brow just like her daddy
Likes the motion of the boat and loves having children aboard
Gave up the pacifier and chews on her fist instead
Readily pacified by talking and being carried around
Grabs her spoon
Greets Darlene with smiles and chatter
First case of constipation
Tracks animals on her mobile and looks at her hands frequently
First real laughter
Very plump from being on baby foods – has doubled birthweight
Holds head up at 45 degrees and quiets when stood up
Inhales and swallows the wind, then laughs openly
Loves arching her back and being upside-down
Quiets to the sound of her own tape-recorded voice
Grasp is preceded by looking at her hands
Tries to insert objects – all objects – in her mouth
Has discovered her feet and is trying to reach them
Arches her back and rocks like a rocking horse when put on tummy
Likes to be rocked to sleep
Still smiling in REM sleep
Middle-of-the-night feedings are the in-thing
Smiles at peek-a-boo and pat-a-cake
Has her own game of tucking her head in your arm, sucking your arm,
  then looking at you and smiling
Likes to suck on noses and fingers – even kids' dirty fingers
Drooling excessively – perhaps teething

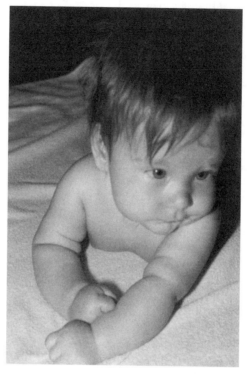

Figure A4 *Getting up there to crawl – fourth month*

End of Tory's Fifth Month

Had her first hissy fit – screamed when surrounded by noisy people
Spends a lot of time looking out of the car window
Pushes with her toes and slides around to reach objects
Can lift her head to 90° from a lying position
First imitation of motor behavior – slapped her ball after I did
Enjoys jolly jumper and looking in her mirror as if at her twin
Puts face under water and comes up looking puzzled
More interested in children than other babies
Betsy & Don insisted we let Tory try crying to sleep rather than rocking
  her to sleep – Brazelton concurred and it worked
Extremely good tempered on boat
Spends a lot of time sucking on Ramona and Katy's swan's bill
Frustrated by unreachable toys

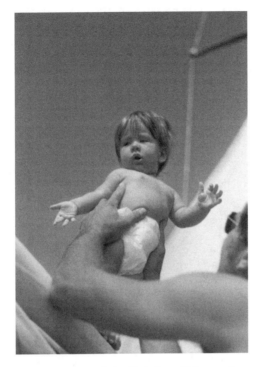

Figure A5 *Standing on mast with Dad's help – fifth month*

Has reverted to several waking periods at night – teething?
Outstretches her arms to be picked up
Loves the freedom of floor play
Rubber swan is her favorite toy – she looks at it, then sucks its bill, then
   looks at it again and vocalizes
Went swimming in Grandma Betty's pool and with some tutoring from
   her kicked her legs, paddled her arms and swallowed great gulps of
   water without a protest
Laughs at Heather's imitation of her
First bath on the boat
Trying to roll over from her back to stomach but much harder than the
   reverse
Smiles at her own face in the mirror
Splashes during her bath very rhythmically with whatever is in her hand
Enjoys being carried face forward now in her carrier
Rolls over from back to stomach finally
Dislikes her pediatrician's office

Very manipulative of people's faces, particularly noses and hair
Enjoys watching TV with Barry, particularly the commercials
Preoccupied with feeling faces – is she exploring or practicing her grasp?
Has near vision – holds her water teether up to her face and watches the
  fish move about
Guides spoon to mouth and plays with her finger food
Cried when Loren fell and cried
Several vowels and some consonants now punctuate her speech
Understands give and take of communication – waits for you to finish
  saying something, then talks during a silent period
Imitates our imitations of sounds already in her own repertoire
Chatters in polysyllabic phrases like hiyahhi
Occasionally breaks into an Aria, chuckling laughter and squealing
  sounds, grunts with a bm and giggles when I push her toes to her mouth
Recognizes her bottle
Rolls onto her side and onto stomach and desperately tries to crawl,
  winging her arms and legs like an airplane

Tory's Sixth Month

Differentially manipulates balls on activator mobile
Inability to crawl highlights intent of reaching things
Can hold bottle by self
First dinghy ride
Has remained a specimen of good health
Feet to her mouth and sucking on each of them in turn
Now laughing a full gutteral, throaty laugh
More patience with overhead toys – plays with those in her crib in the
  early a.m. waiting for us to rise
Squirmed out of her infant seat
First signs of stranger anxiety
Eating adult food – yogurt, mashed chicken liver
Enjoys stroller – watching approaching things and people
Alternate stepping movements in jolly jumper
Eats in a feeder walker
Plays in playpen approximately 20 minutes
Gave teddy bear a hug and kiss
Throws things when tired of them and then groans for something else
Prefers socializing to playing with objects
Laughs uproariously at peek-a-boo
Smiles and laughs almost indiscriminately at people

Figure A6 *Standing alone with boat's help – sixth month*

Ate her first cookie and tried to drink from Tommy Tippie cup
Transfers objects from hand when given another
Looks for object dropped
Slight regression – wants someone else to roll her over and hold her bottle
Loves baths and grandma's swimming pool
Follows trajectory of jet passing overhead
Very sociable
Holds arms out to most people to be held
Teething – rubbing eyes, ears, nose, drooling and fussy
First swim in ocean
Tried to grab ice cream out of cone to eat
Rolls over from back to stomach with relative ease
Curling knees under her preparatory to crawling
Likes playing with kitchen utensils
Gets frustrated playing with a rolling orange
Tory knows her name

Tory's Seventh Month

16 pounds – 26 inches long – 17-inch head circumferencec – 50th percentile

Makes social overtures – reaching, smiling and babbling – to children and adults which often go unnoticed – but doesn't resort to crying – merely tries another trick

Throws objects and wants for them to be retrieved

Much more talkative

Loves every minute of swimming

First two rides on a merry-go-round

All starry-eyed under spray of shower

The world's most traveled 7-month-old

Greeted a new babysitter – Mrs. Thayer – with a big smile

Crawling movements – legs under her, up on arms and plunging forward

Series of Arias just like Loren's

Walking about in walker – moves best sideways and backwards

Figure A7 *An offering for Dad – seventh month*

Sat and stood by herself from bean bag
Approaching plants and grabbing leaves
Loves being around grandma
Continues to enjoy gimbaled infant seat on boat
Pivots about and rolls across room
Jabbers at us in cockpit from seat below
Drinks the wind and loves it
Loves to dance, particularly to the Beatles
Sits without support
Arches back to be in her favorite upside-down position
Up at night teething
Has outgrown pacifying effects of rocker
Difficulty sleeping in strange places
Refused to come to me for first time, preferred to stay with grandma
Reaching out to swimming pool making pleading sounds
Airplane wings flapping in prone wanting to crawl
Eating crackers and ice cream
Polysyllabic cries – wa da da na na no instead of whaaaaa
Practicing her screams
Hand slapping in rhythm on table and in bath
Went to school (infant play cooperative) for first time
Unflappable when poked by more mobile babies
Holding her own cup

Tory's Eighth Month

Chewing on plant leaves when we turned our backs
Miserable cold – first illness – still happy and calm
Swipes at cord of musical crib bird
Stopped breastfeeding
Defends her toys around her British boyfriend Willie
Ate some autumn leaves
Cried inconsolably for the first time – cold and teething
Imitating Willie's crawling motions – up on hands and knees rocking
Watches Willie like a hawk
Pulling at bathroom light cord
Playing in bed waiting for us to rise
Up for 5 hours straight during naptime while at school
Chatters with great abandon
Laughs like a nanny goat

Up on hands and knees rocking, then flops on her tummy
A mere rhythmic wave bye bye
Smiling less – now requiring something funny for a smile or laugh
Continues ballet of her hands while bottlefeeding just as she did during breastfeeding
Wearing leotards, corduroy pants and turtlenecks like a little girl
Enjoyed Eddie pushing her in her walker
Laughs at little kids' antics
Real preference for mommy just developing
Fond of looking in the mirror
Likes dancing to the Beatles
First time showing any ticklishness
Waves bye bye when she feels like it, but only if someone's actually leaving
Crawling backwards – moves knees alternately and slides hands back to meet them
Crawled backwards under dishwasher and into red toy box
Watching falling leaves

Figure A8 *Not willing to relinquish her toy – eighth month*

Enjoys liverwurst
First tooth – lower left – rather protective of her new tooth
Favorite toys are now kitchen utensils
Middle-of-night ride to hospital for mommy – Tory entertains
Kiss on the mouth
Delightfully friendly and happy
Says da da
First sit in a high chair
Looks at stereo speakers when they are emitting voices
Invariable turning to TV commercials
Another tooth – lower right
A little person
Hams it up or fake smiles for photos
Smiles when she's enjoying something

Tory's Ninth Month

Eating hors d'oeuvres – cheese, liverwurst and crackers
Prefers feeding self
Bangs spoon on tray and whimpers when hungry
Another cold from her little playmates
Out to dinner at the Sturbridge Inn with the grandparents and played
  her role well as the head of the table
Has crying jags when she becomes overtired
Has a funny crawl – moves her knees forward, then her hands together
  move forward and all of her flops down on her stomach much to the
  amusement of everyone
Managing to get everywhere slowly with her funny crawl – a very cum-
  bersome way to move about
Likes having her curved spoon filled with food to feed herself
Substances which can't be held – like running water and ice cubes – are
  a continual source of intrigue – we run the sink to overflowing and
  empty ice cube trays for our amusement
Wags her tongue in imitation
Loves to explore faces – grabbing at noses and pulling hair – maybe per-
  sists in doing so since she invariably gets an animated response
Gives us kisses on the lips when we pick her up upon returning
Showing a preference for mommy when she's hurt or tired
Barry plays more games with Tory and I carry her around more
We talk to her and take care of her needs – feed, bathe and change her
  equally as often

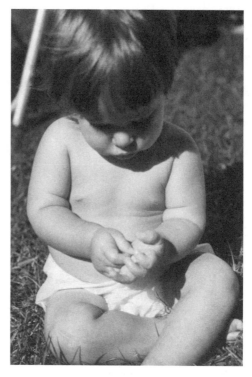

Figure A9 *First splinter – ninth month*

Occasionally refusing to be held by strangers although she smiles and
  talks to them at a distance
Willingly held by grandparents, our boarders (Steve and Jim), and Bob
  (Darlene's husband)
Seems to enjoy our three babysitters, Darlene, Mrs. Thayer and Winnie,
  although they are all very different
Offered food to us for the first time – a soggy already-been-chewed
  cracker
Loves her bath and screams for it as she finishes eating just as she screams
  for her food at the start of a meal
Has found a special playmate at school and laughs when she first sees
  him
Tries very hard to keep up with Collin, her same-age, but more mobile
  playmate

Seems to understand some verbal requests – stops dead in her tracks toward an electric outlet or plant when I say No and turns off the bathroom light upon request

Riding face forward in the car now and wanting to converse with us in between looks at the countryside

Started a walking to and fro routine usually turning back to the other before she reaches the opposite side

Bids for attention by fake cough

Enjoys opening packages more than the contents

Ba ba, ma ma, da da, hi and bye bye fill her conversations

Waving bye bye precipitates the sounds bye bye but not yet the hand wave

Imitates the animal-like sounds she spontaneously emits – then pauses for your imitation of hers in a game-like way

Suddenly started climbing up everything – dishwasher, TV, chairs (even rocking chairs), and peoples' pant legs, but lowers self by falling

When she falls her cry is latent as if she's first stunned or puzzled

Played in the nude after waterplay at school today and seemingly loving the freedom from clothes

Tory and Collin amused themselves for 2 hours and barely noticed my presence behind the video-camera

Very vocal periods during bath and early a.m. (12 hours apart)

Exploring things less by mouth and more by visual and manipulative modes

Searches for your face back and forth into and out of a mirror

Has begun to empty cupboards with utter abandon

Climbs up the side of her crib to greet us when we answer to her post-nap calls

Tory's Tenth Month

Consistently responsive to her name

Looks in mirror for your face when it's turned away from her

Enjoys peek-a-boo-surprise when a face pops out at its original place rather than the other side of the hiding shield

Refuses a mouthful when she catches your eyes

Wants something to do with her hands while being spoonfed

Prefers having meals with us and eating same food

Enjoys looking at picture books

Hiding behind curtains, then smiling as she reappears

Beginning signs of rolling a ball – to Daddy

2 SDs above mean on Bayley mental and 1 SD above mean on Bayley motor but off the scale when correction made for prematurity

Not quite as clever during testing due to tiredness and distractibility – didn't turn pages or use crayon or patacake

Easy baby on Carey temperament questionnaire with low scores on approach, intensity (high) and mood – surprisingly enough since she's typically very social and very cheerful

Continues to offer to us whatever she's eating

No longer likes playpen

Bloodcurdling scream middle-of-night and trembling-stomach cramps or first nightmare?

Waves bye bye spontaneously

Laughs openly at silly things like Daddy throwing snowballs

Climbing up, onto and into things, like the refrigerator

Lowering herself more gracefully from standing position

Enjoys emptying kitchen cupboard or drawer

Likes being crawled after or pursued by a "monster" and beckons you to continue chasing her if and when you stop for a rest

Likes dancing and talking to self in mirror

Hates being put down to be changed – in general doesn't like being repositioned except by her own volition

Beginning to sing – da da up and down scale

Holds things in her mouth while traveling rather like a golden retriever

Looks in receiver of telephone as if expecting to see a face there which belongs to the voice

Likes the sound of her whining – or at least seems to from her repetition

Interrupted sleep

Crawling very agilely

Says bye bye even in anticipation of a leave-taking

Lots of rough and tumble play – with Daddy

Insists on joining us for meals

Splashes gallons of water on kitchen floor from her bath in kitchen sink

Likes to mess with food as if it were fingerpaint

Slightly upset in a.m. when we leave and overjoyed when we return

Stops and looks for a reaction when approaching a No No object like a plant

Stood up by herself from mid floor without support and for the first time

Many more sounds, lots more smiling and laughter and moving around now very freely

Katy gave Tory a cloth football and Tory gave it back to Katy

Figure A10 *Grandpa's golf gear – tenth month*

Walking with support of one hand
Slept through the night
Voluntarily initiated a game of peek-a-boo
Cruising around by hanging onto furniture and standing alone for short
  periods unsupported
Bah bah, baby and bye bye
A step forward to Barry without realizing
Sits straight up, head leaned back and bottle in the air
Loved opening others' Xmas gifts, eating the wrapping paper and ribbon
Tory's first flight – climbed the seat to chat with the folks behind us then
  fell asleep in my lap
Wandered quite a distance from me in the airport on hands and knees
  as if she knew where she was going and I wasn't invited

Tory's Eleventh Month

Climbed first set of stairs – 3 concrete steps behind grandma's house in Florida

Suddenly doing new things and then practicing them over and over again

Enjoys pouring water from a basin with measuring cups

Crawled under a very low bed and got stuck half way under

"Curious George" and into everything

Full swing into container behavior

Snatches ice cubes out of peoples' drinks at cocktail parties, then gives a "fake" grin

Rolling golf balls, fetching and tossing them upon request on grandma's sun porch

Climbing into toy cart, tipping it over and rolling on it like a wheel – discovery of the wheel at such an early age, perhaps she'll be a physicist

Sucking on thumb and forefinger only tentatively, but for the first time initiates tongue clicking sounds to be imitated

Comprehends meaning of bye bye

Has a fake laugh

Empties contents of grandma's car wastebasket every time we go out

Broke into loud joyful sounds at the end of our Marina Jack's restaurant dinner

Third tooth emerged (upper right center)

Tried to eat the sand at the beach

Also enjoyed watching the surf and the gulls finish off our crumbs

Saw her first alligator and two very large turtles as well as many exotic plants (croton, powder puff and bottle brush trees)

Likes sun on her face and wind in her hair

Eats scrambled eggs for breakfast, apples and avocado for lunch

Increasingly difficult to change – crawls very fast off end of bed to get away

Has no real babyisms except that she occasionally wets her pants

Pissed in the grass – first time she wet without a diaper and looked a bit surprised about it

Fourth tooth (upper-left center)

Walked from pole to pole under tables at restaurant, went to a strange waitress without any hesitancy

Played real peek-a-boo – both starting and stopping the game

Squeals with delight when she sees someone she knows several yards away

Throws unwanted food on the floor

Figure A11 *Container behavior – dishes go into and out of dishwasher over and over again – eleventh month*

Laughs lots these days, runs syllables together and occasionally hums
Shows more interest in toddlers than babies
Empties blocks out of pail, then returns them to pail
Claps and rolls her hands to pat-a-cake without prompting
Recognized her babysitters after being away from them for a month
Rocking back and forth, and grinding her teeth
Alternates a knee and opposite foot on stairs
Shakes her head No No when she arrives at a No No like a plant
Second upper-right tooth came through
Says bye bye to everyone
Says Dah a lot when showing you something
Will talk into a phone unless there's a dial tone or a voice on the other
    end

Tory's Twelfth Month

First cold accompanied by a bad cough

Attended baby group and seemed lost without older pre-toddlers

Stands on lap to look out car window, stands on table to look out living room window

Very quiet when exploring a new object, very talkative with a familiar object

Still very friendly with strangers

When mothers are not in playroom with infants, infants are less fussy and play together more cooperatively

Takes a few steps, but then plops down as if she'd changed her mind

Likes variety to her meals – will reject her favorite pickles if she's already had one that day

Anticipates people's leave-taking, waving bye bye as they grab their coats

Waves bye bye to babysitters when we return

Talks herself to sleep these days and talks to herself while waiting for us to get up in a.m.

Latest craze is crawling into drawers – toy drawer in living room, pots and pans drawer in kitchen

Likes climbing up onto dishwasher rack

Likes putting things including herself into and out of containers like drawers and shelves

Tory and Collin are the babies of the pre-toddler group in age, yet the only ones who don't fuss and cry

Tory passed a sneak curve ball to her Daddy today right over her shoulder and down her back just like the pros

Learning to play xylophone

Hardly notices my presence and absence in her class

Loved squeezing Lisa's guinea pig making it squeak

Brushes her own hair when you ask her to

Splashing tons of water out of kitchen sink

Likes her feelie dog book

Books are now her favorite toys

Plays with toys with more concentration of late

Beginning to discern indelible things

Likes going into refrigerator to chew off apple skins

Likes phone calls if there's nobody on the other end

Smacks kisses with her hand

Tries to blow nose into handkerchief

Plays peek-a-boo very adult-like

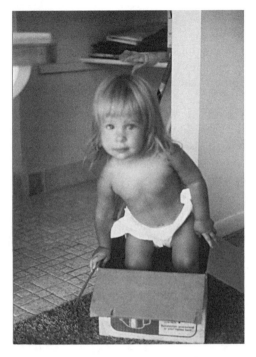

Figure A12 *I can go in and out too – twelfth month*

Picks up phone and jabbers into it

Brushes her teeth with her own toothbrush

Manages to climb down from things like the sofa, the bed, the dishwasher

First fever she's ever had followed by first ear infection

Climbs up her slide, stands up with no hands on the platform, then slides down

Another tooth – lower left of middle teeth

Fairly assertive about hugging – often approaching people with arms open as if to greet them with a big endearing hug

Slithers down beside you, putting her head down on your lap as if to go to sleep

Showing much more awareness of the function of objects, where they go, how they work and don't work

Rarely puts objects in mouth anymore for exploration purposes

Plays with letters on the refrigerator as if she knows they belong there

Is putting things back into containers as often as she removes them

Tory's Thirteenth Month

Tory looked for my earrings on my ears when I'd forgotten to wear them today

She also sponged the kitchen counter from the sink as I have done several times

Beginning to back off things like the couch, bed, dishwasher door, etc.

Also beginning to back down our front stairs (all 30 of them)

Has taken a few steps on her own from time to time, although tentatively

Always perks up for company, particularly children

Shaking her head No No is a built-in routine whenever she even suspects she is in the vicinity of a "No No"

Shrugs her shoulders and opens her arms as if to say "all gone"

Also said "hi Daddy" almost perfectly, hot (to her scrambled eggs), and yeah

Screams bloody murder when Dr. Stewart restrains her

Clinging to me more often and seeming to prefer that I change her, hold her, and carry her around

Walking a few steps to me as Dr. Stewart put her down

Enjoys her rhythm instruments and new spinning top, but still prefers her books

Tory noticed the TV was in the wrong place today, pointed her index finger at it and jabbered at it as if to say "it's in the wrong place"

Whenever Tory wants to make a point, she points her right index finger and raises her voice

Tory sounds a bit like a record running too fast – if we could slow her down and separate the run together speech sounds, we might be able to understand her

Beginning to notice other kids' actions, attends to them when they're crying as if really sympathetic

She does not, however, lend them her toys very often, and frequently grabs and devours their cookies as well

So independent at play group that she hardly notices my presence

Humming in a rather melodic fashion

Perks up and becomes very content when we take her into play group

Trying to wean Tory from a bottle by giving her only a cup during the daytime

Rather agile with a cup and very independent at feeding (eating by hand, and occasionally by spoon tuna, beans, broccoli, etc.) – not a fussy eater

Figure A13 *No stairs in the house, so I will climb the refrigerator – thirteenth month*

Imitates things we repeatedly do such as tongue clicking, animal sounds,
   swaying back and forth, nodding our heads and gives a smile of recognition as she does so
Speech seems at least structurally adult-like, e.g., the length of her sentences and intonation of expressions as well as the organization of
   accompanying nonverbal behaviors like shrugging her shoulders
Greeted everyone entering the play group, saying "hi" to each of them
Tory tends to be somewhat assertive (or aggressive?) snatching toys and
   the like
Was away for 4 days and was greeted very neutrally followed by considerable clinging
Enjoys closing herself in the bathroom and closing refrigerator door

Figure A14 *My first boyfriend at nursery school – fourteenth month*

Has taken up rocking in rocking chairs – climbs up on the chair, then pumps it to make it rock

Tory imitates our dancing motions, our singing, nose blowing, wiping our faces, brushing teeth, etc., and some of the imitations are delayed or in the absence of their modeled behaviors

Glossary on Infant Development and Caregiving

AGGRESSION

Aggression in young children is considered fairly normal. Usually it is their way of trying to get what they want, a toy or attention. Toddlers and preschoolers engage in pushing, shoving, hitting, kicking, yelling, and biting, and infants pull each other's hair and jab fingers in faces, which is not a problem until it is harmful to another child, a parent, or teacher. Lots of the aggressive behaviors happen in the natural course of simply being active on the playground or in the classroom. Typically children "pick themselves up" or go on their way after being assaulted by another child in the course of rough-and-tumble play. Ultimately with modeling from older children and adults they learn to express their feelings verbally instead of physically.

One of the simplest solutions is to simply distract the aggressive child by taking the child's hand and walking toward other toys or interesting the child in other activities. Another common strategy used by teachers is "time out." The idea introduced by behaviorists was to take time away from an activity that was generally satisfying to the child. A general rule of thumb is that time out should last about one minute per year of the child's age. A parent recently told me that "time in" is sometimes more effective: simply asking the aggressive child to hug the other child and then play nicely together, presenting each with a desirable play object.

Aggression is less common in French and Chinese nursery schools than it is in American schools. Even though classrooms in France and China often feature one teacher to 40-some children on the playground or in the classroom, the children are less aggressive. Most aggressions are so minor that they go unnoticed by both the children and the teacher. Interventions by teachers are also very uncommon. This suggests that part of the problem in American schools is apparently the adults' reaction to the aggressive behavior. Aggression may escalate to harmful behavior when a child knows that this will achieve a teacher's attention. If there is less attention available from teachers, children seem not to escalate their aggression, and they resolve their own difficulties.

Another reason there may be less aggression in French children in particular is that families in France touch each other more than in the US. The US Center for Disease Control statistics show France on the bottom of a bar graph and the US on the top of a bar graph depicting the incidence of homicides by 20- to 29-year-old males. In contrast, France is on the top of a bar graph and the US on the bottom of a bar graph depicting the amount of touching that goes on in those societies. A related study on 49 cultures shows that there is less adult violence in societies that display more physical affection toward their infants and young children, and more violence in societies that feature less physical affection toward children. Many monkey experiments show monkeys becoming violent as they are deprived of physical contact.

Even physical affection from other children stops aggressive behavior. In a recent study in Paris only two teacher interventions were noted following 40 hours of observation on a preschool playground of 48 children and one teacher. The teacher intervened as two children shoved a third child onto the ground. The teacher simply grabbed the hands of the two aggressive children, led them to the knocked down child and asked them to hug and kiss that child. Those hugs and kisses ended the fight very quickly.

ANGER
Expressions of anger can be seen as early as the newborn period in crying outbursts by an uncomfortable newborn whose needs are not being met. The temper tantrums of a 2-year-old occur for the same reasons: discomfort and not getting what is wanted or needed. In the preschool years, transgressions against a child either for his possessions or against his person, as in shoving, pushing, hitting, and kicking, sometimes cause anger at having been made uncomfortable or having their feelings hurt.

ANXIETY
Children, like adults, have a host of stresses and anxieties that make their lives uncomfortable. Anxiety can cause sleep disturbances and illness as well as learning problems. The anxieties are different at different developmental stages. Infants and toddlers, for example, experience the stress of separation anxiety and stranger anxiety. Infants also experience frustration during developmental milestone periods such as crawling and walking, although anxiety is difficult to measure at those ages.

Preschooler anxieties are more likely related to being hospitalized or starting school.

Children who are particularly prone to anxiety are those who are temperamentally shy and have difficulty making transitions. To help with the transitions various comfort objects such as pacifiers at the younger age and blankies and stuffed animals at the older age are helpful. Other solutions are unique to the different type of anxiety. For example, for separation anxiety, which is typically related to the infant not realizing that you are going to come back, the infant can be reassured that you are just going to get something and will return shortly. For stranger anxiety, a goodbye ritual helps, particularly if it is brief and upbeat. Sometimes play acting these leave-takings with the child by using dolls and making the babysitter come and go in fantasy play helps. Also spending a little time in the presence of the babysitter before leaving until the child becomes familiar helps a great deal.

Most anxieties are very normal and pass with the developmental stage, except for separation anxiety, which seems to persist. Most children do not particularly like their parents leaving them (until they reach adolescence and want to leave their parents). Separation anxiety in its extreme form, where the child will not leave the parent and develops symptoms such as headaches and stomach aches, may be a more serious form of anxiety, enough for it to be labeled separation anxiety disorder.

Massage therapy invariably helps. A 10-minute back rub on a daily basis invariably reduces anxiety. This can be observed as reduced agitation and nervous behavior, or it can be measured by decreased stress hormones such as cortisol taken from saliva samples.

ATTENTION-SEEKING

Attention-seeking is probably one of the most important motivating factors behind child behavior, second only to curiosity/exploration/learning. From the time infants discover that they can make something happen, at around 3 months when they can reach, grab onto something, and pull it towards them, to the time that they can move from one side of the room crawling to the other, to the time they can walk by holding onto furniture, they are discovering that they can do things. Typically the infant looks to whoever is in the near vicinity to see their reaction. The infant is innately a social being, and social interactions from the beginning of life involve getting attention and paying attention.

The problem is that as the world becomes busier and parents are juggling a thousand things, it is simply hard to pay attention to all the positive behaviors and all the accomplishments of the child. Doling out hugs and praise is time consuming, can sometimes lead to dependency if given too often, and therefore is at odds with our general cultural childrearing agenda, which is facilitating autonomy (self-reliance). But children will inevitably get attention from someone by some behavior and often that is negative behavior such as temper tantrums, interrupting, complaining, whining, breaking things, having accidents. The child is impatient and wants attention when he or she wants it.

If possible, diverting the child's attention, mimicking the whining (babies stop crying when you imitate their crying), or attempting to ignore it and trying to engage the child in your activity (talking on the phone or laying out the lunches), will sometimes suffice. Escalations into full-blown temper tantrums, particularly when they are in public places like restaurants, call for moving the child from the situation and having a time out.

ATTRACTIVENESS
Attractive infants and children typically receive better treatment by adults, including their parents. In studies comparing the misbehavior of attractive and unattractive children, the transgression was viewed more negatively if it was committed by an unattractive compared with an attractive child, and the suggested punishment by the adults was more severe for the unattractive children despite the children's identical misbehavior. This apparently starts very early in life, as mothers of "cute newborns" were more affectionate and maintained more eye contact. Fathers' participation in caregiving for the 3-month-olds in another study was significantly and positively correlated with infant attractiveness assessed when the babies were newborns. In still another study mothers of more attractive 3-month-old infants were more affectionate and playful compared to mothers of less attractive infants. In contrast, the mothers of less attractive infants were more likely to be attentive to other people rather than to their infant and to engage in routine caregiving rather than affectionate behavior.

I recall my own daughter, who had a very large head of hair and a very winning smile as early as the newborn period, and how the nurses exclaimed about her cuteness and in turn spent more time with her rather than several other babies. Thus, there must be something to the expression attributed to Queen Victoria, who had nine children, and was quoted as saying "an ugly baby is a very nasty object."

These findings are perhaps not surprising inasmuch as adults commonly show a preference for other attractive adults and attractiveness has been correlated with popularity. It seems, though, that if parents appreciate that they also show this preference towards their very young infants and children (rather than assuming that attractiveness makes no difference) they will reduce the amount of deferential treatment and perhaps try to compensate in their treatment toward children who are less attractive.

AUTISM

Autism has a variety of genetic and nongenetic causes with the etiology (development) being unknown in the majority of children. Boys are more frequently affected than girls, and autism first becomes apparent in the preschool years. It always affects sociability, communication, and the child's repertoire of activities and interests. Autism encompasses a broad range of severities and a variety of other signs of brain dysfunction. These include motor signs, notably stereotypes such as head banging and flapping of hands. Abnormal responses to a variety of sensory stimuli occur, and the children have very severe attention problems and problems showing their emotions. A significant number of autistic children experience epileptic seizures and have abnormal EEGs. Magnetic resonance imaging (MRI) has revealed abnormalities of brain development in some autistic children. The level of intelligence may range from profound mental deficiencies to giftedness. The pattern of cognitive skills is likely to be uneven, typically with better nonverbal than verbal skills. In the preschool years, autistic children have a language disorder. Verbal expression may range from total lack of language to being extremely verbose (some even have echolalia, which is endless talking). Comprehension and language use are invariably impaired. While there are no specific drugs that can reduce the symptoms of attention disorder and seizures, the autistic features can change with maturation and appropriate intervention. Communication skills and sociability remain deficient but improved for all but the most severely affected children. The children can be positively affected by early interventions focused on the development of appropriate social skills and meaningful communication.

Autism is a particularly difficult problem because the child is unresponsive. As early as infancy, autistic children are noted to arch their backs when held, to make very little eye contact, and to simply dislike physical affection. At the preschool stage or as young children they prefer to play by themselves and often sit and do nothing, staring into space. Their difficulty staying on-task and their autistic behaviors, such as flapping their hands and whirling around, spinning things, or rocking and banging their heads, is very disruptive behavior and often wins them no friends at school.

The number of autistic children has increased dramatically over the past several years, probably because screening techniques are more sensitive but less specific so that more children are labeled autistic (and many more who are not really autistic). Thus this is a "waste-basket" diagnosis, as some clinicians call it. Many schools are now providing special classes for autistic children, and even some schools serve only autistic children. Statistically, approximately one in every 1,000 children is affected, with males being affected four times as often as females. Generally the disorder is thought to be inherited. However, so many theories have been advanced about neurological and neurotransmitter causes that an entire journal is now devoted to autism. Medical conditions associated with autism include epilepsy, hearing deficits, speech and language impairments, and eyesight problems. A comprehensive medical work-up is required in all cases with pervasive autistic symptomatology.

Autistic children have very little language and tend to repeat words, sometimes memorizing paragraphs of TV guides and reiterating them and in general speaking inappropriately. One study showed that using baby-talk-like language (motherese) was more effective in gaining the attention of autistic children than using simple "conversational tones." Many therapy attempts have focused on physical interactions such as wrapping the children in blankets and holding them to enhance their attentiveness. Although these children are also thought to have an aversion to touch, we were able to successfully perform a massage therapy study with them recently. In this study the children who received massage therapy a couple of times a week for a month showed less off-task behavior, they had fewer autistic mannerisms, and they related more positively to their teachers, suggesting at least that they did not find touch aversive. Rather, they found it calming. This may be a technique that parents could use as a way of being physically more intimate with their typically rejecting autistic children and as a way of enhancing their attentiveness. In addition, we have used imitation therapy to help the parents and children interact. The parents imitate the child's behaviors, and the child becomes more social.

AUTONOMY

Autonomy is probably the primary goal of childhood. It generally happens by the end of childhood, and then ensues the long struggle for adolescents to have complete autonomy. Teaching children how to take care of themselves, how to monitor and control their own behavior, how to relate to other people in a socially effective way, how to express their emotions and how to achieve their potential is what we call the package of parenting. The developmental course in autonomy proceeds from the infant who cries at 6 months when you stifle their crawling attempts or remove a desired object, to the child who wants to walk unassisted, to the "terrible twos" when the child wants to have everything plus power over parents. Developing all those skills from motor to cognitive to social are all in the service of achieving some autonomy.

Problems that get in the way of developing autonomy include deficits in the child, temperament problems such as inhibition and unwillingness to have commerce with the world, limited time and patience of parents, who might find it easier to do things for the child, and inability on the parents' part to allow the child to fail in trial-and-error learning. The frustration is felt on all sides but ultimately the child will be autonomous and the parent will be proud. Even the terrible twos are a small price to pay. Actually this is where the parent can have more fun, enjoying the slapstick-like humor of the child's clumsiness as he achieves the milestones of autonomy.

BABBLING
Babbling is the child's first attempt at conversation and consists of long strings of sounds formed with the lips and tongue, including *baba* and *dada* and arias of cooing that make the child seem musically talented. These sounds are universal and gradually become differentiated into, say, American versus Japanese sounds as the child is further exposed to his unique speech environment. Importantly, babbling reinforces the parent's attempts to talk to the child. In the first conversations the parent says something, the child babbles, and the parent says "Oh is that so," as if the child has truly participated in the conversation.

BABYSITTERS
Having a babysitter even from the newborn period is a great break for parents and their needed time together. Finding someone who has experience, who loves taking care of babies, and who comes with good references from people you know, is generally the best way to choose. On the first few occasions it is important to be there for a while until the babysitter becomes comfortable in the environment and familiar with the baby. Watching how the babysitter relates to your child and cares for your child in those few hours of getting acquainted is one way to develop confidence in the babysitter.

BATHING
Bathing is typically one of those end of the day activities where the parent has prime time with the child. From very early in infancy bath time is a favorite activity of the child. It becomes a family ritual and is intended not only for cleaning but also relaxing the child at bedtime. Children love the kicking and splashing, sliding under the water, exploring the taste of the shampoo, and even turning on the hot water faucets without realizing they could burn. The most critical thing to remember is not

only to have fun playing with the child and his bathtub toys but that the child should never be left unattended in the bathtub. The one inch of water in the bottom of the bathtub is the leading cause of drownings.

BAYLEY SCALES

The Bayley Scales were created by Nancy Bayley in 1963 (and revised in 1993) to assess the infant's mental and motor development. They can be given to children from about 3 months of age to about age 4 years. Typically the child is seated on the parent's lap while the Bayley Scales are given, and usually they last approximately 40 minutes. Developmental age-appropriate items are given, such as a red ring dangled in front of a 3-month-old infant's face, and pegs and peg boards are given at a slightly older toddler age. Motor skills are assessed by watching the child's natural motor behavior and offering more challenging tests at a later age such as climbing stairs and walking on a rail. These scales yield a score with an average being at about 100. They are used simply to give the pediatrician or developmental professional a sense of how the child's mental and motor development are progressing and whether there are any areas that need work.

BEDTIME PROBLEMS

Bedtime is one of those quality times for parents and children. It needs to be a happy time even though children can fret or procrastinate. Having a bedtime ritual that the child looks forward to is often helpful. The teddybear gets tucked in, the child hears a story, and then a backrub helps a child get to sleep. A recent study in our lab suggested that backrubs were more effective than rocking from early infancy through early toddlerhood. In the case of rocking, the child goes to sleep during the rocking but awakens as soon as he is carried to bed. In the case of backrubs, the child is awake during the backrub and goes to sleep in that position shortly thereafter.

BITING

Biting is perhaps the most difficult problem parents and teachers have with toddlers. Unfortunately, very little is known about how to prevent it because it is not a favorite topic for research. Generally a child uses biting when other behaviors do not manage to get him what he wants from his playmates. Pushing another child often escalates into slapping which escalates into biting. Biting attracts more attention from teachers because teeth marks are generally more alarming and potentially more dangerous than scrapes and bruises. Unfortunately, one child's biting often leads to an epidemic of biting where several children follow the lead and the problem becomes unmanageable. Biting occurs most often in the mid-morning, randomly throughout the week, probably because children are more active mid-morning, and most often in September, probably because this is a back-to-school period which is a frustrating transition for children.

Generally teachers will "special" a child, paying additional attention to the biting child and trying to predict when the child will bite. The teachers will typically intervene when they think the child is about to bite and attempt to distract the child with toys before the biting occurs. Other situations in which the child might resort to biting are when he is extremely tired, frustrated, or overexcited. If the child learns that he does not have to resort to biting to get what he wants (teacher provides the "wanted object" as warnings occur that are less worrisome), the child will probably no longer resort to biting. If the child appears to be compulsively biting, then more extreme measures may be necessary, such as providing a stuffed animal as a substitute for biting another child (it being less dangerous to bite the stuffed animal than another child). Another measure that may be used is "time out." Usually a minute per year of the child's age is sufficient. Often the child will see what he is missing during the time out and will learn to control his behavior. Another effective measure is giving the child lemon juice. Most bites are minor and can be treated by washing, applying cold compresses, and comforting the child.

The advice of a child psychologist is that the best thing for an adult to do when one child bites another is to remain calm, take the child to a time out area, telling him "no biting" and that he should remain there until you return, console the bitee but not make a big deal of the injury. If the bite has broken the skin, administer a topical antibiotic and call a pediatrician. Then without appearing that you are "on the alert for another incident" be aware of signals that the child is "working himself up to a bite," move in, and either remove him from the playing field or distract him. Research suggests that there is no connection between parenting style and biting, nor is biting indicative of psychological problems or predictive of later problems getting along with other children.

Because this behavior problem, more than virtually any other behavior problem, distresses parents, it needs special attention immediately. Parents become extremely emotional about this problem. For example, a thoracic surgeon parent was recently so hysterical about his child being bitten that he claimed the biting child could have pierced his child's lung (if he were being objective he would have remembered that he was a thoracic surgeon and knew very well that the rib cage stands outside the lung and would protect the lung from biting).

CARRIERS

Carriers come in many varieties for various kinds of carrying positions. For example, in a recent study we observed that carrying the baby in a front-to-front position led to infant sleep, while carrying the infant faced outwards led to more wakeful and exploratory behavior. The optimal carrier might allow for both positions. Being carried by the parent has a long history in evolution and is popular in many cultures, probably because it provides additional stimulation for the baby, enables the mother to closely monitor the baby, and lets her work unencumbered with hands free. This arrangement might also allow for less heat loss and the conservation of energy.

CHILDPROOFING

Childproofing offers the opportunity to simplify your environment and it can even be fun to convert your living room to a playroom where the whole family can enjoy playing together. The obvious safety precautions are removing sharp objects, poison substances, plastic bags, and anything that can injure or anything small that can lead to choking or suffocation, placing guards on stairs, safety latches on cupboards, plugs on electric outlets, locked front doors, and certainly locking up guns. For many years children do not know the difference between reality and fantasy, and for that reason alone guns should be under lock and key. Choking on foreign bodies is the cause of death for more than 300 children each year in the United States. A review of the records of 548 children (aged 4 months to 18 years) was undertaken to identify factors important in diagnosis. A wide variety of objects was recovered, the most common being peanuts, organic material, other nuts, popcorn, seeds, plastic objects, and pins.

Airway obstruction from aspiration of a foreign body should be suspected in all infants and children who have swallowing or respiratory difficulties. If the patient is unable to clear the airway by coughing, the Heimlich maneuver should be attempted. Parents can help to prevent airway obstruction by keeping small objects away from infants and children and by teaching them to chew food thoroughly. Whenever the child is approaching a forbidden object or something dangerous it is best to simply remove the child or distract him with a similar object or activity rather than saying no and expecting the child to leave the area. Saying "No" for most young children is simply a challenge and escalates into a struggle. Simply carrying or taking the child by the hand and moving him to another area where he can be distracted is more effective.

CLINGING

Clinging is a fairly normal activity for young children when they are hesitant about new places and people. Clinging or "holding on to the mother's apron strings," as they once called it, gives the child a sense of reassurance about the situation. Clinging is also fairly common during developmental milestone periods, for example, around 1 year when the child is learning to walk and separation and stranger anxiety are occurring, and again during the time of the "terrible twos." Situations during which children may cling are during leave-takings at preschool and following special events like the birth of a sibling. This behavior occurs most frequently in temperamentally shy, slow-to-warm-up children who have difficulty making transitions to new situations.

Not showing your own anxiety about your child's anxious behavior will help. In addition, engaging your child in play may help her adjust to the new situation. For example, when leaving her off at preschool, letting her have her stuffed animal or whatever makes her comfortable should help reduce clinging.

COLIC

Colic is a syndrome of persistent crying in young infants. Colic is one of the most common problems in infancy (the incidence ranging from 10 to 35%). Researchers disagree about the definition and clinical criteria for colic and some pediatricians suggest that "colic does not exist." This presents a very confusing picture to parents.

The word "colic" is derived from the Greek word *kolikos*, the adjective of *kolon*, meaning the large intestine. Colic also goes by the labels "infantile colic" and "paroxysmal fussing." Colic has been described as intermittent and unexplained crying during the first 3 months of life by infants who are otherwise well fed and healthy. Colic usually starts during the second or third week of life and spontaneously disappears at around 3 months. The crying is generally intense and typically lasts from 30 minutes to 3 hours, often occurring in the late afternoon or evening, followed by difficulty falling asleep. The crying may also occur intermittently and last for several hours at any time of the day or night, although the crying episodes tend to recur at the same time of day.

In most cases crying is considered normal infant behavior and can be treated with reassurance and counseling about appropriate parental responses. In a minority of cases, the crying pattern and other infant behaviors may suggest a gastrointestinal problem that may require treatment. Fussiness and crying are not easy to tolerate by most adults, which probably explains why colic is the most frequent problem presented to pediatricians. Although colic ends almost abruptly at 3 months, irritability and excessive crying have been known to recur during frustrating developmental milestones such as sitting, crawling, walking, and virtually any learning stage.

Some clinicians accept the definition of colic as full-force crying for at least 3 hours per day, for 3 or more days per week, for 3 weeks. Colic begins with a sudden onset of crying. The cry is often high pitched and accompanied by facial grimacing, suggesting that the infant is experiencing severe pain. The crying is accompanied by increased motor activity, flexion of the elbows, clenched fists, hypertonicity (for example, the knees are drawn up or the legs are stiff and extended), and the abdomen is tense and distended. The infant's eyes are either tightly closed or wide open, the back is arched, the feet are often cold, bowel sounds can be heard, infants may hold their breath for brief periods of time, and they may resist soothing.

Several factors may be involved in infant colic, including biological factors such as temperament and sleep-state organization and environmental factors, for example, overstimulation by parents. Biological factors include hypertonicity, gastrointestinal and allergic factors, and an immature central nervous system. Although gastrointestinal factors have typically been described for colic, serial radiographs suggest a normal amount of gas in the GI tracts of colic infants.

Breast milk, cow's milk, and soy milk have also been implicated in colic. Digestion of milk and soy protein produces excessive intestinal gas and peristalsis which can result in colic. However, colic occurs as commonly in breastfed as in formula-fed infants.

Feeding patterns have been implicated as a potential contributor to colic. Short interfeed intervals resulted in less crying. Infants who were carried more frequently did not cry at the usual 6-week crying peak, and the crying and fussing that tended to occur in the early evenings decreased. Overstimulation also contributes to colic. This became clear when infants who were hospitalized for colic cried less once they were hospitalized. Other overstimulating factors are excessive noise, bright lights, and irritating blankets or clothing. Colic may cease around 3 months because infants can now use self-comforting techniques such as gaze aversion, thumb sucking, turning over, reaching, and grasping to avoid or remove the annoying stimulation. Having schedules for feeding, bathing, and sleeping routines is very effective. In addition, providing soothing stimulation such as massaging the infant, rocking or swinging, and playing classical music or white noise can also be extremely effective.

CONVERSATION SKILLS

Conversation skills start developing as early as birth when babies have face-to-face interactions with their parents. These are particularly frequent and become exciting interactions at around 3 to 6 months, when babies not only have frequent eye contact but also smile, make a lot of funny faces, coo and make funny sounds. Early conversations have been analyzed in detail by psychologists, who note that these conversations have many prespeech sounds (the vowels and consonants), all the universal facial expressions (which occur as early as 5 months in utero), and many expressive gestures of the hands. When the timing of speech and pauses in speech and looking and looking away are studied, the baby's behavior is very much like an adult's. For example, the baby looks at his interaction partner when listening and looks away when talking, as if to concentrate on what he is saying. Occasionally both speak at the same time, and occasionally there are interruptions just as in adult conversation. But the turn-taking and the turn-taking signals are already fairly well developed.

Much of the infant's learning of these skills appears to come from imitation which frequently happens during parent–infant interactions. Like a game, the parent imitates the infant and the infant imitates the parent. In fact, one of the easiest ways to get an infant to stop crying is to imitate that crying. The infant stops crying and pays close attention to the ridiculous-sounding adult. Another game parents often play is providing the words for the infant. The mother says "I like your hat" and the baby coos and the mother says "Oh, you like your hat too," as if providing the words for the baby. An important rule the parents learn immediately is to respect the infant's looking away. This indicates (as it does in adult conversations) that the infant is either bored, tired, or has had enough of that conversation. Repeating the child's speech sounds and adding to his words helps as the infant becomes older. By toddlerhood children have conversations with the world, with themselves, and with their imaginary playmates. At that stage the silence at bedtime is a welcome relief.

CRAWLING (or creeping)

Crawling tends to occur at around 6 to 9 months, although some babies never crawl, and those babies sometimes walk at an earlier age. Every baby seems to have her own style of crawling, with some tending to crawl backwards, some sideways, and some straight ahead. Some crawl on their hands and knees, while others do it on their hands with bended legs. Generally speaking, it seems an awkward way to get from one place to another, and it looks like hard work, so it is perhaps not surprising that there has to be something the baby really wants to reach for crawling to occur. A recent study was conducted on motor skill development in crawlers and noncrawlers during early infancy. The noncrawlers showed slower motor skill development, suggesting that those who do not crawl may develop motor skills more slowly.

A parent recently expressed concern that her child was retarded because she was not crawling at 9 months. After reminding the parent that some babies never crawl, I placed my keys on the carpet, and the baby proceeded to crawl directly to them. The mother, who typically carried her infant on her hip around the house for hours at a time, expressed amazement that all it took was placing her child on the floor with something desirable in view, and her child was no longer "retarded."

CRYING

The most common causes of crying in infants and young children are fatigue, hunger, indigestion, soiling, wetness, and pain. The most common psychological reason is a parent's leaving. Very soon after birth parents come to recognize the cry sounds of their infant. The frequency, intensity, and intonation of cry sounds are different for all of these problems. For example, fussy cries are less tense than hungry or pain-induced cries. Parents will often assure themselves that all of these problems are taken care of before letting the child "cry it out." Sometimes when a child is overstimulated and, thus, overexhausted, crying serves as a kind of stimulus barrier to ward off all other sounds in the environment.

The parent may be able to stop crying by rocking or walking or driving the infant around, but often the crying will start again when the infant is put to bed. This could become a pattern of crying for the parent to come and comfort. The simplest method for solving this problem seems to be letting the infant cry it out. For the first night the crying may persist for 20 to 30 minutes, and when there is no rescue from the parents the infant finally falls asleep. The second night the crying may last only 10 minutes and by the third night there usually is no crying. Getting up for every cry not only overstimulates and ultimately tires the infant but certainly tires the parent. A recent study suggests that when parents pick up a crying child at bedtime, the child's crying becomes a routine pattern that does not stop until the child is picked up.

DAYCARE

Early daycare helps develop a child's social and intellectual skills, but only if it is quality care. Penelope Leach, in her book *Children First*, and others have claimed that full-time daycare can have harmful effects.

However, their concerns relate to poor-quality daycare. In contrast, the average daycare that most middle-class kids get is considered helpful for cognitive and social development, according to the National Research Council and a 1993 survey conducted by the Child Care Action Campaign and *Working Mother* magazine.

Quality care can be hard to define, but knowing what to look for in a daycare center helps. US state and federal governments have licensing requirements that ensure the provision of adequate space and safety features (for example, smoke alarms and sprinkler jets). These requirements also ensure optimal teacher–student ratios and class sizes. For example, quality programs in Florida have no less than 1 teacher for every 4 infants, 1 teacher for every 6 toddlers, and 1 teacher for every 10 preschoolers in classrooms with no more than 20 infants, 30 toddlers, and 40 preschoolers. These figures, however, are meaningless if sufficient space is not provided (approximately 35 sq. ft. for indoor space and 50 sq. ft. for outdoor space per child).

Most parents know when they have discovered a quality daycare setting. It will be immediately apparent that the teachers are nurturant and the children are happy. Children will be involved in creative activities and the environment will be organized, colorful, and rich with interesting materials and play opportunities. A class schedule with designated times for show and tell, snacks, naps, free play, expressive arts, along with free time for fantasy play, and "gross motor" play (play which uses muscles) is also an important part of quality daycare. Outdoor play areas will include moving vehicles, sand play, and structures for climbing. Parents should ask questions about how long the teachers have been with the center (stability of the teachers is very important) and how much experience they have had.

Some of the highest quality centers are found in university lab schools because they are partially subsidized by the universities. Some of the benefits of a laboratory school include active research and teacher training programs affiliated with their early childhood education and psychology departments. Religious centers (e.g., churches and synagogues), hospitals, corporate centers, and Montessori schools also provide quality daycare. Specific listings are often provided by early childhood education departments at universities. In a study on skills needed by preschool children for success in daycare, teachers assigned the highest ratings to communication and independence. More specifically these included children's ability to respond to their names, ask for help from an adult, stay out of restricted areas and respond to adults' questions. The teachers rated skills in the area of pre-academics (including sitting cross-legged in a circle and cutting with scissors) the lowest.

DEPRESSION

Infants can have symptoms that mimic adult depression, including withdrawal and listlessness around other children, sad facial expressions, a monotone voice, whining and complaining. The child might also show eating problems such as overeating or undereating and toileting regressions, difficulty going to sleep, frequent nightwakings, and difficulty getting up in the morning. Symptoms of illness include respiratory problems, constipation, and diarrhea. Illness probably occurs because the immune system is negatively affected by high stress levels accompanying depression.

DISCIPLINE

Affection and discipline are two of the most important aspects of parenting. Children growing up in the wild without parents become like wild animals because they are missing affection and discipline. In addition to needing the affection for growth and development, children need discipline for their behavior to be organized and self-regulated. While some choices can be left to the child, for example, what the child wishes to wear, other matters that are critical to survival, such as not playing in the street and not being cruel to other children, require very firm limits. A parent should not ask a child if the child wants to hold their hand while crossing the street. This is not a safe choice for a child to make. Having an intellectual discussion on the reasons why hurting someone is bad is also not effective. I recall a teacher in a model preschool quietly leaving the room after having been hurt by a flying block only to return several minutes later to have an intellectual discussion with the children about the "negative aspects of flying blocks." A better lesson would have been reacting normally to being hurt so the children would know the consequences of their actions.

Another problem with discipline is its frequent inconsistency. Recent reviews of the literature on behavior problems and on child abuse suggest that the most predictive factor is inconsistent discipline, such as parents being inconsistent from one time to the next or from one parent to the other. In societies where discipline is consistent within and across parents and between parents and teachers, such as in France and China, children have fewer behavior problems, and the incidence of child abuse is very low. Socially accepted forms of discipline are practiced by parents and teachers alike. Thus, the child is never seen "driving the parent up the wall" and the parent losing control.

A recent study revealed that verbal and physical discipline are not substitutes but, instead, are commonly used together. Parents who yelled frequently were the ones most likely to hit frequently. Respondents who were spanked (yelled at) frequently as children were more prone to frequently spank (yell at) their own children. Harsh parental discipline occurring early in life was associated with later aggression in children. The good news was that most people were able to break out of the cross-generational cycle of punitive childrearing, although physical punishment is still quite common. In a recent survey 19% of mothers believed that there are times when it is appropriate to spank a child less than 1 year old and 74% believed this about children 1 to 3 years old. Forty-two percent reported that they had spanked their own child in the past week. Mothers believed more strongly in spanking for dangerous misbehaviors than for annoying ones. Other traditional disciplinary methods include rewards for good behavior and punishment for unacceptable behavior. The most common rewards are verbal praise, a smile, special attention or activities, or physical affection. Usual kinds of punishment include verbal disapproval, an unhappy look, ignoring the behavior (extinction), or temporary isolation (time out). Rewards are typically cited as being more effective than punishment.

EAR INFECTIONS
Ears could be considered more vulnerable sense organs because it is difficult to close them to unwanted noise. Ears are also a source of major discomfort to many young children because they experience ear-aches from inner and middle ear infections. Excessive pulling on the ears, irritability, and signs of difficulty hearing can mean another ear infection. After dozens of these infections and antibiotic treatments, pediatricians often refer the child for a myringotomy. This procedure involves piercing holes in the eardrums to enable the fluid to drain and is considered a minor procedure, although anesthesia is typically required and that is certainly not minor. Treatment is critical because there are data showing that repeated, prolonged ear infections contribute to delays in language development and learning difficulties at school. For example, children with inner ear infections (*otitis media*) have significantly lower expressive language scores, suggesting impairments in language expression. They also have deficits in processing auditory information and spelling skills, and are noted to receive more special education services during school age. Despite these problems, their academic achievement tests do not appear to suffer, and by later childhood their early language delays are no longer present.

EATING PROBLEMS
Eating problems can range from food refusals and minor conflicts with parents to eating disorders. The minor food refusals are sometimes just the child being finicky about food preferences, although very little is

known about children's food preferences because all the nutritious foods are bottled in baby food form, with very little choice being given the child until such time as she can select from her own lunch box or the school cafeteria menu. In addition to very little being known about taste preferences, very little is known about food textures that children prefer. In a recent study we were surprised to find that very young infants preferred chunky applesauce if they are given the choice before the designated age for chunky applesauce.

Other reasons for food refusals are the child's own power in struggles that happen as early as the "terrible twos," when children simply want to be autonomous and do what they want to do when they want to do it. These can continue into preschool and grade school when children do not have the "good models" of their parents for food preferences but the fads of what other children are eating. At this time full lunch boxes might simply mean the child has eaten someone else's more desirable lunch.

Although playing with food is a good way to learn the art of eating at the infancy and toddler stage, by preschool the child should be learning appropriate restaurant eating habits. Around this time the child learns that mealtimes are a social time for the family, not a time for reading or watching TV. Unfortunately, because this is often the family's only time together, mealtimes can become times for conflict and conflict resolution. This can contribute to digestive problems and the association between food and anxiety or sadness. The association of food with joy is perhaps also not good, as it may come to be used as a way of solving problems and warding off depression.

EMOTIONAL EXPRESSIONS

The necessary muscles for the universal emotional expressions are present very early in fetal development (3 months' gestation). These universal expressions include happy, interest, surprise, sad, angry, fearful, and disgusted. Although the expressions seem exaggerated during early development when children laugh without restraint as well as cry sometimes incessantly, the expressions become socialized with development and you begin to see blends of expressions such as a combination of surprise and sadness when feelings are hurt. Some children are noted to display their emotions, as in the expression "wearing their heart on their sleeve," and others tend to be more "poker-faced" and show very little emotion. These extremes, sometimes labeled extroversion and introversion, appear in children as early as the newborn stage. In a study we conducted on newborns' imitations of facial expressions, about 20% of infants showed very exaggerated facial expressions and very little heart rate change, while the other extreme 20% showed emotional responses in their heart rate changes but were "poker-faced." Most children (like most adults) show their emotions not only on their face but in their physiological responses as well, for example in a racing heart, sweaty hands, or a blushed face.

EMPATHY
Some form of empathy is apparent as early as birth, when newborns cry at the sound of other babies crying. A typical situation that is used to study empathy in toddlers and preschoolers is asking a mother to pretend she is crying. Almost always the child will show some signs of attempting to comfort the mother. However, some children, who, for example, have depressed mothers or have been prenatally exposed to drugs, show no empathy. Some recent research in our lab suggests that there are different forms of nonempathetic behavior including sad and angry responses. In the mother pretend-crying situation, for example, some preschoolers showed nonempathetic angry behavior including kicking their "crying" mother or yelling at her, while other children showed nonempathetic sad behavior by simply ignoring the mother's "crying."

EXPLORATION
This is usually the precursor to playful behavior. The child explores objects to learn what the object can do and what the child can do to the object. One of the earliest forms of exploration is the newborn sucking on its mother's breast. For the next 6 months everything gets explored by mouth, and much is learned (for example, the shapes of things) by exploring with the mouth. The hands take over and then exploration seems almost an obsession as infants make messes with their finger foods, throw objects on the ground for adults to retrieve, and take everything out of drawers and put them back in again (container behavior), as they explore and learn the properties of things. As exploration proceeds the child's behavior becomes more playful, with actions being repeated over and over usually to the sounds and facial expressions of sheer joy. Stifling exploration should be avoided at all costs, as it would in turn stifle curiosity, creativity, and the entire learning process. Extremes of babyproofing or childproofing the house can seriously interfere with exploration.

EYE CONTACT
Eye contact is present as early as birth and is one of the most important features of social interactions. Without eye contact, it is extremely difficult to communicate with people. Infants and older children will sometimes turn off their eye contact or show gaze aversion when they are being overstimulated and need to process the information, much like

taking a break from a conversation. However, excessive gaze aversion or the absence of eye contact early in infancy is often considered a sign of autism and should be further evaluated if this problem persists. A recent study on children age 2–6 noted that children who had averted gaze from their parents in the first month of life (1) developed a maladaptive relationship in terms of their interactions by 2 years; (2) showed behavior problems and developmental delays for up to 6 years; and (3) had less favorable development during the preschool years.

FATHERS

In most studies people have found fathers to be more playful and stimulating and mothers to provide more caregiving and comforting. We found an exception to this when we studied fathers who were primary caregivers. The stay-at-home-fathers turned out to be more like mothers than fathers, and the mothers who were the "breadwinners" were more like the stereotypical father. We suggested that this meant that more caregiving is provided by the person who knows the infant best and more playfulness by the parent who knows the infant least.

In a sense the more stimulating, rough-and-tumble play of the fathers is complementary to the more soothing, comforting behavior of mothers. In a similar light, mothers tend to view their infants as being more difficult (perhaps because they are in a comforting role) and fathers are reported to enjoy their infants more (again because they engage in more play with them). Across the first several years, fathers are more involved in social interaction than in caregiving, and mothers continue to provide more of the caregiving. Although the differences between mothers and fathers has lessened over the years as more mothers have joined the workforce, some differences have continued, showing the mother providing more caregiving and the father more playful stimulation.

Despite the differences in their behaviors, infants and young children are noted to be equally attached to both parents. It may not appear that way, as infants and young children often protest their mothers leaving them at preschool and barely notice their fathers leaving. This is probably because fathers matter-of-factly leave, saying they will see their child later, while mothers make a greater fuss about leaving their children and express more reassurance about their returning, which seems to draw out this fussing behavior. The children's ambivalence about leaving their mothers is also displayed upon her return, whereas infants greet fathers as they return with intense, brief displays of positive emotion.

FLASHCARDS

The flashcard method was designed by a "better baby" school in Philadelphia to teach children music, language, science, and virtually anything that can be taught on flashcards to infants and toddlers. The school has repeatedly made great claims that 2-year-olds can learn physics, violin, and the classification of insects, for example. This is done by repeated drilling with flashcards, typically at home by the parent. None of these claims, however, have been supported by research, and the directors of the school are reluctant to have their methods tested. It is also not clear why a parent would want their child to know all this by the time they enter school, only to present the potential problem that the child would be rejected as "weird" by his peers. Certainly the child who is busily learning flashcard skills has very little time to learn social skills and how to get along with his peers, which is certainly a more important priority at the preschool stage.

FOOD PREFERENCES
As early as birth infants appear to have food preferences. Studies on newborns show that they make different faces to different tastes, with sweet flavors being accompanied by happy faces and quinine or rotten egg flavors being accompanied by grimacing. This seems to happen whether the food is tasted or simply smelled. Of course, the amniotic fluid which engulfs the fetus contains all of the basic flavors, especially the more salty/bitter taste. Newborns will readily take glucose but tend to reject salty water. Taste preferences then shift across age. Very little is known about young children's food texture preferences, although foods prepared for infants and young children tend to be pureed at first and only later have considerable texture. Their preferences for hot and cold foods is also relatively unknown.

Studies show that monozygotic ("identical") twins have more similar food preferences than dizygotic (nonidentical) twins, suggesting a strong genetic determination of food preferences. Many children will follow parental likes and dislikes, particularly dislikes after seeing an adult grimace at the thought of eating a particular food. On the other hand, parents who expose their children to wide varieties of foods have children who are not fussy eaters and who are willing to try new foods.

FRIENDS
Friendships develop at a very early stage in life, which we perhaps never knew until our children started attending infant daycare. In the nursery school my research group runs, we can no longer graduate infants at 12 months to the toddler nursery without also transferring their best friend with them. Parents told us very early on that they wanted their child to wait until they could move with their best friend, but it was only after studying this phenomenon that we appreciated that even infants experience anxiety and depression when separated from their best friends. In

our study the infants who were transferred without their friends experienced sleep problems, eating problems (either more or less), toileting problems (constipation or diarrhea), and sometimes even illness (typically upper respiratory infections). Thus, friendship starts at a very early age.

In our studies where parents were absent for a meeting or for the birth of another child, the preschoolers who remained in daycare with their friends were less depressed. In the early stages because of a child's shyness and less-developed social skills, parents may need to set the stage for developing relationships. This can be arranged through shared babysitting, remembering to invite a peer along for special activities, and trying to facilitate cooperative play between the children by giving them the same opportunities to engage in the same activity and by having play materials in twos, ensuring that each child has a play object or a book, so fighting is less likely to occur.

GAMEPLAYING

Gameplaying punctuates the early interactions between parents and their infants. Infant games such as "pat-a-cake" and "peek-a-boo" appear with such frequency that they are "universally" recognized as infant games. The importance of early gameplaying has been underscored by a number of early interaction researchers who suggest that gameplaying provides a context for learning one of the most important rules of conversation, that of turn-taking. Infant games are highly repetitive with simple and stereotyped roles for both participants. As such they exemplify the structure of conversational give and take or turn-taking. Even when the infant is still too young to assume an active role, the structure of these repetitive games may enable the infant to assimilate the turn-taking nature of interaction.

Other important features of early games include the "contingency experience" they provide (i.e., learning to react to and innovate in changing situations) and the facilitation of positive emotion. An illustration of the contingent responsivity provided by a game can be seen in one of the most popular early games, called "Tell Me a Story." The words are provided by the parent who treats the infants' vocalizations as if they too were words. The parent asks "Do you want to tell me a story?" The infant coos, the parent responds "Oh yeah? And then what happened?" The infant coos again and the parent replies "Oh, that's funny." The infant contingently responds to the parent's words by his cooing, and the parent contingently responds to infant cooing by further elaborations of the games.

The game "I'm Gonna Get You" is an illustration of the way in which games facilitate positive emotion. The parent repeatedly looms toward the infant, rubbing his or her head into the lap of the infant, tickling and jostling the infant, and accompanying each repetition with verbalizations such as "Ah, boom!" or "I'm gonna get you." These repetitious behaviors elicit infant smiles, vocalizations, and sometimes laughter. The parents contingently respond to these infant behaviors by playing more of the same game. The game ceases at the point at which it no longer elicits contented responses, and the parent moves on to another game.

Thus, early gameplaying provides an affective, contingency experience during which infants may learn important rules of communication such as turn-taking. When games are missing from the interaction or age-inappropriate games are played, the interaction appears to be badly timed, disorganized, or disturbed. When a mother plays age-inappropriate games or games which are too complex for a given age of infant, for example peek-a-boo with a 6-week-old infant, the interaction lacks positive emotion and is not sustained.

The early interactions of developmentally delayed, "atypical," or failure-to-thrive infants and mothers feature very few games. These mothers do not appear to "enjoy" playing games and do not as frequently play games, particularly age-appropriate games, with their infants, probably because their infants are less responsive.

In one of our studies, the types and frequency of "universally" recognized infant games were observed during face-to-face interactions of normal and high-risk infants and parents when the infants were 4 months old. Approximately six different games were played for approximately one-third of the interaction time. Fathers played with normal male infants more often, and the high-risk infants and parents played games less frequently than the normal infants and parents.

GRANDPARENTS

Grandparents have a number of positive effects on child development. Children are often more able to explore and try their skills around grandparents when not around their own parents. They seem to recognize a certain autonomy around grandparents, in contrast to their dependence around parents. This may be a two-sided process, as grandparents appear more relaxed and less overprotective around their grandchildren than parents do. They apparently also have a lesser need to set limits than parents, as typically children seem more self-regulated in their presence. Part of this phenomenon may relate to grandparents giving children their undivided attention, whereas parents are oftentimes busy trying to juggle children and other activities at the same time. It could be that the child's more demanding and less compliant behavior in the parents' presence is attention-getting behavior. It could also be that the children sense greater demands being placed on them by their parents and higher expectations for performance. Combined experience with parents and grandparents, in any case, would appear to be optimal for any child.

HANDEDNESS

Handedness, right or left hand preference, develops very early in infancy and can be determined by placing a desirable object in front of the infant and determining which hand leads to grasp the object. The dominant hand will invariably be preferred for fine-motor, dexterity activities. However, a recent study highlights the important staging and guiding function of the nondominant hand from very early in infancy. Left-handedness is more frequent in twins than in single born children and in males than in females.

The literature is very mixed about the association between handedness and problems. For example, in one study handedness and dyslexia (a learning disability) were significantly related, but handedness was only weakly associated with immune problems. In another study auto-immune disorders were more prevalent in lefthanders. In a third study lefthanders had nearly three times as many immune disorders as righthanders, the relatives of the lefthanders suffered from the same conditions, there was a higher frequency of learning disabilities such as dyslexia, stuttering, and autism in the lefthanders, and lefthanders had migraine headaches more often. One of the theories for lefthandedness, aside from the genetics theory, is that during fetal development testosterone slows the growth of the left hemisphere. When testosterone (the predominant male hormone) is elevated, it is more likely to produce left-handedness, and, in extreme cases, to lead to alterations in the left hemisphere that may be responsible for learning disorders such as dyslexia. Excessive testosterone levels can also alter immune function, which can then lead to immune problems such as eczema, psoriasis, and asthma.

In the earlier days attempts were made to shift children from being lefthanded to righthanded so that penmanship and scissors and virtually all hand-held devices (which are designed for right-handed people) would be more easily mastered. Today, parents and teachers do not attempt to alter handedness because of the undocumented theory that shifting handedness in itself may lead to learning disabilities.

HEAD BANGING

Head banging was once considered a very pathological activity that only handicapped or emotionally disturbed children showed. However, recent studies on rhythmic behaviors of infants and toddlers suggest that many children engage in these rhythmic activities as part of normal development. These include behaviors like head banging, rocking, lip biting, and thumb sucking. They generally happen when the infant/toddler is otherwise unoccupied and appears to be bored. In this case, these rhythmic activities may be a source of substitute stimulation. Other times they occur when the child is extremely tired, and at those times they seem to pacify and quiet the child. Generally they will disappear after a short period of time, so they are probably best ignored. If the child shows any of these behaviors excessively and is actually hurting himself, it may be important to get a professional evaluation.

IMITATION

Until very recently people thought that imitation did not occur until around the end of the first year of life. This concept of imitation was advanced by the famous child psychologist, Jean Piaget, who based his ideas on observations of his own two children. More recently several researchers have shown that even a newborn can imitate exaggerated facial expressions made by adults. These expressions include tongue protrusion (sticking the tongue out), an exaggerated smile, surprised face, and sad face. Of course not all children show imitative behaviors as early as the newborn stage. In fact, some newborns have been described as "poker-faced" and merely stare inquiringly as you model these faces. In the study we conducted on newborn imitation we made sure that first the newborn was awake and bright eyed. Then we held the baby in front of our face and bobbed up and down with a couple of knee bends to make sure the newborn's eyes were open, and then made a couple of tongue clicks to make sure the newborn was looking directly at our faces. We then put an exaggerated expression on our faces, leaving it there until the infant looked away. We would then repeat the action with the same or a different expression. When a baby was in a very alert state and in the mood for this game we saw very interesting imitative behavior. Later, at around 3 months, mothers almost invariably imitate their baby's cooing sounds during face-to-face games, and the baby in turn imitates the mother. This game goes back and forth for many rounds. A little while later infants imitate gestures and fine-motor behaviors. Although much of what infants show us they can do seems to be hardwired and occurs on some predetermined developmental schedule, imitation like other skills improves with experience.

INTELLIGENCE TESTS

Intelligence is still a hotly debated issue particularly for infants and young children. Although there are now scales that are considered infant

IQ tests, such as the Brazelton Scale and the Bayley Scales for Infant Development, these have very little stability over time. For example, some children score high early in infancy because of their precocious motor development, but then score poorly at a later age because of their limited language environment. The scales seem to focus more on motor skills at an early infancy stage and language skills in early childhood stage. Also, scores are significantly affected by many environmental conditions, suggesting that performance is not strictly determined by genetic factors.

INTERACTION COACHING

When parents, most typically mothers, are having difficulty interacting with their infants, they can be given interaction coaching which helps modify the behavior of the parent, and, in turn, the behavior of the infant. Typically mothers and infants are seated in a face-to-face position with the infant positioned in an infant seat. The mothers are given instructions in order to slow down their behavior. For example, they slow down when they are asked to imitate their infants' behaviors and they provide more stimulation when they are asked to "keep their infants' attention." Having to imitate the baby's behaviors slows down the mother's behavior simply because infant behaviors are slow in time. The infants usually delight at being imitated, and before long, mothers and infants are engaging in a back and forth imitation game. Another way that mothers learn to modify their behaviors is by being given video feedback on their interactions. By watching the videotapes, mothers can usually see the immediate effects of their behaviors and will show change almost immediately.

LEAVE-TAKINGS

Leave-takings are increasingly common, given the increasing numbers of infants, toddlers, and preschoolers attending nursery schools. Research suggests that different children have different leave-taking styles. In one study, children who cried during the early morning separations showed either a slow approach or no response except looking at the mother when she returned from her day's work. Those children who left their mothers quickly in the mornings typically continued playing and showed things to the mother when she returned in the afternoon. The mothers of children who cried during separations more often "slipped out" of the room. The authors of this study suggested that much of the separation/reunion behavior is determined by the child, with the mother merely being in a "responding mode" at these times, mainly waiting to receive and act on signals from her child. However, in a study we conducted we thought that the parents were very influential on the leave-takings.

We studied the leave-taking and the reunion behaviors of the infants, toddlers, preschoolers, and their parents as the children were dropped off and picked up at their nursery school each day. On arrival at their classroom, infants and toddlers related primarily to their parents, whereas preschoolers related to their teachers. Girls more frequently engaged in interaction with their teachers, and boys more frequently approached the children's play activities. Toddlers showed the most distress behaviors during the parents' departures, and the toddlers' parents hovered about them and "sneaked out of the room" more frequently. When mothers dropped off the children, the children showed more attention-getting behavior and crying than when the children were dropped off by their fathers. Mothers engaged in more "distracting-the-child" behaviors and took a longer time to leave the classroom than fathers. Giving a verbal explanation, distracting the child, lingering in the classroom, and "sneaking out of the room" were accompanied by more crying. We noted that some children had difficulty making transitions, and those children not only showed difficulty leaving their parents in the morning but difficulty leaving their classroom in the afternoon. In addition we noted that fathers were much more "nonchalant" in their behavior, and the children were less distressed when they were dropped off by their fathers. Thus, the rather business-like style of leave-taking by the fathers seems to work better if parents want to avoid the stress of seeing their children's distress.

MASSAGE THERAPY

Massage therapy has been noted to help infants and children in many ways. When we gave hospitalized premature infants three 15-minute massages a day for 10 days they gained 47% more weight, were hospitalized for 6 fewer days (at a hospital cost savings of approximately $10,000), and were more responsive to social stimulation. Eight months later they still showed a growth advantage and their performance on mental and motor developmental tests was superior. Massage therapy used with normal infants led to less irritability, more alertness, and better sleep patterns. Normal infants also gained weight following 5 weeks of massage. When compared to a group of infants who were rocked, the massaged infants were awake while they were being massaged and quickly went to sleep following the massage, while the rocked infants slept during the rocking but awakened as the rocking ended. This suggests that massage is a more effective way for parents to help their infants go to sleep.

Although the underlying mechanism for the effectiveness of massage is not clear, it seems to put infants and children in a more relaxed state.

In that state their stress hormones (cortisol levels) are reduced and they are more alert. The reduction in stress hormones improves the functioning of the immune system.

Infant massage classes are being started in many places in the US to teach parents how to massage their children. In at least one study we have shown that the person giving the massage benefits as much as the person receiving the massage. In that study we trained grandparent volunteers to massage babies, and after a month of massaging babies they showed several changes including fewer trips to the doctor, more social calls, fewer cups of coffee, less depression, and greater self-esteem. Although mothers are typically given the training, researchers have also observed fathers as massage therapists. For example, in one study Australian fathers were taught to give massages during bath time for 4 weeks after the infants were born. By 3 months the infants were greeting their fathers with more eye contact, smiling, vocalizing, reaching, and orienting responses, and showed less avoidance behavior. At this time the fathers who had been in the massage group also showed greater involvement with their infants. Thus, massage therapy has many benefits for both parents and their children.

MATERNAL DEPRESSION

Mothers who are depressed or who have symptoms of depression such as flat affect (showing little emotion) and listless behavior tend to have a difficult time interacting and being responsive to their infants. The infants in turn develop flat affect and low activity levels. If the mother remains depressed over the first 6 months of life, the infant will begin to show growth and developmental delays by one year. By 3 years children of depressed mothers developed behavior problems such as depression and conduct problems. If mothers are simply depressed postpartum and the depression does not continue, the infants do not experience long-term effects.

Fathers and substitute caregivers such as infant nursery teachers can buffer some of these effects. Infants of depressed mothers often appear normal when interacting with their nondepressed fathers and infant nursery teachers. Other effective interventions are the use of mood inductions with the mothers, such as music therapy and massage therapy. Interaction coaching to help the mother be more active and responsive to their infants, such as playing peek-a-boo and imitation games, helps them improve their interactions. Teaching depressed mothers to massage their infants also helps improve the mothers' mood and reduce stress in the infants.

MOVING

Moving is one of the most stress-producing and growth-producing experiences in childhood. Whether the move is from classroom to classroom, neighborhood to neighborhood, city to city, or country to country, the source of stress is losing one's friends. Separation from peers leads to symptoms very much like those that occur following separation from parents. The child becomes agitated and then depressed. Sleep is most affected by moving, with nightwakings and night terrors frequently happening. The child's behavior fluctuates between being aggressive and withdrawn, and like depression in adults, eating habits change (overeating or undereating occurs). The children experience constipation or diarrhea, and sometimes they get sick because of immune problems. We have observed these changes in studies on moves to new classrooms and moves to new schools. Even as young as one year of age, we are having to move children's best friends with them when they graduate from infancy classes to toddler classes so that they will not experience these symptoms. The children who are left behind often experience more severe symptoms, perhaps because they are remaining in the same environment where they are reminded of their long-lost friends.

MUSIC

Music is noted to have profound effects as early as birth. Studies on premature infants, for example, show that following repeated exposure to music, the infants grow and develop better. In a study on preschoolers, performance on cognitive tasks was superior following exposure to music. Much of these effects may be attributed to music's ability to relax infants and young children. When heart rate and blood pressure are recorded, for example, they are lower following music. When infants or children are distressed, they typically show greater EEG activity in the right frontal area of the brain (activity in this region is typically associated with negative emotions and mood states). Exposure to music can actually shift EEG activity from the right to the left side of the brain.

PACIFIERS

Pacifier and thumb-sucking is often viewed with disdain, and it is discouraged to the extent that premature infants in some hospitals require a physician's prescription for a pacifier. Yet documented and anecdotal reports show infants' sucking pacifiers helps calm them during uncomfortable procedures, and toddlers are made more comfortable for adapting to unfamiliar situations. Pacifiers provide comfort, promote physiological tranquillity, and help in growth and development. In one study, we used pacifiers during painful hospital procedures. The infants who were allowed to suck on pacifiers cried significantly less, and their heart rate and respiration were slower. Pacifiers used during circumcisions reduced crying by 40%. It is not clear whether pacifier use reduces pain associated with invasive procedures or if the sucking is just incompatible with crying and therefore crying occurs less often. It is also possible that sucking on pacifiers releases pain-alleviating chemicals like serotonin. Sucking on pacifiers has also been used for weight gain, particularly with premature babies. In a study we conducted on preemies, those who were allowed to use pacifiers gained weight more rapidly and were discharged from the hospital 6 days earlier than those not using pacifiers, at savings of approximately $3,000 per infant. These infants also performed better on the newborn assessment scale.

Given the positive effects of sucking, it is very fortunate that infants are inclined instinctively to engage in sucking behavior. That predisposition emerges very early in gestation, with fetuses as young as 5 months appearing to suck on their own hands in utero. During the first day of life, infants have been observed sucking as often as 30 minutes per hour. This does not appear to vary with the feeding experience. One survey found that 89% of parents introduced pacifiers to soothe their infants. Most studies in the literature concur that sucking is the most common method for soothing an infant. In another study pacifiers were compared with rocking. Pacifiers produced sleep states and rocking produced alert states. Pacifiers also reduced heart rate levels significantly more than rocking. Thus pacifiers seem to be more soothing than rocking.

Sucking is also used for exploration and learning. Babies in one study sucked harder to hear their mothers' voice than their fathers' voice, probably because they were more familiar with the vibrations of their mothers' voice in utero. Sucking is used in this and many studies to determine whether infants hear, see, make discriminations, and demonstrate sophisticated skills such as performing small math problems, discriminating different colors, and learning musical scales as early as the newborn period. Other investigators have noted how much learning occurs during infants' exploration by mouth. For example, infants are able to show that they can differentiate two different nipples (one with a rough surface and one with a smooth surface) simply by having experienced sucking on the nipple and then looking longer at the picture of the nipple they had sucked, showing their preference for that familiar nipple.

Even if infants do not have nipples to suck on, they frequently suck on their hands or other objects. As early as 5 months' gestation, fetuses explore their hands with their mouths. This persists through early infancy, when the mouth explores the hands, fist, and fingers. Similarly, for at least the first 6 months of life, everything the infant grasps goes into the mouth. In a recent court hearing I was asked how a 5-month-old infant could stuff a rather unpleasant-tasting alcohol wipe in his/her mouth. Invariably every 5-month-old I filmed for the hearing did exactly that. When babies have something more interesting to suck on, such as a nipple or rattle, they do not choose alcohol wipes. Infants prefer toys, because of their interesting textures of softness, hardness, and firmness. Toys also give the infant information about features such as shape. Infants have individual preferences as well. Some infants enjoy sucking their soft toes, and others enjoy hard, firm plastic toys. Thus, sucking is a predominant activity during the first 6 months of life, just as walking is at one year, and it clearly provides a very basic learning function.

If sucking is so critical for reducing stress and facilitating growth and development, most especially cognitive (mental) development, and if sucking does not appear to have any negative effects, why should anyone want to eventually discourage the habit? One reason is that as a child develops, sucking on a pacifier or thumb may be incompatible with vocalizing and talking, just as it is incompatible with crying during the newborn stage. When infants become preschoolers they may experience rejection by peers for engaging in "baby behavior." Thus pacifier use at preschool is probably not desirable. In one study pacifier use declined in a voluntary way between 3 and 24 months, suggesting that for most children, the attachment to a pacifier declines naturally. However, for others, sucking is a type of "security blanket" which becomes difficult to relinquish.

To prevent pacifier overuse parents should not get into the habit of popping pacifiers into their babies' mouth when the baby doesn't need pacifying. It is important to learn to tune in and appropriately respond to your babies' cues and prevent pacifier overuse. Older babies should only be given a pacifier for true pacifying, soothing, and calming.

As an aside, parents often ask whether sucking on a pacifier or thumb can mean that the child will need to wear braces. For most children this is not a problem. Pacifier and thumb-sucking has very little effect on a child's oral–facial development and on the primary teeth and position of the jaw when it is done periodically. If the child continues to do it when the permanent teeth are coming in, pacifier or thumb-sucking could cause movement of the teeth and bones, and orthodontic treatment might be needed.

PLAY

Play and pretend play are critical to a child's development. Playfulness is measured by physical, social, and cognitive (mental) spontaneity, by joy and a sense of humor. Much of this develops in the child through experience of playing, starting in preschool, when a child's entire agenda is play, and tapering off as children get older and have less time for play. In one study on individual differences in young children's pretend play, early social pretend play was significantly related to the child's developing understanding of other people's feelings and beliefs. These data provide strong support for the notion that early experience in pretend play is associated with mastery of relations between mental life and real life. Parents need to orchestrate some of the play of their children inasmuch as the natural opportunities for play, such as neighborhood playgrounds, have become more rare in very busy and unsafe cities. Oftentimes all it takes is arranging a child's friend to visit, gathering together the props, and getting the pretend play started. Once they get started, children are very good at pretend play.

PREMATURITY

Infants who are born prematurely have a number of problems in infancy suggesting delayed growth and development. Long-term follow-ups suggest sleep-related problems and more accidents in the case of 1- to 3-year-olds; and inferior eye and hand coordination, and less practical reasoning, more delayed language development, visual and hearing disorders, and more hospital care over the first 4 years, according to a second study. In a third study significant delays were noted in cognitive (mental) functioning only until 6 years of age. The data analysis showed that environmental factors accounted for more variation in their cognitive development than perinatal factors. Preterm children exhibited a self-righting tendency during early childhood, so that eventually environmental influence overshadowed biological influences.

QUALITY TIME

In today's world of dual-career families parents are concerned about snatching as much time as they can with their children. Often this leads to children staying up late and sacrificing the quality time they spend in daycare. Quality time, the time parents give their undivided attention to their children, is key – not quantity of time.

REGRESSIONS

Regressions often occur at times when developmental strides are being made. This seems like one step forward and two steps backward. Probably the most disturbing are the regressions accompanying the birth of the next child. Language regressions and toilet training regressions are commonly seen at this time. They are probably best ignored and treated as a sign of the child needing more positive reinforcement at this time.

ROCKING

Rocking is a classic technique used by parents to calm their children and probably themselves as well. Recent studies suggest that pacifiers and massage are more effective at calming children and getting them to sleep, although rocking may very well serve the purpose of calming the parents. And for that reason alone, its popularity may well continue.

SCHEDULE

The importance of a schedule cannot be overrated. From the time of birth, newborns need to be on sleeping and feeding schedules so that they can organize their own internal clock and have sustained periods of sleeping and ultimately sustained periods of playfulness. Having periods of consolidated sleep including deep sleep is critical for children to sustain their activities, attentiveness, and interest in their play. Without having a schedule when they are growing up, children can have serious difficulties organizing themselves and often will become hyperactive and develop learning disabilities.

I remember one of our "laid back" nursery school teachers who believed that every infant should have his or her own schedule, and she operated her infant nursery class on that premise. The infants were extremely fussy, often spitting up and not being able to focus their attention on any activities. Being on 16 different schedules, the 4 nursery teachers also became very exhausted and irritable. The teacher who replaced her ran the infant nursery like an army sergeant and had all the infants on the same schedule within a week. Parents were at first resistant but came to appreciate that their infants were much less irritable. The need for a schedule continues through childhood, which is why children typically do much better in a school setting than they do on weekends when everyone is on a different schedule.

SECURITY BLANKETS

Security blankets have their place in infancy and toddlerhood, as children can more securely leave their mother (father leave-takings are typically less difficult). However, beyond the toddler stage, security blankets may be a source of embarrassment for the children when their peers make fun of their security objects. Bringing toys to school may be less a source of embarrassment, but that often leads to little wars for possessing each other's objects. For that reason most teachers prefer that children leave their toys at home.

SEPARATION ANXIETY

Temporary separations from parents during hospitalizations of the parent or child or from parents during conference trips, and more permanent separation from peers associated with moves to other schools, are relatively stressful for young children. In a study that we conducted on toddlers and preschool children's responses to separation from the mother during the birth of another child, the children were agitated during the mother's hospitalization and then depressed after the mother's return. During her hospitalization the children were irritable, hyperactive, and were unable to sleep. When the mother returned the children showed depressed emotion, changes in eating and toileting, continuing sleep disturbances, and illnesses including constipation and upper respiratory problems (all characteristic of adult depression). The children were clearly agitated by separation from the mother, even though they visited her at the hospital during this period and their fathers cared for them. The depression following her return from the hospital may have related to the mother's depression or exhausted behavior. This lesser animation of the mother, together with the arrival of a new sibling, seemed to alter the relationship the mother and child had previously experienced. Examples of the child's disturbance over this altered relationship were provided by the parents in comments such as the child "remained close to the parent," "the child wanted to be rocked and held," "reverted to baby talk, whining, and screaming for attention," "destroyed his playroom," "threatened to run a truck across the baby's head." In addition, increased fantasy play in the children was characterized by a number of scenes which involved aggression against the new sibling. For example, the children's preschool lego constructions were made to "fall on the baby," "run over the baby," or "drive the baby to a high bridge and throw the baby in the water."

Some children did not seem to suffer separation stress as much as others. Those who seemed to suffer least were those who continued attending preschool while the mothers were hospitalized, as opposed to those who stayed at home with the grandmother or babysitter during the mother's hospitalization. Keeping the child's daily routine seemed to help buffer the effect of children's separations from their mothers.

In a subsequent study we observed children's responses to repeated separations from their mothers who were attending conferences throughout the year. Although we were concerned that there may be cumulative effects that made each separation worse than the last, we found that children became accustomed to these separations, and after a few of them were no longer showing the extreme behavioral and physiological changes as well as illness that accompanied the first and second separations.

Although most parents (and psychologists alike) had assumed that separation stress only occurs when parents are missing (because parents are supposedly the primary attachment figures), separation stress is also experienced over the loss of a teacher or favorite peer. Parents in our nursery school used to tell us that they wanted their infant or toddler to wait to graduate to the next class when their best friend was also ready to graduate. Sometimes parents actually transferred schools when their child's best friend transferred. In a recent study, preschool children who were transferring to new schools were observed during the 2 weeks prior to their leaving. The children showed increased fantasy play, physical contact, negative statements, fussiness, hyperactivity, and illness, as well as changes in eating and sleeping patterns. Shortly after the children left, those who left the school showed less agitated behavior but those who remained behind showed increased agitated behavior. Apparently the remaining children were being reminded of their lost friends by staying in the same environment. As in a divorced couple, the person remaining in the old house often has more difficulty because of reminders of the old relationship.

In another study we explored infants' and toddlers' reactions to being graduated to the next classroom with and without their best friends. Infants and toddlers who transferred without their best friend showed increased activity, negative emotion, fussiness, and changes in eating and sleep patterns. Some children ate too much and some children ate too little; some children slept all the time and others slept not at all. Those who transferred with close friends did not experience the stressful effects of the transition period.

It is clear from these studies that children have difficulty with loss from a very early age, so that the loss of the old relationship with mother after a new sibling arrives or loss of the peer friend can be the most stressful. At those times consistent routine (e.g., remaining in school versus staying at home) can alleviate some of the stress. Otherwise parents simply need to "ride it out" and recognize that these are normal responses to loss and change. Having a familiar routine may help not only because it is familiar but also because it provides distraction and opportunities for the child to actively cope with the stress.

SEX DIFFERENCES

Sex differences are present from birth. Research suggests that for most assessments, whether it is responding to social stimulation, discriminating faces and voices, or simple learning tasks, females are more skilled. This sexual advantage for girls persists until at least school age. Although it is widely known that boys are physically at a disadvantage at birth, often being smaller birthweight and having more perinatal complications, very little is known about the origins of boys' slower development. This is particularly a problem when parents compare their boy child to their girl child and conclude that the slower language development, for example in the boy, is suggestive of developmental delays or retardation. Parents need to have more moderate expectations of their male children, particularly in the early preschool years. Sometime later in children's schooling, female children lose their gains, often as they develop diffidence and experience more limited expectations for academic performance from adults.

There are, of course, many other sex differences that emerge, for example in the expression of empathy and social interests. While most people like to believe that these are socially determined, such as the introduction of dolls to girls and guns to boys, many of these preferences are apparent before the socializing experiences. For example, in a recent study on 12-month-old infants, girl infants presented with the choice of a toy airplane or a doll more often reached for the doll, while boy infants more often reached for the airplane. An anecdote highlights a similar response. When a teacher carried her baby into the preschool, the boy children rushed to the block corner and the girl children rushed to the teacher's baby, much to the chagrin of the teacher, who had tried very hard to encourage unisex activities and behavior in her preschool classroom.

SHYNESS

A significant body of research suggests that shyness is one of the strongest temperamental traits in children. Research from our lab shows that even newborns show behaviors that look like shyness. Approximately 20% of newborns show shy, introverted behavior such as limited responses to social stimulation. We have called that being "poker-faced." At the other extreme, approximately 20% of children are extremely extroverted or "wear their heart on their sleeve." Approximately 60% of newborns and children lie somewhere in the middle of those extremes. In our study we found that when a child seemed to be born with a shy temperament but had extroverted parents, there was often a shift towards being somewhere in the middle. Thus, although this seems to be an inborn trait (particularly because we saw shyness more often being shared by identical than nonidentical twins), the environmental influences (such as shyness or no-shyness in the parents) are also very strong.

Data also show that children who tend to be shy also have unique physiological characteristics such as greater reactivity of heart rate and different brain waves. Sometimes they have very strong physiological responses to emotional situations and their shyness or social withdrawal might be seen as a way of providing a barrier to the excessive stimulation. If a child is socially withdrawn, there is often a tendency for people to respect the child's shyness and let the child take the initiative. Often the shy, slow-to-warm-up child will be most comfortable with making his or her own overtures and contacts.

Researchers at Harvard found that children, who were timid during infancy and as toddlers, tended to be socially inhibited at age 7. They estimated that 15 percent of children, significantly more girls than boys, are born shy. Although, they found that many outgrew their shyness.

SLEEP DISTURBANCES

Sleeplessness, in the form of difficulty falling asleep and/or nighttime waking, is a very common pediatric problem, affecting some 15 to 35% of infants and toddlers. Sleep problems as early as infancy may relate to physiological factors, temperamental features of the infants, and parents' responses to difficult sleep patterns. In recent years the rate of sleep disorders has supposedly increased, possibly because parents are increasingly less tolerant or more worried about sleep disturbances and how disruptive they are to the dual-career family, or possibly due to more sophisticated methods of monitoring sleep and knowledge about the development of sleep patterns. Various methods have been developed to study infant sleep, including facial muscle activity (EMG), EEG, heart rate, and respiration. In addition, diaries are frequently kept by parents to record information on duration of sleep, crying, and other activities.

The infants' wakeful time gradually increases from an average of 8 hours at birth to 12 hours at 6 months. By the time the infant is 3 months old, sleep predominantly occurs during the nighttime hours, with the infant tending to remain awake during the later afternoon and early evening hours. By 6 months the time awake has increased from a mean of 2 hours at 3 months to about $3\frac{1}{2}$ hours, and the longest waking period is about one-third of the total awake time. Although a diurnal (normal) sleep–wake pattern is established by this time and the infant is capable of sustaining sleep during the nighttime hours, many infants continue to wake during the night. Also, at this time the amount of time the infant takes to fall asleep increases, and parents begin to establish bedtime routines and the use of blankies and other self-comforting objects to facilitate earlier sleeping.

Once infants are put to bed, there is a large variation in the amount of time required for sleep onset depending on age. For example, 2-month-olds are thought to require approximately 28 minutes and 9-month-olds only 6 minutes to fall asleep. Nightwakings occur in approximately 29% of infants during the third month, 17% by the sixth month, and 10% at the end of the first year. Once asleep, newborns typically sleep approximately 17 hours per day, and by the sixth month they are sleeping only approximately 14 hours (including naps), which remains the same across the first 2 years.

Temperamental features reported for sleep disturbances include low sensory thresholds, difficulty establishing regular routines, and reluctance to move from one activity to another. Given that infants who are stimulated less seem to organize their sleep states sooner, overstimulation by parents may be disruptive to infant sleep. A study on healthy infants suggests that most children need something to assist them to fall asleep. In this study, regular use of a transitional object such as a blanket or toy was described for 44% of the children, bedtime sucking for 22%, and both for 14%, leaving only 20% of the children who fell asleep without assistance.

Parents use a number of comforting techniques to induce sleep in young infants, including swaddling, rocking, and sounds such as white noise or classical music. Others advocate letting the child cry or taking the child into the parents' bed or supplying toys. In addition, infants use their own bodies to self-comfort, including sucking on hands, and rocking or head banging in a rhythmic way.

More formal procedures have been tried in studies giving parents instructions. These have mostly involved having the parents find a consistent sleeping place, a regular bedtime, and a bedtime ritual. In one study parents were asked to try a quiet play routine before bed in which they used soothing and relaxing techniques such as massage and pleasant music. They were asked to refrain from using a light, changing diapers, and talking during their nighttime interactions. The majority of infants showed improvement during the first few weeks of treatment. Whenever parents are present at the time of sleep onset, there are more frequent nightwakings.

We recently used massage therapy to help infants sleep. The infants who experienced massage therapy compared to infants who were rocked cried less and had lower stress hormones (salivary cortisol levels), suggesting lower stress. After the massage versus the rocking sessions, the infants spent less time in an active awake state, suggesting that massage may be more effective than rocking for inducing sleep. Over the 6-week period the massage therapy infants gained more weight, showed greater improvement on emotionality, sociability, and soothability temperament dimensions, and had greater decreases in stress hormones.

SLEEP PROBLEMS
Sleep problems are a milder, less chronic form of sleep disturbance that most children experience for brief periods at the different transitions of

childhood. They tend to occur whenever the child is disturbed by virtually anything. All other behaviors may be fine but the child experiences difficulty falling asleep, waking up early, and frequent nightwakings. Disorganized sleep and the lack of deep sleep may lead to an illness such as upper respiratory infection. Problems that almost invariably lead to sleep difficulties are separations from parents, the loss of a pet or a friend, and squabbles with peers. Other times that sleep difficulties occur are during developmental milestones when children are extremely frustrated, such as when they are learning to walk and talk, and when they are being toilet trained. Being new at different schools at different stages of childhood is also stressful, with sleep problems often occurring around those transitions.

Aside from different stressful events and developmental stages, as many as 20% of children experience significant sleep problems. During infancy and early childhood (between the ages of 1 and 4) as many as one-third of children have difficulties sleeping. Most infants do not develop an organized sleep/wake cycle until they are about 3 to 6 months of age, and then they do not sleep through the night until approximately 6 to 8 months of age. About one-third of babies also experience colic, which often wakes them during the night. Allergies and ear infections also contribute to difficulty sleeping.

Those who have conducted research on interventions to help children sleep suggest that the best intervention is having a bedtime routine or a naptime routine when the child hears a story or has a backrub. Then the parent's expectation is clear that the child is intended to go to bed, and the parent does not linger or continually return to the child's protestations and cries. Some have suggested that the infant can be weaned from protest crying by the parent going to the child after increasingly long periods of crying, maybe a couple of minutes the first night, a few minutes the second night, five minutes the third night, until the child realizes that his cries are not associated with the parent coming to him. Typically the child's crying is related to excessive stimulation and exhaustion, and the parent's rocking or playing with the child further increases the child's arousal level, leading to difficulty unwinding and settling down.

Sometimes parents feel that it is necessary to take their child to bed with them, for example when the child is sick or when the child is having nightmares. Around about preschool age children develop vivid imaginations and worry about monsters and other creatures in the night. Sometimes that is related to television, movies, or fairytales they have been hearing. Most parents, however, are uncomfortable with routine co-sleeping arrangements, as children are extremely active in their sleep (often night talking), making it very difficult to experience deep sleep.

Deep sleep (also called quiet sleep or restorative sleep) is considered essential for growth. It is during this type of sleep that growth hormone is released in children, and immune function is compromised in both children and adults when robbed of deep sleep.

STIMULATION

Optimal parenting is often discussed in the context of providing the right amount of stimulation. This is particularly true for the infancy and toddler stages, when children need some help monitoring and regulating the amount of stimulation they receive. Different children by virtue of having different temperaments have different thresholds for the amounts and kinds of stimulation they desire. Matching the kind of stimulation to the personality is critical because either too much or too little stimulation will not enhance growth and development. Sometimes parents provide too little stimulation because they are tired, depressed or preoccupied by their own problems. Other times, for example when children are unresponsive or slow in doing things, parents will be overstimulating and they try to get a response or an action.

Finding the optimal amount and kind of stimulation a child needs is one of the most difficult tasks of parenting. Probably the most effective approach is to take the cues from the child. When interacting with infants, it is easy to tell whether they are getting the kind of stimulation they want or need. Infants will gaze avert, turn their head, arch their back, and, at the extreme, fuss and cry when they are either getting too little or too much stimulation. Slightly older children may go into a shell and seemingly ignore their parents' attempts to engage them. From very early infancy, children have conversation skills such as turn-taking and paying attention or ignoring. These skills can be used as signals that the parent is doing "the right thing" and the child is interested. Just like adults, children need breaks not only to process information from the conversation as well as to formulate a response, but also to take rests and have some down time periods for thinking and imagining things.

STRANGER ANXIETY

Stranger anxiety starts at approximately 9 months of age after a rather extended period of infants loving to be held and played with by strangers. It is not clear why it emerges at this time, because even newborns have been shown to recognize the difference between their own mother and women who are strangers. In a study we conducted, newborns showed that they preferred their mothers by looking longer at them than at women who were strangers. This was surprising because they had had only 4 hours of contact with their mothers. Equally surprising is their ability to identify their mother by her smell. Recognition of mother by her voice is probably less surprising since newborns would have had experience with the mother's voice in utero.

Nonetheless, even though infants recognize their mothers as early as the newborn stage, they do not appear to show stranger anxiety until approximately 9 months. This takes the form of fussing and showing fearful faces in the presence of the stranger, whether at a distance or when being handed to a stranger. This persists for anywhere between 3 months and a couple of years, in part depending on whether the infant remains at home with the mother or attends an infant nursery school. When an infant has experience with several adults, the infant shows less stranger fear and sometimes no fear. It is not clear what function the stranger fear serves. It certainly would not prevent kidnapping at this early helpless stage of life, and were it to happen any earlier it might even interfere with parents returning to work or having babysitters for any reason. Fortunately, it is a stage that disappears as quickly as it appears.

STUTTERING

Approximately 8% of children stutter at some time, most usually between about $1\frac{1}{2}$ and 6 years of age, when the child is learning to talk, and later when the child begins school. Other statistics suggest that approximately three times as many boys as girls stutter, and stutterers are also more often lefthanded and have blond hair and blue eyes. Approximately 75% of children who stutter stop stuttering at around 12 or 13 years of age.

Typically stutterers are delayed in their expressive language skills, not their receptive language skills, lending support for the hypothesis that language deficits observed in stuttering children result at least in part from their attempts to simplify verbal responses as a means of coping with their stuttering. A recent study suggested that stutterers also show more nonspeech behavior during stuttered words than nonstutterers show during similar words. For example, they turn their heads to the left, blink and raise their upper lip excessively. Some evidence suggests a genetic predisposition for stuttering, and some researchers have found that the EEG of stutterers differs from those of nonstutterers, suggesting a disturbance of interhemispheric relationships. This may be a significant factor in the development of stuttering. Stressful events like the birth of siblings or transitions to new schools or new places can exaggerate the stuttering. The most difficult aspect of this problem is the embarrassment it causes the child, and the delay it causes in language development.

Parents can help by not drawing attention to the stuttering, trying to ignore it, and certainly not speaking for the child. When children stutter, the tendency is to provide words for them rather than let the child complete his sentences. If the problem becomes so serious that the child cannot be understood, a speech therapist might be helpful. Often the therapist will work with the child to speak more slowly and to practice various breathing techniques that help the child become less stressed.

SWADDLING

Swaddling or the tight wrapping of babies (typically with a blanket) is done for a very limited period of time in the United States. Usually parents swaddle their babies to calm them down or help them go to sleep, and sometimes to make it easier to carry them. Although swaddling is more common in other cultures, such as American Indians wrapping infants tightly to carrying boards, it is discouraged in our country as a baby care practice because it is considered limiting to the development of hand–eye motor coordination.

TASTE

Newborns are born with very sophisticated abilities to discriminate different tastes, probably because the amniotic fluid is comprised of all tastes including sweetness, salty, and bitter. This has been observed in many studies based on newborns' facial expressions in response to different tastes. For example, disgust faces are noted following the baby tasting quinine and other bitter tastes, whereas contented faces are noted following a sweet taste. Compared to older infants, however, they do not seem to reject salty and bitter substances, perhaps because those were extremely familiar in utero. Slightly older infants seem to prefer novel tastes. For example, in one study, infants spent more time breastfeeding after their mothers ate garlic, as compared to those infants whose mothers repeatedly consumed garlic. Clearly, though, the sweetest substances are preferred from the first day of life. In fact, sucrose has been used as an analgesic during painful procedures in the newborn nursery. Newborns who were given sucrose solutions to suck on during blood draws, for example, cried less following the procedure. Children who are introduced to new tastes and new foods in early childhood tend to enjoy a variety of different foods later, whereas those with a limited diet tend to have negative reactions to new foods.

TEETHING

Teething or the breaking through of new teeth can be uncomfortable for infants and distressful for parents. Parents' favorite treatment is probably the rubbing of gums with a bit of liqueur. Both the rubbing action and the liqueur have analgesic effects.

TELEVISION

The American Academy of Pediatrics recommends that children under the age of 2 not watch any television. Yet several surveys indicate high numbers of infants routinely watching, including 17% of 0- to 11-month-old infants and 48% of 12- to 23-month-old toddlers in a large US study, and even larger numbers in a Japanese study (30% of 3-month-olds, and 90% of 12-month-olds). Exposure is also high, at an average 44 minutes per day in American 4-month-old infants, increasing to 62 minutes per day in 12-month-old infants; and again, there is higher exposure in Japan. In one study, 92% of exposure of 4-month-olds was to adult TV. Some view TV exposure as a cognitive (mental) learning experience, but others are concerned that infants are imitating TV models, both immediately, and, days later, remembering and mimicking the model's actions. They also are taking directions from TV. For example, in one study, 10- to 12-month-old infants who watched an actress respond to a toy with fear, then avoided playing with it themselves, and they were more likely to appear worried and cry.

Children are first exposed to the audio and video stimulation of TV shortly after birth to the age of 2 months. They then begin to have an interest in and glance at or watch the TV screen at 4 to 5 months of age. When they are able to crawl at around 6 months, they approach and investigate the TV set. At 7 to 8 months they enjoy switching channels, and then they become interested in and speak to the on-screen characters at 10 to 11 months. At 12 to 14 months of age they have favorite TV characters and programs, and enjoy TV as "ordinary TV viewers," move their bodies with the music and mimic the actors on-screen, smile and ask questions of parents. They fix the information from TV in their memory, and they are pleased to see the things they like on TV. Even the fetus is affected by TV, showing heart rate acceleration or deceleration and fetal movement when the mother is watching TV. The other negative effect cited for infants may also pertain to fetuses, that is, the disruption of sleep patterns. For some, though – for example, infants of depressed mothers – selected children's TV may provide more adequate stimulation.

TEMPERAMENT

For most of history parents have blamed themselves for their children's temperaments. More recently considerable research suggests that infants come into the world with a temperament that is only then slightly modified by parents' temperament and things that happen in the environment. Parents will still blame themselves, but now they will do so for transmitting temperament traits by their genes rather than by their childrearing. Temperament researchers have described babies, for example, as easy or difficult from the start, and they have based their conclusions on parents' reports and on observations of several characteristics they call temperament traits. These include the child's activity level, adaptability, distractibility, intensity, mood, persistence, regularity or rhythmicity, sensitivity, and weariness. Different temperament traits combine to determine whether a child is easy or difficult. In one of our studies, we noted that newborns in the first hours of life could be placed somewhere on a continuum between being extraverted and being introverted. The extraverted newborns showed very expressive faces and were not very reactive when we measured heart rate. In contrast, at the other extreme the introverted newborns were "poker-faced" but showed considerable physiological reactivity as recorded by their heart rate. Most newborns (approximately 60%) fell in between these two extremes, being both facially expressive and physiologically reactive. When we looked at these behaviors in identical and nonidentical twins we found that there was more similarity in the personality types of identical than nonidentical twins, suggesting again that there was some genetic component to these personality profiles. Observing these infants over the first few years of life we noted that if an extraverted infant was born to introverted parents the extraverted infant moved toward the middle of the continuum, while if the extraverted infant was born to extraverted parents, she more likely continued to be extraverted. Thus the interplay between genetics and environmental influences became clear.

Extraverted and introverted children have very different ways of interacting with the world. Extraverted children are more exploratory and risk-taking and therefore likely to excel in development. On the other hand, if the parent is aware of the temperamental traits of the introverted child and tries to match parenting strategies to that style, the child may end up being exploratory in spite of his introversion. Several researchers have tracked the development of temperament traits to determine whether they are stable over time and which traits seem to contribute to superior development. In one study, activity level was most predictive of effective coping as observed in grade school. Dimensions of temperament that were most closely associated with less difficult responses to stress, fewer behavior problems, and lower stress were predictability, positive mood, adaptability, higher approach, lower intensity reaction, and lower responsiveness threshold.

Because of the stability of temperamental traits over development, psychiatrists have been concerned about the relation between those traits and behavioral syndromes in later childhood. In one study, for example, both high emotionality and low sociability predicted high scores on an anxiety/depression scale. In another study, a high degree of psycho-pathology was associated with high activity and low rhythmicity.

TEMPER TANTRUMS

Temper tantrums occur at frustrating stages in development. They are considered a mark of the child's attempts to become independent, for example around the "terrible twos" when the child has power struggles with parents and because of limited language development has difficulty expressing his/her frustration except by tantrums. Temper tantrums typically arise from children's thwarted efforts to exercise mastery and autonomy. They occur more frequently in the active, determined child who has abundant energy. They may also occur in children who are hypersensitive to sounds, lights, and other stimulating features of the environment. Although these are considered normal behaviors, it is also clear that for a number of children temper tantrums turn into more difficult behavior problems.

In one study, tantrums were reported in about 25% of children and most commonly at 2 to 5 years, becoming less common at 6 to 8 years. Children showing tantrums had a higher incidence of postnatal trauma. Parental overprotection and marital discord were stress factors in a greater number of boys than girls, and parental negligence was a significant stress factor for girls. Behavior problems that accompanied temper tantrums included thumb-sucking, bedwetting, tics, head banging, and sleep disturbances. In another study, 52% of those who showed temper tantrums had multiple behavior problems. Factors independently associated with the tantrums included maternal depression and irritability, use of physical punishment, marital stress, childcare provided exclusively by the mother and poor child health.

After having established that the child's temper tantrum is not simply related to his discomfort, it is important to look at how the tantrum is being treated. Parenting practices that may encourage tantrums include inconsistency, unreasonable expectations, excessive strictness, overprotectiveness and overindulgence. The child might also be bored, fatigued, hungry, or ill, thus reducing his tolerance for frustration. In those situations it would obviously be important to distract the child or interest him in something less boring. Beyond these attempts, temper tantrums are probably best handled by ignoring the outburst and saving attention for the post-tantrum, as well as helping the child learn to express negative feelings in less annoying ways.

TERRIBLE TWOS

The 2-year-old stage has become so notorious for its difficulties that it is now classified as the terrible twos. This is the first of many autonomy-setting stages of the child's life, and may be the worst (next to adolescence) because it is the first. Parents have come to totally enjoy their lovely child when all of a sudden they find themselves faced with a little monster. Every other word is no and every other action is forbidden and accompanied by looks toward the parent of "I dare you." Language has emerged and with that the child acts as if he's smarter than the parents. That might be true, as the child repeatedly outwits them. Because of the autonomy-establishing ways of the child at this age, it's important that parents not get into power struggles with their child over the child's behavior. For example, many children who have not been toilet trained by 2, use toilet training as grounds for power struggles with their parents. Waiting until 2 virtually means waiting until at least 3, when autonomy issues are not as great. Thus, the terrible twos combined with toilet training can dramatically exacerbate the problems of the terrible twos.

Aside from trying not to save important developmental milestones for this stage, such as toilet training, parents are probably best advised not to get into verbal power struggles, but to simply move the child from the source of altercation (like an electric socket or restaurant where he has resorted to temper tantrums) or to attempt to distract by activities that the child can clearly dominate. Parents' attempts to explain their "unpopular" position typically fall on deaf ears and accelerate the conflict. It is probably not surprising that this is an increasingly popular age for parents to begin children at school. There the children can have their terrible two struggles with teachers and other terrible 2-year-olds.

THUMB-SUCKING

Thumb-sucking in newborns and young infants is considered a very sophisticated, self-soothing behavior. Except for unusually shy children, most stop thumb-sucking at around the preschool stage. After that, thumb-sucking typically occurs only during times of stress and going to sleep. If this behavior continues into grade school, it is problematic because of peer rejection. In a study on 7-year-olds, for example, children viewed photos of boys and girls in thumb-sucking and nonthumb-sucking poses and rated the pictures. The results indicated that children in a thumb-sucking pose were rated as less intelligent, happy, attractive, likable, and fun and less desirable as a friend, playmate, seat mate, classmate, and neighbor than when they were in the nonthumb-sucking pose. Thus the risk of losing social acceptance is real at this stage. Typically thumb-sucking subsides unless it is negatively reinforced. A parent's simple expression of concern that their child will be teased by his friends is enough warning for the child. Other times simply having distracters or substitute activities that are more interesting than thumb-sucking can solve the problem.

TOILET TRAINING
Toilet training is typically treated as an individual readiness phenomenon by pediatricians, although most children are toilet trained (according to a recent study) by $2\frac{1}{2}$ years, with physicians beginning to discuss toilet training with parents at around 12 to 18 months of age. Waiting to start toilet training at age 2 is particularly problematic because the "terrible twos" involve power struggles between parents and children that make toilet training extremely difficult.

Placing a child in training pants and trying not to use diapers except during nighttime sleep is an effective introduction to toilet training. Buying the child his own seat also gives the child a sense of control over his own activity. Children seem to learn faster when they are attending preschool, probably because the older children model more mature toileting behavior. Taking a child frequently to the toilet will give him the idea whether at home or at school that there are designated periods when all kids have bathroom time.

TOUCHING
In a recent study on the touching behavior of mothers and fathers with their newborn infants, both mothers and fathers touched their infant for an equal amount of time and frequency, but mothers touched/stroked their infants more than they patted/moved them. Fathers did not show a preference for either type of touching. Mothers preferentially touched their infant's hand and face more than the body, while fathers preferred to touch their infant's hand. The authors suggest that this is consistent with mothers' inclination to caretake their infants, and fathers' tendency to play with their infants more often. Another study conducted on touching premature newborns in intensive care suggested that touching occurs 63% of the observation time, and 69% of the touching was treatment oriented, 15% was caregiving-oriented and 16% simply comforting touch. The majority of touching was done by the nurses.

TWINS
Twins can come as a shock to any family, even though they seem to run in families. Senior family members try to prepare first time parents for that possibility. Most parents also have part of pregnancy as preparation, in that ultrasound and other prenatal tests typically reveal twins sometime during pregnancy. The downside is that you need two of everything and it is twice as much work, but the upside is that you can have

twice the joy in half the time. Identical twins have quite amazing similarities as early as birth. For example, in a study we conducted on newborns, identical twins were almost identical in the amount of time they looked at faces and mimicked faces, while nonidentical or fraternal twins were very different in their facial expressions and their attentiveness. Fraternal twins are often perplexing because they seem no more alike than nontwins in the same family. Despite their similar experiences at the same time in development they can behave and develop very differently.

WALKING

Children typically start walking at around 10 months of age and are pretty proficient by the time they are toddlers at around 16 to 18 months. Temperamental differences occur in the time of onset, so that one often sees children who are risk-takers and exploratory starting earlier than children who are shy and slow-to-warm-up. Although scientists have shown that walking can occur very early if it is practiced, there has been some concern that early walking may slow down the development of other skills such as talking. Typically, children are focusing on one skill at a time, and those seem to be prewired developmentally to occur at specific times. Crawling and walking, of course, give a child more freedom to explore and get into trouble when the environment isn't childproof. Although walkers seem to be very effective in helping children develop walking skills, they are coming under increasing criticism because of their use as "babysitters" and some serious falls reported in the literature. Jolly jumpers or hanging harnesses from door frames are also very helpful for learning balance and walking movements. Whether walkers or jolly jumpers are used, all children seem to walk about the same time. If walking is delayed, other functions may also be delayed. In one study, slow walking and slow talking were predictive of lower IQ scores and reading difficulties, but this is only if they started walking after 18 months, and only half the children who walked after 18 months later had low IQs and reading difficulties.

Bibliography

Abravanel, E. & De Yong, N.G. (1997). Exploring the roles of peer and adult video models for infant imitation. *Journal of Genetic Psychology, 158*, 133–50.

Adachi, K., Shimada, M. & Usui, A. (2003). The Relationship Between the Parturient's Positions and Perceptions of Labor Pain Intensity. *Nursing Research, 52*, 47–51.

Adams, R.J. (1995). Further exploration of human neonatal chromatic–achromatic discrimination. *Journal of Experimental Child Psychology, 60*, 344–60.

Adams, R.J. & Courage, M.L. (1995). Development of chromatic discrimination in early infancy. *Behavioral Brain Research, 67*, 99–101.

Adams, R.J. & Courage, M.L. (1998). Human newborn color vision: Measurement with chromatic stimuli varying in excitation purity. *Journal of Experimental Child Psychology, 68*, 22–34.

Adams, R.J., Maurer, D. & Davis, M. (1986). Newborns' discrimination of chromatic and achromatic stimuli. *Journal of Experimental Child Psychology, 41*, 267–81.

Adams, S.M., Jones, D.R., Esmail, A. & Mitchell, E.A. (2004). What affects the age of first sleeping through the night? *Journal of Paediatrics and Child Health, 40*, 96–101.

Adamson, L.B. & Frick, J.E. (2003). The still-face: A history of a shared experimental paradigm. A target article. *Infancy, 4*, 451–73.

Ahnert, L., Gunnar, M.R., Lamb, M.E. & Barthel, M. (2004). Transition to child care: Associations with infant–mother attachment, infant negative emotion, and cortisol elevations. *Child Development, 75*, 639–50.

Aina, O.F. & Morakinyo, O. (2005). Normative data on mental and motor development in Nigerian children. *West African Journal of Medicine, 24*, 151–6.

Ainsworth, M., Blehar, M., Waters, E. & Wall, S. (1978). *Patterns of attachment. A psychological study of the strange situation.* New Jersey: Hillside.

Akman, I., Ozek, E., Bilgen, H., Ozdogan, T. & Cebeci, D. (2002). Sweet solutions and pacifiers for pain relief in newborn infants. *Journal of Pain, 3*, 199–202.

Alexander, R.T. & Radisch, D. (2005). Sudden infant death syndrome risk factors with regards to sleep position, sleep surface, and co-sleeping. *Journal of Forensic Science, 50,* 147–51.

Almerigi, J.B., Carbary, T.J. & Harris, L.J. (2002). Most adults show opposite-sided biases in the imagined holding of infants and objects. *Brain and Cognition, 48,* 258–63.

Andersson, L., Sundström-Poromaa, I., Wulff, M., Åström, M. & Bixo, M. (2004). Implications of antenatal depression and anxiety for obstetric outcome. *Obstetrics & Gynecology, 104,* 467–76.

Arita, A., Hiraki, K., Kanda, T. & Ishiguro, H. (2005). Can we talk to robots? Ten-month-old infants expected interactive humanoid robots to be talked to by persons. *Cognition, 95,* B49–57.

Ashman, S.B., Dawson, G., Panagiotides, H., Yamada, E. & Wilkinson, C.W. (2002). Stress hormone levels of children of depressed mothers. *Developmental Psychopathology, 14,* 333–49.

Auerbach, J., Faroy, M., Ebstein, R., Kahana, M. & Levine, J. (1998). The association of the dopamine D4 receptor gene (DRD4) and the serotonin transporter promoter gene (5-HTTLPR) with temperament in 12-month-old infants. *Journal of Child Psychology and Psychiatry, 42,* 777–83.

Auerbach, J., Geller, V., Lezer, S., Shinwell, E., Belmaker, R.H., Levine, J. & Ebstein, R. (1999). Dopamine D4 receptor (D4DR) and serotonin transporter promoter (5-HTTLPR) polymorphisms in the determination of temperament in 2-month-old infants. *Molecular Psychiatry, 4,* 369–73.

Austin, A.M. & Peery, J.C. (1983). Analysis of adult–neonate synchrony during speech and non-speech. *Perception of Motor Skills, 57,* 455–9.

Austin, M.P., Hadzi-Pavlovic, D., Leader, L., Saint, K. & Parker, G. (2005). Maternal trait anxiety, depression and life event stress in pregnancy: relationships with infant temperament. *Early Human Development, 81,* 183–90.

Ayalon, L. & Young, M.A. (2003). A comparison of depressive symptoms in African Americans and Caucasian Americans. *Journal of Cross-Cultural Psychology, 34,* 111–24.

Ayoun, C. (1998). Maternal responsiveness and search for hidden objects and contingency learning by infants. *Early Development and Parenting, 7,* 61–72.

Badr, L., Abdallah, B. & Mahmoud, A. (2005). Precursors of preterm birth: Comparison of three ethnic groups in the Middle East and the United States. *Journal of Obstetric, Gynecologic, and Neonatal Nursing, 34,* 444.

Bahrick, L.E., Hernandez-Reif, M. & Flom, R. (2005). The development of infant learning about specific face–voice relation. *Developmental Psychology, 41,* 541–52.

Bahrick, L.E. & Lickliter, R. (2004). Infants' perception of rhythm and tempo in unimodal and multimodal stimulation: A developmental test of the intersensory redundancy hypothesis. *Cognitive and Affective Behavioral Neuroscience, 4,* 137–47.

Bahrick, L.E. & Pickens, J.N. (1995). Infant memory for object motion across a period of three months: Implications for a four-phase attention function. *Journal of Experimental Child Psychology*, *59*, 343–71.

Bailey, B., Delaney-Black, V., Covington, C., Ager, J., Janisse, J., Hannigan, J. & Sokol, R. (2004). Prenatal exposure to binge drinking and cognitive and behavioral outcomes at age 7 years. *American Journal of Obstetrics and Gynecology*, *191*, 1037–43.

Ball, H.L. (2002). Triadic bed-sharing and infant temperature. *Child: Care, Health and Development*, *28*, 55–8.

Ball, H.L., Hooker, E. & Kelly, P.J. (2000). Parent–infant co-sleeping: Fathers' roles and perspectives. *Infant and Child Development*, *9*, 67–74.

Balleyguier, G. & Melhuish, E.C. (1996). The relationship between infant day care and socio-emotional development with French children aged 3–4 years. *European Journal of Psychology of Education*, *11*, 193–9.

Banos, J.E., Ruiz, G. & Guardiola, E. (2001). An analysis of articles on neonatal pain published from 1965 to 1999. *Pain Research and Management*, *6*, 45–50.

Barglow, P., Contreras, J., Kavesh, L. & Vaughn, B.E. (1998). Developmental follow-up of 6–7 year old children of mothers employed during their infancies. *Child Psychiatry*, *29*, 3–20.

Barnett, B., Schaafsma, M.F., Guzman, A.M. & Parker, G.B. (1991). Maternal anxiety: A 5-year review of an intervention study. *Journal of Child Psychology and Psychiatry & Allied Disciplines*, *32*, 423–38.

Barone, C.M. (2002). Mother–infant sleep behaviors in solitary and bed-sharing conditions. *Dissertation Abstracts International: Section B: The Sciences and Engineering*, *62*, 3416.

Barr, H. & Streissguth, A. (2001). Identifying maternal self-reported alcohol use associated with fetal alcohol spectrum disorders. *Alcohol, Clinical and Experimental Research*, *25*, 237–8.

Barr, R., Viera, A. & Rovee-Collier, C. (2001). Mediated imitation in 6-month-olds: Remembering by association. *Journal of Experimental Child Psychology*, *79*, 229–52.

Bartochuk, L.M. & Beauchamp, G.K. (1994). Chemical senses. *Annual Review of Psychology*, *45*, 419–49.

Batki, A., Baron-Cohen, S., Wheelwright, S., Connellan, J. & Ahluwalia, J. (2000). Is there an innate gaze module? Evidence from human neonates. *Infant Behavior and Development*, *23*, 223–9.

Bauer, P.J., Wiebe, S.A., Carver, L.J., Waters, J.M. & Nelson, C.A. (2003). Developments in long-term explicit memory late in the first year of life: Behavioral and electrophysiological indices. *Psychological Science*, *14*, 629–35.

Bebib, R. & Baudonniere, P.M. (2000). Vocal imitation in 3-month-old infants: A releasing stimulus or a releasing context? *Behaviour, Brain and Cognition*, *2*, 79–93.

Beckett, C., Maughan, B., Rutter, M., Castle, J., Colvert, E., Groothues, C., Kreppner, J., Stevens, S., O'Connor, T.G. & Sonuga-Barke, E.J. (2006). Do the effects of early severe deprivation on cognition persist into early adolescence? Findings from

English and Romanian adoptees study. *Child Development*, 77, 696–711.

Behne, T., Carpenter, M., Call, J. & Tomasello, M. (2005). Unwilling versus unable: Infants' understanding of intentional action. *Developmental Psychology*, 41, 328–37.

Belsky, J. (1990). Developmental risks associated with infant day care: Attachment insecurity, noncompliance, and aggression? In S.S. Chehrazi (Ed.), *Psychosocial issues in day care* (pp. 37–68). Washington, DC: American Psychiatric Press.

Belsky, J. & Braungart, J.M. (1991). Are insecure–avoidant infants with extensive day-care experience less stressed by and more independent in the strange situation? *Child Development*, 62, 567–71.

Bendell-Estroff, D., Greenfield, D.B., Hogan, A.E. & Claussen, A.H. (1989). Early assessment of sensorimotor and cognitive development in high-risk infants. *Journal of Pediatric Psychology*, 14, 549–57.

Benhamou, I. (2000). Sleep disorders of early childhood: A review. *Israel Annals Journal of Psychiatry and Related Sciences*, 37, 190–6.

Ben-Meir, A., Schenker, J.G. & Ezra, Y. (2005). Cesarean section upon request: Is it appropriate for everybody? *Journal of Perinatal Medicine*, 33, 106–11.

Bergeson, T.R. & Trehub, S.E. (2002). Absolute pitch and tempo in mothers' songs to infants. *Psychology and Science*, 13, 72–5.

Berthier, N.E., Bertenthal, B.I., Seaks, J.D., Sylvia, M.R., Johnson, R.L. & Clifton, R.K. (2001). Using object knowledge in visual tracking and reaching. *Infancy*, 2, 257–84.

Bertoncini, J., Floccia, C., Nazzi, T. & Mehler, J. (1995). Morae and syllables: Rhythmical basis of speech representations in neonates. *Language Speech*, 38, 311–29.

Blackburn, C., Bonas, S., Spencer, N., Dolan, A., Coe, C. & Moy, R. (2005). Smoking behavior change among fathers of new infants. *Social Science Medicine*, 61, 517–26.

Blair, P., Ward Platt, M.P., Smith, I.J. & Fleming, P.J. (2005). Sudden Infant Death Syndrome and sleeping position in pre-term and low birthweight infants: An opportunity for targeted intervention. *Archives of Disease in Childhood*, 91(2), 101–6.

Blass, E.M. (1999). Savoring sucrose and suckling milk: Easing pain, savoring calories and learning about mother. In M. Lewis et al. (Eds.), *Soothing and stress* (pp. 79–107). Mahwah, NJ: Lawrence Erlbaum.

Blass, E.M. & Camp, C.A. (2004). The ontogeny of face identity; I. Eight- to 21-week-old infants use internal and external face features in identity. *Cognition*, 92, 305–27.

Blass, E.M. & Shah, A. (1995). Pain-reducing properties of sucrose in humans newborns. *Chemical Senses*, 20, 29–35.

Bloom, L. (1998). Language acquisition in its developmental context. In W. Damon, D. Kuhn & R. Siegler (Eds.), *Child Psychology* (5th ed., pp. 309–70). New York: Wiley.

Bohnhorst, B., Heyne, T., Peter, C.S. & Poets, C.F. (2001). Skin-to-skin (kangaroo) care, respiratory control, and thermoregulation. *Journal of Pediatrics*, 138, 193–7.

Boller, K. (1997). Preexposure effects on infant learning and memory.

Developmental Psychobiology, 31, 93–105.

Borge, A.I.H., Rutter, M., Cote, S. & Tremblay, R.E. (2004). Early childcare and physical aggression: differentiating social selection and social causation. *Journal of Child Psychology and Psychiatry*, 45, 367–76.

Borkowski, M.M. (2002). Infant sleep and feeding: A telephone survey of Hispanic Americans. *Dissertation Abstracts International: Section B: The Sciences and Engineering*, 62, 4204.

Borkowski, M.M., Hunter, K.E. & Johnson, C.M. (2001). White noise and scheduled bedtime routines to reduce infant and childhood sleep disturbances. *Behavior and Therapist*, 24, 29–37.

Bornstein, M.H. (2002). Measurement variability in infant and maternal behavioral assessment. *Infant Behavior and Development*, 25, 413–32.

Bornstein, M.H., Arterberry, M.E. & Mash, C. (2004). Long-term memory for an emotional interpersonal interaction occurring at 5 months of age. *Infancy*, 6, 40.

Bortfeld, H., Morgan, J.L., Golinkoff, R.M. & Rathbun, K. (2005). Mommy and me: Familiar names help launch babies into speech-stream segmentation. *Psychological Science*, 16, 298–304.

Bosch, L. & Sebastián-Gallés, N. (2001). Evidence of early language discrimination abilities in infants from bilingual environments. *Infancy*, 2, 29–49.

Bower, T.G.R. (1989). *The rational infant: Learning in infancy*. New York: W.H. Freeman.

Brand, R.J., Baldwin, D.A. & Ashburn, L.A. (2002). Evidence for "motionese": Modifications in mothers' infant-directed action. *Developmental Science*, 5, 72–83.

Brandon, D.H., Holditch-Davis, D. & Winchester, D.M. (2005). Factors affecting early neurobehavioral and sleep outcomes in preterm infants. *Infant Behavior and Development*, 28, 206–19.

Brazelton, T.B. (1983). *Infants and mothers: Differences in development*. New York: Random House.

Breazeal, C. & Scassellati, B. (2000). Infant-like social interactions between a robot and a human caregiver. *Adaptive Behavior*, 8, 49–74.

Bremner, J.G., Johnson, S.P., Slater, A., Mason, U., Foster, K., Cheshire, A. & Spring, J. (2005). Conditions for young infants' perception of object trajectories. *Child Development*, 76, 1029–43.

Brennan, P.A., Hammen, C., Katz, A.R. & Le Brocque, R.M. (2002). Maternal depression, paternal psychopathology, and adolescent diagnostic outcomes. *Journal of Consultant Clinical Psychology*, 70, 1075–85.

Brenner, R.A., Simons-Morton, B.G., Bhaskar, B., Revenis, M., Das, A. & Clemens, J.D. (2003). Infant–parent bed sharing in an inner-city population. *Archive of Pediatric and Adolescent*, 157, 33–9.

Brookes, H., Slater, A.M., Quinn, P.C., Lewkowicz, D.J., Hayes, R.A. & Brown, E. (2001). Three-month-old infants learn arbitrary auditory–visual parings between voices and faces. *Infant and Child Development*, 10, 75–82.

Brouwers, E., van Baar, A. & Pop, V. (2001). Does the Edinburgh Postnatal Depression Scale measure anxiety? *Journal of Psychosomatic Research*, 51, 659–63.

Browning, C. (2001). Music therapy in childbirth: Research in practice. *Music Therapy Perspectives*, 19, 74–81.

Bryden, M.P. & Steenhuis, R. (1991). The assessment of handedness in children. In J.E. Obrzut & G.W. Hynd (Eds.), *Neuropsychological foundations of learning disabilities: A handbook of issues, methods, and practices* (pp. 411–36). San Diego, CA: Academic Press.

Buitelaar, J.K., Huizink, A.C., Mulder, E.J., de Medina, P.G. & Visser, G.H. (2003). Prenatal stress and cognitive development and temperament in infants. *Neurobiology Aging*, 24, 53–60.

Burchinal, M.R., Bryant, D.M., Lee, M.W. & Ramey, C.T. (1992). Early daycare, infant–mother attachment, and maternal responsiveness in the infant's first year. *Early Childhood Research Quarterly*, 17, 235–43.

Burd, L., Cotsonas-Hassler, T.M., Martsolf, J.T. & Kerbeshian, J. (2003). Recognition and management of fetal alcohol syndrome. *Neurotoxicology and Teratology*, 25, 681–8.

Burgess, K.B., Marshall, P.J., Rubin, K.H. & Fox, N.A. (2003). Infant attachment and temperament as predictors of subsequent externalizing problems and cardiac physiology. *Journal of Child Psychology and Psychiatry*, 44, 819–31.

Bushnell, I.W.R. (2001). Mother's face recognition in newborn infants: learning and memory. *Infant and Child Development*, 10, 67–74.

Bushnell, I.W.R., Sai, F. & Mullin, J.T. (1989). Neonatal recognition of the mother's face. *British Journal of Developmental Psychology*, 7, 3–15.

Buss, K.A., Schumacher, J.R., Dolski, I., Kalian, N.H., Goldsmith, H.H. & Davison, R.J. (2003). Right frontal brain activity, cortisol, and withdrawal behavior in 6-month-old infants. *Behavioral Neurosciences*, 117, 11–20.

Butterfield, E.C. & Cairns, G.F. (1974). Discussion summary – Infant reception research. In R.L. Schiefelbusch & L.L. Lloyd (Eds.), *Language perspectives – Acquisition, retardation and intervention*. Baltimore: University Park Press.

Butterworth, B. (2005). The development of arithmetical abilities. *Journal of Child Psychology and Psychiatry*, 46, 3–18.

Cairns, G.F. & Butterfield, E.C. (1975). Assessing infants' auditory functioning. In B.Z. Friedlander, G.M. Sterritt & G. Kirk (Eds.), *The exceptional infant: Assessment and intervention*. New York: Brunner/Mazel, vol. 3.

Caley, L., Kramer, C. & Robinson, L. (2005). Fetal alcohol spectrum disorder. *Journal of School Nursing*, 21, 139–46.

Calkins, S.D., Dedmon, S.E., Gill, K.L., Lomax, L.E. & Johnson, L.M. (2002). Frustration in infancy: Implications for emotion regulation, physiological processes, and temperament. *Infancy*, 3, 175–97.

Caravale, B., Tozzi, C., Albino, G. & Vicari, S. (2005). Cognitive development in low risk preterm infants at 3–4 years of life. *Archives of disease in childhood. Fetal and neonatal edition*, 90, 474–9.

Carey, W. & McDevitt, S. (1978). Revision of the infant temperament questionnaire. *Pediatrics*, *61*, 735–9.

Carpenter, M., Call, J. & Tomasello, M. (2005). Twelve- and 18-month-olds copy actions in terms of goals. *Developmental science*, *8*, F13–20.

Carvajal, F. & Iglesias, J. (2001). The Duchenne smile with open mouth in infants with Down syndrome. *Infant Behavior & Development*, *24*, 341–46.

Carver, L.J. & Bauer, P.J. (2001). The dawning of a past: The emergence of long-term explicit memory in infancy. *Journal of Experimental Psychology Gen*, *130*, 726–45.

Casper, R., Fleisher, B., Lee-Ancajas, J., Gilles, A., Gaylor, E., DeBattista, A. & Hoyme, H. (2003). Follow-up of children of depressed mothers exposed or not exposed to anti-depressant drugs during pregnancy. *Journal of Pediatrics*, *142*, 402–8.

Catherwood, D. (1994). Exploring the seminal phase in infant memory for color and shape. *Infant Behavior and Development*, *17*, 235–43.

Ceponiene, R., Kushnerenko, E., Fellman, V., Renlund, M., Suominen, K. & Näätänen, R. (2002). Event-related potential features indexing central auditory discrimination by newborns. *Brain Research: Cognitive Brain Research*, *13*, 101–13.

Cernack, J.M. & Porter, R.H. (1985). Recognition of maternal axillary odors by infants. *Child Development*, *56*, 1593–8.

Cernadas, J.M., Noceda, G., Barrera, L., Martinez, A.M. & Garsd, A. (2003). Maternal and perinatal factors influencing the duration of exclusive breastfeeding during the first 6 months of life. *Journal of Human Lactation*, *19*, 136–44.

Charpak, N., Ruiz-Pelaez, J.G., Figueroa, C.Z. & Charpak, Y. (2001). A randomized, controlled trial of Kangaroo mother care: Results of follow-up at 1 year of corrected age. *Pediatrics*, *108*, 1072–9.

Chatoor, I., Ganiban, J., Hirsch, R., Borman-Spurrell, E. & Mrazek, D.A. (2000). Maternal characteristics and toddler temperament in infantile anorexia. *Journal of American Academic Children and Adolescent Psychiatry*, *39*, 743–51.

Chaudron, L.H., Kitzman, H.J., Peifer, K.L., Morrow, S., Perez, L.M. & Newman, M.C. (2005). Prevalence of maternal depressive symptoms in low-income Hispanic women. *Journal of Clinical Psychiatry*, *66*, 418–23.

Chen, X., Striano, T. & Rakoczy, H. (2004). Auditory–oral matching behavior in newborns. *Developmental Science*, *7*, 42–7.

Cheour, M., Kushnerenko, E., Ceponiene, R., Fellman, V. & Näätänen, R. (2002). Electric brain responses obtained from newborn infants to changes in duration in complex harmonic tones. *Developmental Neuropsychology*, *22*, 471–9.

Chung, T.K.H., Lau, T.K., Yip, A.S.K., Chiu, H.F.K. & Lee, D.T.S. (2001). Antepartum depressive symptomatology is associated with adverse obstetric and neonatal outcomes. *Psychosomatic Medicine*, *63*, 830–34.

Cianfarani, S., Geremia, C., Scott, C.D. & Germani, D. (2002). Growth, IGF system, and cortisol in children with intrauterine growth retardation: Is catch-up growth affected by reprogramming of the hypothalamic–pituitary–adrenal axis? *Pediatric Research, 51,* 94–9.

Cicero, T.J. (1994). Effects of paternal exposure to alcohol on offspring development. *Alcohol Health and Research World, 18,* 37–41.

Cigales, M., Field, T., Hossain, Z., Pelaez-Nogueras, M. & Gewirtz, J. (1996). Touch among children at nursery school. *Early Child Development & Care, 126,* 101–10.

Cintas, H.M. (1988). Cross-cultural variation in infant motor development. *Physical and Occupational Therapy in Pediatrics, 8,* 1–20.

Clark, H.H. (1995). *Using language.* Cambridge: Cambridge University Press.

Clark, K.M., Castillo, M., Calatroni, A., Walter, T., Cayazzo, M., Pino, P. & Lozoff, B. (2006). Breast-feeding and mental and motor development at $5\frac{1}{2}$ years. *Ambulatory Pediatrics, 6,* 65–71.

Clarke-Stewart, K.A., Fitzpatrick, M.J., Allhusen, V.D. & Goldberg, W.A. (2000). Measuring difficult temperament the easy way. *Journal of Deviant Behavior Pediatrics, 21,* 221–3.

Clearfield, M.W. (2004). The role of crawling and walking experience in infant spatial memory. *Journal of Experimental Child Psychology, 89,* 214–41.

Cluett, E., Nikodem, V., McCandlish, R. & Burns, E. (2004). Immersion in water in pregnancy, labour and birth. *Cochrane Database System Revue, 2.*

Coe, C.L. & Crispen, H.R. (2000). Social stress in pregnant squirrel monkeys (*Saimiri boliviensis peruviensis*) differentially affects placental transfer of maternal antibody to male and female infants. *Health Psychology, 19,* 554–9.

Cohen, L.B. & Cashon, C.H. (2001). Do 7-month-old infants process independent features or facial configurations? *Infant and Child Development, 10,* 83–92.

Cohen, M.M. (2000). A meta-analysis of the predictive ability of attachment: is the emperor wearing any clothes? *Dissertation Abstracts International: Section B: The Sciences and Engineering, 60,* 4926.

Cohen, N.J., Lojkasek, M., Muir, E., Muir, R. & Parker, C.J. (2002). Six-month follow-up of two mother–infant psychotherapies: Convergence of therapeutic outcomes. *Infant Mental Health Journal, 23,* 361–80.

Colombo, J. & Richman, W. (2002). Infant timekeeping: Attention and temporal estimation in 4-month-olds. *Psychological Science, 13,* 475–9.

Connellan, J., Baron-Cohen, S., Wheelwright, S., Batki, A. & Ahluwalia, J. (2000). Sex differences in human neonatal social perception. *Infant Behavior and Development, 23,* 113–18.

Coubet, N., Rattaz, C., Pierrat, V., Bullinger, A. & Lequien, P. (2003). Olfactory experience mediates response to pain in preterm newborns. *Developmental Psychobiology, 42,* 171–80.

Couturier-Fagan, D.A. (1996). Neonatal responses to tongue protrusion and mouth opening modeling. *Dissertation Abstracts International: Section B: The Sciences and Engineering, 57,* 2173.

Cowan, M.J. (2001). Maternal depression and comorbidity: Predicting early parenting, attachment security, and toddlers social-emotional problems and competencies. *Journal of the American Academy of Child and Adolescent Psychiatry*, 40, 18–26.

Crockenberg, S. & Leerkes, E.M. (2005). Infant temperament moderates associations between childcare type and quantity and externalizing and internalizing behaviors at $2\frac{1}{2}$ years. *Infant behavior & Development*, 28, 20–35.

Crook, C.K. (1978). Taste perception in the newborn infant. *Infant Behavior and Development*, 1, 52–69.

Cuevas, K.D., Silver, D.R., Brooten, D., Youngblut, J.M. & Bobo, C.M. (2005). The cost of prematurity: Hospital charges at birth and frequency of rehospitalizations and acute care visits over the first year of life: A comparison by gestational age and birth weight. *American Journal of Nursing*, 105, 56–64.

Cullen, C., Field, T., Escalona, A. & Hartshorn, K. (2000). Father–infant interactions are enhanced by massage therapy. *Early Child Development and Care*, 164, 41–7.

Curtis, W.J., Lindeke, L.L., Georgieff, M.K. & Nelson, C.A. (2002). Neurobehavioural functioning in neonatal intensive care unit graduates in late childhood and early adolescence. *Brain*, 125, 1646–59.

Cyna, A., McAuliffe, G. & Andrew, M. (2004). Hypnosis for pain relief in labour and childbirth: A systematic review. *British Journal of Anaesthesia*, 93, 505–11.

Davis, E., Snidman, N., Wadhwa, P., Glynn, L., Schetter, C. & Sandman, C. (2002). Prenatal maternal anxiety and depression predict negative behavioral reactivity in infancy. *Infancy*, 6, 319–31.

De Schipper, E., Riksen-Walraven, J. & Geurts, S. (2002). Effects of child–caregiver ratio on the interactions between caregivers and children in childcare centers: An experimental study. *Child Development*, 77, 861.

De Vicente, J., Perez, A., Garcia, M. & Reinoso, F. *Preoperative evaluation of the pediatric patient. General concepts*. Pediatrika: Alpe Editores SA, 2005.

de Vries, A.M. & de Groot, L. (2002). Transient dystonias revisited: A comparative study of preterm and term children at $2\frac{1}{2}$ years of age. *Developmental Medicine and Child Neurology*, 44, 415–21.

De Weerth, C., van Hees, Y. & Buitelaar, J.K. (2003). Prenatal maternal cortisol levels and infant behavior during the first 5 months. *Early Human Development*, 74, 139–51.

De Weerth, C., Zijl, R.H. & Buitelaar, J.K. (2003). Development of cortisol circadian rhythm in infancy. *Early Human Development*, 73, 39–52.

DeCasper, A.J. & Fifer, W.P. (1980). Of human bonding: Newborns prefer their mothers' voices. *Science*, 208, 1174–6.

DeCasper, A.J., Lecanuet, J.P., Busnel, M.C., Granier-Deferre, C. & Maugeais, R. (1994). Fetal reactions to recurrent maternal speech. *Infant Behavior and Development*, 17, 159–64.

DeCasper, A.J. & Prescott, P.A. (1984). Human newborns' perception of male voices: Preference, discrimination and reinforcing value.

Developmental Psychobiology, 17, 481–91.

DeCasper, A.J. & Spence, M.J. (1986). Prenatal maternal speech influences newborns' perception of speech sounds. *Infant Behavior and Development*, 9, 133–50.

Decety, J. & Jackson, P.L. (2004). The functional architecture of human empathy. *Behavioral Cognitive and Neuroscience Review*, 3, 71–100.

Dehaene-Lambertz, G., Dehaene, S. & Hertz-Pannier, L. (2002). Functional neuroimaging of speech perception in infants. *Science*, 298, 2013–15.

Delgado, C.E.F., Messinger, D.S. & Yale, M.E. (2002). Infant responses to direction of parental gaze: A comparison of two still-face conditions. *Infant Behavior and Development*, 25, 311–18.

DeLuca, A., Rizzardi, M., Torrente, I., Alessandroni, R., Salvioli, G., Filograsso, N., Dallapiccola, B. & Novelli, G. (2001). Dopamine D4 receptor (DRD4) polymorphism and adaptability trait during infancy: A longitudinal study in 1- to 5-month-old neonates. *Neurogenetics*, 3, 79–82.

Denham, S., et al. (1995). Continuity and change in emotional components of infant temperament. *Child Study Journal*, 25, 289–308.

Dennis, C.L. & Ross, L. (2005). Relationships among infant sleep patterns, maternal fatigue, and development of depressive symptomatology. *Birth*, 32, 187–93.

Dennis, C.L.E. & Stewart, D.E. (2004). Treatment of postpartum depression, Part 1: A critical review of biological interventions. *Journal of Clinical Psychiatry*, 65, 1242–51.

DeRegnier, R.A., Wewerka, S., Georgieff, M.K., Mattia, F. & Nelson, C.A. (2002). Influences of postconceptional age and postnatal experience on the development of auditory recognition memory in the newborn infant. *Developmental Psychology*, 41, 216–25.

Diego, M., Field, T., Jones, N.A., Hernandez-Reif, M., Cullen, C., Schanberg, S. & Kuhn, C. (2004). EEG responses to mock facial expressions by infants of depressed mothers. *Infant Behavior and Development*, 27, 150–62.

Diego, M.A., Field, T., Hart, S., Hernandez-Reif, M., Jones, N., Cullen, C., Schanberg, S. & Kuhn, C. (2002). Facial expressions and EEG in infants of intrusive and withdrawn mothers with depressive symptoms. *Depression and Anxiety*, 15, 10–17.

Diego, M.A., Jones, N.A., Field, T. & Hernandez-Reif, M. (1998). Aromatherapy reduces anxiety and enhances EEG patterns associated with positive mood and alertness. *International Journal of Neuroscience*, 96, 217–24.

Dieter, J., Field, T., Hernandez-Reif, M., Jones, N.A., Lecanuet, J.P., Salman, F.A. & Redzepi, M. (2001). Maternal depression and increased fetal activity. *Journal of Obstetrics and Gynaecology*, 21, 468–73.

Dieter, J.N.I., Field, T., Hernandez-Reif, M., Emory, E.K. & Redzepi, M. (2003). Stable preterm infants gain more weight and sleep less after five days of massage therapy. *Journal of Pediatric Psychology*, 28, 403–11.

DiPasquale, D.J., Moran, M.K., Horge, E.O. & Dajani, A.N. (2001).

Pregnancy anxieties and natural recognition in baby-switching. *British Journal of Nursing, 10,* 718–26.

DiPietro, J.A., Bornstein, M.H., Costigan, K.A., Pressman, E.K., Hahn, C.S., Painter, K., Smith, B.A. & Yi, L.J. (2002). What does fetal movement predict about behavior during the first two years of life? *Development Psychobiology, 40,* 358–71.

DiPietro, J., Hodgson, D., Costigan, K. & Johnson, T. (1996). Fetal antecedents of infant temperament. *Child Development, 67,* 2568–83.

Dixon, W.E. & Smith, P.H. (2003). Who's controlling whom? Infant contributions to maternal play behavior. *Infant and Child Development, 12,* 177–95.

Dodd, J.M., Crowther, C.A., Cincotta, R., Flenady, V. & Robinson, J.S. (2005). Progesterone supplementation for preventing preterm birth: a systematic review and meta-analysis. *Acta Obstetrica et Gymecologica Scandinavica, 84,* 526–33.

Dodd, V.L. (2004). Effects of kangaroo care in preterm infants. *Dissertation Abstracts International, Section A: Humanities and Social Sciences, 64,* 2777.

Dondi, M., Costabile, A., Rabissoni, M., Gianfranchi, C., Lombardi, O. & Corchia, C. (2004). Smiles of premature neonates: An exploratory investigation/Il sorriso del neonato prematuro: Una recerca esplorativa. *Giornale Italiano di Psicologia, 31,* 377–99.

Dondi, M., Simion, F. & Caltran, G. (1999). Can newborns discriminate between their own cry and the cry of another newborn infant? *Developmental Psychology, 35,* 418–26.

Doussard-Roosevelt, J.A., Porges, S.W., Scanlon, J.W., Alemi, B. & Scanlon, K.B. (1997). Vagal regulation of heart rate in the prediction of developmental outcome for very low birth weight preterm infants. *Child Development, 66,* 474–85.

Draghi-Lorenz, R., Reddy, V. & Costall, A. (2001). Rethinking the development of "nonbasic" emotions: A critical review of existing theories. *Developmental Review, 21,* 263–304.

Easterbrook, M.A., Kisilevsky, B.S., Hains, S.M.J. & Muir, D.W. (1999). Faceness or complexity: Evidence from newborn visual tracking of facelike stimuli. *Infant Behavior and Development, 22,* 17–35.

Ebstein, R., Levine, J., Geller, V., Auerbach, J., Gritsenko, I. & Belmaker, R. (1998). Dopamine D4 receptor and serotonin transporter promoter in the determination of neonatal temperament. *Molecular Psychiatry, 3,* 238–46.

Edhborg, M., Lundh, W., Semyr, L. & Widstrom, A.M. (2001). The long-term impact of postnatal depressed mood on mother–child interaction: A preliminary study. *Journal of Reproductive and Infant Psychology, 19,* 61–71.

Edhborg, M., Lundh, W., Semyr, L. & Widstrom, A.M. (2003). The parent–child relationship in the context of maternal depressive mood. *Archives of Women Mental Heath, 6,* 211–16.

Egeland, B. & Hiester, M. (1995). The long-term consequences of infant day-care and mother–infant attachment. *Child Development, 66,* 474–85.

Ehrenkraz, R.A., Dusick, A.M., Vohr, B.R., Wright, L.L., Wrage, L.A. & Poole, W.K. (2006). Growth in the neonatal intensive care unit influences neurodevelopmental and growth outcomes of extremely low birth weight infants. *Pediatrics, 117,* 1253–61.

Eichstedt, J.A., Serbin, L.A., Poulin-Dubois, D. & Sen, M.G. (2002). Of bears and men: Infants' knowledge of conventional and metaphorical gender stereotypes. *Infant Behavior & Development, 25,* 296–310.

Einarson, A., Selby, P. & Koren, G. (2001). Abrupt discontinuation of psychotropic drugs during pregnancy: Fear of teratogenic risk and impact of counseling. *Journal of Psychiatry and Neuroscience, 26,* 44–8.

Engen, T. & Lipsitt, L.P. (1965). Decrement and recovery of responses to olfactory stimuli in the human neonate. *Journal of Comparative Physiological Psychology, 56,* 73–7.

Erber, N.L., Almerigi, J.B., Carbary, T.J. & Harris, L.J. (2002). The contribution of postural bias to lateral preferences for holding human infants. *Brain and Cognition, 48,* 352–6.

Essex, M.J., Klein, M.H., Cho, E. & Kalin, N.H. (2002). Maternal stress beginning in infancy may sensitize children to later stress exposure: effects on cortisol and behavior. *Biology and Psychiatry, 15,* 776–84.

Fabes, R., Martin, C., Hanish, L. & Updegraff, K. (2000). Criteria for evaluating the significance of developmental research in the twenty-first century: Force and counterforce. *Child Development, 71(1),* 212–21.

Farroni, T., Johnson, M.H. & Csibra, G. (2004). Mechanisms of eye gaze perception during infancy. *Journal of Cognitive Neuroscience, 16,* 1320–6.

Fazzi, E., Farinotti, L., Scelsa, B., Gerola, O. & Bollani, L. (1996). Response to pain in a group of healthy term newborns: Behavioral and physiological aspects. *Functional Neurology: New Trends in Adaptive and Behavioral Disorders, 11,* 35–43.

Feldman, R. & Eidelman, A.I. (2003). Skin-to-skin contact (kangaroo care) accelerates autonomic and neuro-behavioral maturation in preterm infants. *Developmental Medicine of Child Neurology, 45,* 274–81.

Feldman, R., Eidelman, A.I., Sirota, L. & Weller, A. (2002). Comparison of skin-to-skin (Kangaroo) and traditional care: Parenting outcomes and preterm infant development. *Pediatrics, 110,* 16–26.

Ferber, S.G., Feldman, R., Kohelet, D., Kuint, J., Dollberg, S., Arbel, E. & Weller, A. (2004). Massage therapy facilitates mother–infant interaction in premature infants. *Infant Behavior and Development, 28,* 74–81.

Ferber, S.G. & Makhoul, I.R. (2004). The effect of skin-to-skin contact (kangaroo care) shortly after birth on the neurobehavioral responses of the term newborn: A randomized, controlled trial. *Pediatrics, 113,* 858–65.

Fernandez, M., Blass, E.M., Hernandez-Reif, M., Field, T., Diego, M. & Sanders, C. (2003). Sucrose attenuates a negative electroencephalographic response to an aversive stimulus for newborns. *Journal of*

Developmental and Behavioral Pediatrics, 24, 261–6.

Fernandez, M., Hernandez-Reif, M., Field, T., Diego, M., Sanders, C. & Roca, A. (2001). EEG during lavender and rosemary exposure in infants of depressed and non-depressed mothers. *Infant Behavior and Development*, 27, 91–100.

Field, T. (1977). Effects of early separation, interactive deficits, and experimental manipulations on infant–mother face-to-face interaction. *Child Development*, 48, 763–71.

Field, T. (1979). Differential behavioral and cardiac responses of 3-month-old infants to a mirror and peer. *Infant Behavior and Development*, 2, 179–84.

Field, T. (1985). Attachment as psychobiological attunement: Being on the same wavelength. In M. Reite & T. Field (Eds.), *Psychobiology of attachment*. New York: Academic Press.

Field, T. (1990). *Infancy (the developing child)*. Cambridge, MA: Harvard University Press.

Field, T. (1990). Touch and massage in early childhood development. In L. Moyer Mileur (Ed.), *Optimizing growth and bone mass in premature infants: Are diet and physical movement the answer?* Johnson and Johnson Pediatric Institute, LLC, 2004, 167–80.

Field, T. & Brazelton, T.B. (Eds.) (1990). *Advances in touch*. Skillman, NJ: Johnson & Johnson.

Field, T., Cohen, D., Garcia, R. & Greenberg, R. (1984). Mother–stranger face discrimination by the newborn. *Infant Behavior and Development*, 7, 19–25.

Field, T., Dempsey, J., Hallock, N. & Shuman, H.H. (1978). The mother's assessment of the behavior of her infant. *Infant Behavior and Development*, 1, 156–67.

Field, T., Diego, M. & Hernandez-Reif, M. (2001). Newborns' EEG responses to lavender bath oil (unpublished manuscript).

Field, T., Diego, M., Hernandez-Reif, M., Salman, F., Schanberg, S., Kuhn, C., Yando, R. & Bendell, D. (2002). Prenatal anger effects on the fetus and neonate. *Journal of Obstetrics and Gynaecology*, 22, 260–6.

Field, T., Diego, M., Hernandez-Reif, M., Schanberg, S. & Kuhn, C. (2002a). Right frontal EEG and pregnancy/neonatal outcomes. *Psychiatry*, 65, 35–47.

Field, T., Diego, M., Hernandez-Reif, M., Schanberg, S. & Kuhn, C. (2002b). Relative right versus left frontal EEG in neonates. *Developmental Psychobiology*, 41(2), 147–55.

Field, T., Diego, M., Hernandez-Reif, M., Schanberg, S. & Kuhn, C. (2003). Depressed mothers who are "good interaction" partners versus those who are withdrawn or intrusive. *Infant Behavior and Development*, 26, 238–52.

Field, T., Diego, M., Hernandez-Reif, M., Schanberg, S., Kuhn, C., Yando, R. & Bendell, D. (2003). Pregnancy anxiety and comorbid depression and anger: effects on the fetus and neonate. *Depression and Anxiety*, 17, 140–51.

Field, T., Diego, M., Hernandez-Reif, M., Vera, Y., Gil, K., Schanberg, S., Kuhn, C. & Gonzalez-Garcia, A. (2004a). Prenatal predictors of maternal and newborn EEG. *Infant*

Behavior and Development, 27, 533–6.

Field, T., Diego, M., Hernandez-Reif, M., Vera, Y., Gil, K., Schanberg, S., Kuhn, C. & Gonzalez-Garcia, A. (2004b). Prenatal maternal biochemistry predicts neonatal biochemistry. *International Journal of Neuroscience*, 114, 933–45.

Field, T. & Goldson, E. (1984). Pacifying effects of nonnutritive sucking on term and preterm neonates during heelstick procedures. *Pediatrics*, 74, 1012–15.

Field, T., Harding, J., Soliday, B., Lasko, D., Gonzalez, N. & Valdeon, C. (1994). Touching in infant, toddler & preschool nurseries. *Early Child Development and Care*, 98, 113–20.

Field, T., Hernandez-Reif, M., Taylor, S., Quintino, O. & Burman, I. (1997). Labor pain is reduced by massage therapy. *Journal of Psychosomatic Obstetrics and Gynecology*, 18, 286–91.

Field, T., Hernandez-Reif, M., Vera, Y., Gil, K., Diego, M., Bendell, D. & Yando, R. (2004). Anxiety and anger effects on depressed mother–infant spontaneous and imitative interactions. *Infant Behavior and Development*, 28, 1–9.

Field, T., Hernandez-Reif, M., Vera, Y., Gil, K., Diego, M. & Sanders, C. (2005). Infants of depressed mothers facing a mirror versus their mother. *Infant Behavior and Development*, 28, 48–53.

Field, T., Pickens, J., Prodromidis, M., Malphrus, J., Fox, N., Bendell, D., Yando, R., Schanberg, S. & Kuhn, C. (2000). Targeting adolescent mothers with depressive symptoms for early intervention. *Adolescence*, 35, 381–414.

Field, T. & Reite, M. (1984). Children's responses to separation from mother during the birth of another child. *Child Development*, 55, 1308–16.

Field, T., Sandberg, D., Quetel, T.A., Garcia, R. & Rosario, M. (1985). Effects of ultrasound feedback on pregnancy anxiety, fetal activity and neonatal outcome. *Obstetrics and Gynecology*, 66(4), 525–8.

Fifer, W.P. & Moon, C.M. (1994). The role of mother's voice in the organization of brain function in the newborn. *Acta Paediatrica Supplement*, 397, 86–93.

Finster, M. & Wood, M. (2005). The Apgar score has survived the test of time. *Anesthesiology*, 102, 855–7.

Fleckenstein, L.K. & Fagen, J.W. (1994). Reactivation of infant memory following crying-produced forgetting. *Infant Behavior and Development*, 17, 215–20.

Fleming, A.S., Corter, C., Stallings, J. & Steiner, M. (2002). Testosterone and prolactin are associated with emotional responses to infant cries in new fathers. *Hormones and Behavior*, 42, 399–413.

Foley, D., Pickles, A., Simonoff, E., Maes, H., Silberg, J., Hewitt, J. & Eaves, L. (2001). Parental concordance and comorbidity for psychiatric disorder and associate risks for current psychiatric symptoms and disorders in a community sample of juvenile twins. *Journal of Child Psychology and Psychiatry*, 42, 381–94.

Forcada-Guex, M., Pierrehumbert, B., Borghini, A., Moessinger, A. & Muller-Nix, C. (2006). Early dyadic patterns of mother–infant interactions and outcomes of prematurity at 18 months. *Pediatrics*, *118*, 107–14.

Fox, N.A. (1994). Dynamic cerebral processes underlying emotion regulation. In N.A. Fox (Ed.), *The development of emotion regulation: Behavioral and biological considerations* (Vol. 23, Serial No. 240, pp. 152–66): Monographs of the Society for Research in Child Development, *59*.

Fox, N.A. & Clakins, S.D. (2003). The development of self-control of emotion: Intrinsic and extrinsic influences. *Motivation and Emotion*, *27*, 7–26.

Fox, N.A., Henderson, H.A., Marshall, P.J., Nichols, K.E. & Ghera, M.M. (2005). Behavioral inhibition: Linking biology and behavior within a developmental framework. *Annual Review of Psychobiology*, *56*, 235–62.

Fox, N.A., Henderson, H.A., Rubin, K.H., Calkins, S.D. & Schmidt, L.A. (2001). Continuity and discontinuity of behavior inhibition and exuberance: psychophysiological and behavioral influences across the first four years of life. *Child Development*, *72*, 1–21.

Fox, N.A., Kimmerly, N.L. & Schafer, W.D. (1991). Attachment to mother/attachment to father: Meta-analysis. *Child Development*, *62*, 210–25.

Franco, P., Chabanski, S., Scaillet, S., Groswasser, J. & Kahn, A. (2004). Pacifier use modifies infant's cardiac autonomic controls during sleep. *Early Human Development*, *77*, 99–108.

Franco, P., Seret, N., Van Hees, J.N., Lanquart, J.P., Jr. Groswasser, J. & Kahn, A. (2003). Cardiac changes during sleep in sleep-deprived infants. *Sleep*, *26*, 845–8.

Franco, P., Seret, N., Van Hees, J.N., Scaillet, S., Groswasser, J. & Kahn. A. (2005). Influence of swaddling on sleep and arousal characteristics of healthy infants. *Pediatrics*, *115*, 1307–11.

Franco, P., Szliwowski, H., Dramaix, M. & Kahn. A. (2000). Influences of ambient temperature on sleep characteristics and autonomic nervous control in healthy infants. *Sleep: Journal of Sleep Research and Sleep Medicine*, *23*, 401–7.

Franklin, A., Pilling, M. & Davies, I. (2005). The nature of infant color categorization: Evidence from eye movements on a target detection task. *Experimental Children Psychology*, *91*, 227–48.

Freudigman, K.A. (1996). Neonatal sleep as an indicator of perinatal events and as a predictor of later developmental status. *Dissertation Abstracts International: Section B: The Sciences and Engineering*, *56*, 4602.

Frick, J.E. & Richards, J.E. (2001). Individual differences in infants' recognition of briefly presented visual stimuli. *Infancy*, *2*, 331–52.

Fujisaki, A. (2002). Owners' understanding of their pets' internal states. *The Japanese Journal of Developmental Psychology*, *13*, 109–21.

Fuller, B.F. (2002). Infant gender differences regarding acute established pain. *Clinical Nursing Research*, *11*, 190–203.

Gal, P., Kissling, G.E., Young, W.O., Dunaway, K.K., Marsh, V.A., Jones, S.M., Shockley, D.H., Weaver, N.L., Carlos, R.Q. & Ransom, J.L. (2005). Efficacy of sucrose to reduce pain in premature infants during eye examinations for retinopathy of prematurity. *Annals of Pharmacotherapy*, *39*, 1029–33.

Galler, J.R., Robert, H.H., Ramsey, F., Butler, S. & Forde, V. (2004). Postpartum maternal mood, feeding practices, and infant temperament in Barbados. *Infant Behavior and Development*, *27*, 267–87.

Ganchrow, J.R., Steiner, J.E. & Daher, M. (1983). Neonatal facial expressions in response to different qualities and intensities of gustatory stimuli. *Infant Behavior and Development*, *6*, 473–84.

Gannon, J.N. (1999). So happy together: Co-bedding multiples boosts growth and development enhanced bonding. *Neonatal Network*, *18*, 39–40.

Garrett, M., McElroy, A.M. & Stains, A. (2002). Locomotor milestones and babywalkers: Cross sectional study. *British Medical Journal*, *324*, 1494.

Geissbuehler, V. & Eberhard, J. (2002). Fear of childbirth during pregnancy: A study of more than 8000 pregnant women. *Journal of Psychosomatic Obstetrics and Gynaecology*, *23*, 229–35.

Gentile, S. (2005). SSRIs in pregnancy and lactation: emphasis on neurodevelopmental outcome. *CNS Drugs*, *19*, 623–33.

Geva, R., Gardner, J.M. & Karmel, B.Z. (1999). Feeding-based arousal effects on visual recognition memory in early infancy. *Developmental Psychology*, *35*, 640–50.

Gibson, E., Dembofsky, C.A., Rubin, S. & Greenspan, J.S. (2000). Infant sleep position practices 2 years into the "Back to Sleep" campaign. *Clinical Pediatrics*, *39*, 285–9.

Gingras, J.L., Mitchell, E.A. & Grattan, K.E. (2005). Fetal homologue of infant crying. *Archives of Disease in Childhood: Fetal Neonatal*, *90(5)*, 415–18.

Godding, V., Bonnier, C., Fiasse, L., Michel, M., Longueville, E., Lebecque, P., Robert, A. & Galanti, L. (2004). Does in utero exposure to heavy maternal smoking induce nicotine withdrawal symptoms in neonates? *Pediatric Research*, *55*, 645–51.

Goebel, P.W. (2002). Fathers' touch in low birthweight infants. *Dissertation Abstracts International: Section B: The Sciences and Engineering*, *62*, 3553.

Goldberg, S., Levitan, R., Leung, E., Masellis, M., Basile, V.S. & Nemeroff, C.B. (2003). Cortisol concentrations in 12- to 18-month-old infants: Stability over time, location, and stressor. *Bological Psychiatry*, *54*, 719–26.

Goldman, H.I. (2001). Parental reports of "MAMA" sounds in infants: An exploratory study. *Journal of child Language*, *28*, 497–506.

Goldsmith, H. & Lemery, K. (2000). Linking temperamental fearfulness and anxiety symptoms: A behavior-genetic perspective. *Biology and Psychiatry*, *48*, 1199–209.

Goldsmith, H.H., Lemery, K.S., Buss, K.A. & Campos, J.J. (1999). Genetic analyses of focal aspects of infant temperament. *Developmental Psychology*, *35*, 972–85.

Goldstein, M.H. (2002). Social mechanisms of vocal learning in human infants. *Dissertation Abstracts International: Section B: The Sciences and Engineering, 62*, 3828.

Goldstein, M.H., King, A.P. & West, M.J. (2003). Social interaction shapes babbling: Testing parallels between birdsong and speech. *Proceedings of the National Academy of Science USA, 100*, 9645–6.

Goodlin-Jones, B.L., Burnham, M.M., Gaylord, E.E. & Anders, T.F. (2001). Night walking, sleep–wake organization, and self soothing in the first year of life. *Journal of Developmental and Behavioral Pediatrics, 22*, 226–33.

Goodman, J.H. (2004). Paternal postpartum depression, its relationship to maternal postpartum depression, and implications for family health. *Journal of Advance Nursing, 45*, 26–35.

Gormally, S., Barr, R.G., Wertheim, L., Alkawaf, R., Calinoiu, N. & Young, S.N. (2001). Contact and nutrient caregiving effects on newborn infant pain responses. *Developmental Medicine and Child Neurology, 43*, 28–38.

Gorman, K.J. (2002). Breastfeeding and cosleeping: A correlational assessment. *Dissertation Abstract International: Section B: Science and Engineering, 62*, 4273.

Goubet, N., Rattaz, C., Pierrat, V., Bullinger, A. & Lequien, P. (2003). Olfactory experience mediates response to pain in preterm newborns. *Development Psychobiology, 42*, 171–80.

Gradin, M. & Schollin, J. (2005). The role of endogenous opioids in mediating pain reduction by orally administered glucose among newborns. *Pediatrics, 115*, 1004–7.

Graham, F.K. & Clifton, R.K. (1966). Heart rate change as a component of the orienting response. *Psychological Bulletin, 65*, 305–20.

Greenberg, C.S. (2002). A sugar-coated pacifier reduces procedural pain in newborns. *Pediatrics Nursing, 28*, 271–7.

Groer, M., Davis, M., Casey, K., Short, B., Smith, K. & Groer, S. (2005). Neuroendocrine and immune relationships in postpartum fatigue. *American Journal of Maternal and Child Nursing, 30*, 133–8.

Groome, L.J., Mooney, D.M., Holland, S.B., Smith, Y.D., Atterbury, J.L. & Dykman, R.A. (2000). Temporal pattern and spectral complexity as stimulus parameters for eliciting a cardiac orienting reflex in human fetuses. *Perception and Psychophysics, 62*, 313–20.

Groome, L.J., Swiber, M., Holland, S., Bentz, L., Atterbury, J. & Trimm, R. (2001). Spontaneous motor activity in the perinatal infant before and after birth: stability in individual differences. *Developmental Psychobiology, 35*, 15–24.

Grunau, R.E., Holsti, L., Haley, D.W., Oberlander, T.F., Weinberg, J., Solimano, A., Whitfield, M.F., Fitzgerald, C. & Yu, W. (2005). Neonatal procedural pain exposure predicts lower cortisol and behavioral reactivity in preterm infants in the NICU. *Pain, 113*, 293–300.

Grunau, R.E., Oberlander, T.F., Whitfield, M.F., Morison, S.J. & Saul, J.P. (2001). Pain reactivity in former extremely low birth weight infants at corrected age 8 months compared with term born controls. *Infant*

Behavior and Development, 24, 41–55.

Grunau, R.E., Whitfield, M.F., Fay, T., Holsti, L., Oberlander, T. & Rogers, M.L. (2006). *Developmental Medicine and Child Neurology, 48,* 471–6.

Gunner, M.R., Larson, M.C., Hertsgaard, L. & Harris, M. (1992). The stressfulness of separation among nine-month-old infants: Effects of social context variables and infant temperament. *Child Development, 63,* 290–303.

Gutteling, B.M., de Weerth, C., Willmesen-Swinkels, S.H., Huizink, A.C., Mulder, E.J., Visser, G.H. & Buitelaar, J.K. (2005). The effects of prenatal stress on temperament and problem behavior of 27-month-old toddlers. *European Child Adolescent Psychiatry, 14,* 41–51.

Hadders-Algra, M. (2005). Development of postural control during the first 18 months of life. *Neural Palsticity, 12,* 99–108.

Haley, D.W. & Stansbury, K. (2003). Infant stress and parent responsiveness: Regulation of physiology and behavior during still-face and reunion. *Child Development, 74,* 1534–46.

Hallemans, A., De Clercq, D., Otten, B. & Aerts, P. (2005). 3D joint dynamics of walking in toddlers: A cross-sectional study spanning the first rapid development phase of walking. *Gait Posture, 22,* 107–18.

Hannigan, J.H. (1995). Effects of prenatal exposure to alcohol plus caffeine in rats: Pregnancy outcome and early offspring development. *Alcoholism: Clinical and Experimental Research, 19,* 238–46.

Harris, L.J. (2002). Lateral biases for holding infants: Early opinions, observations, and explanations with some possible lessons for theory and research today. *Brain and Cognition, 48,* 392–4.

Harrison, L.J. & Ungerer, J.A. (2002). Maternal employment and infant–mother attachment security at 12 months postpartum. *Developmental Psychology, 38,* 758–73.

Hart, S., Field, T., Hernandez-Reif, M. & Lundy, B. (1998). Preschoolers' cognitive performance improves following massage. *Early Child Development & Care, 143,* 59–64.

Hart, S., Field, T. & Nearing, G. (1998). Depressed mothers' neonates improve following the MABI and a Brazelton demonstration. *Journal of Pediatric Psychology, 23,* 351–6.

Hartshorn, K. & Rovee-Collier, C. (1997). Infant learning and long-term memory at 6 months: A confirming analysis. *Developmental Psychobiology, 30,* 71–85.

Harvey, J. (2004). Cocaine effects on the developing brain: Current status. *Neuroscience and Behavioral Review, 27,* 751–64.

Hayes, R.A., Slater, A. & Brown, E. (2000). Infants' ability to categorise on the basis of rhyme. *Cognitive Development, 15,* 405–19.

Hayne, H., Herbert, J. & Simcock, G. (2003). Imitation from television by 24- and 30-month-olds. *Developmental Science, 6,* 254–61.

Hayne, H. & Rovee-Collier, C. (1995). The organization of reactivated memory in infancy. *Child Development, 66,* 893–906.

Hayne, H., Rovee-Collier, C. & Borza, M.A. (1991). Infant memory for place information. *Memory & Cognition*, *19*, 378–86.

Hedberg, A., Carlberg, E.B., Forssberg, H. & Hadders-Algra, M. (2005). Development of postural adjustments in sitting position during the first half year of life. *Developmental Medicine and Child Neurology*, *47*, 312–20.

Heimann, M. & Ulistadius, E. (1999). Neonatal imitation and imitation among children with autism and Down's syndrome. In J. Nadel et al. (Eds.), *Imitation in infancy. Cambridge studies in cognitive perceptual development*. New York: Cambridge University Press, pp. 235–53.

Hellstrom-Westas, L., Inghammar, M., Isaksson, K., Rosen, I. & Stjernqvist, K. (2001). Short-term effects of incubator covers on quiet sleep in stable premature infants. *Acta Paediatrica*, *90*, 1004–8.

Henderson, L.M., Yoder, P.J., Yale, M.E. & McDuffie, A. (2002). Getting the point: Electrophysiological correlates of protodeclarative pointing. *International Journal of Developmental Neuroscience*, *20*, 449–58.

Hernandez-Reif, M., Field, T., del Pino, N. & Diego, M. (2000). Less exploring by mouth occurs in newborns of depressed mothers. *Infant Mental Health Journal*. In Press.

Hernandez-Reif, M., Field, T. & Diego, M. (2004). Differential sucking by neonates of depressed versus non-depressed mothers. *Infant Behavior and Development*, *27*, 465–76.

Hernandez-Reif, M., Field, T., Diego, M. & Largie, S. (2001). Weight perception by newborns of depressed versus non-depressed mothers. *Infant Behavior and Development*, *24*, 305–16.

Hernandez-Reif, M., Field, T., Diego, M. & Largie, S. (2002). Depressed mothers' newborns show inferior face discrimination. *Infant Behavior & Development*, *23*, 643–53.

Hernandez-Reif, M., Field, T., Diego, M. & Largie, S. (2003). Haptic habituation to temperature is slower in newborns of depressed mothers. *Infancy*, *4*, 47–63.

Hill, W.L., Borovsky, D. & Rovee-Collier, C. (1988). Continuities in infant memory development. *Developmental Psychobiology*, *21*, 43–62.

Hiscock, H. & Wake, M. (2002). Randomised controlled trial of behavioural infant sleep intervention to improve infant sleep and maternal mood. *British Medical Journal*, *324*, 1062–5.

Hofberg, K. & Brockington, I. (2000). Tokophobia: An unreasoning dread of childbirth. A series of 26 cases. *British Journal of Psychiatry*, *176*, 83–5.

Hoff, M.P., Nadler, R.D., Hoff, K.T. & Maple, T.L. (1994). Separation and depression in infant gorillas. *Developmental Psychobiology*, *27*, 439–52.

Hollich, G., Newman, R.S. & Jusczyk, P.W. (2005). Infants' use of synchronized visual information to separate streams of speech. *Child Development*, *76*, 598–613.

Holst, M., Eswaran, H., Lowery, C., Murphy, P., Norton, J. & Preissl, H. (2005). Development of auditory evoked fields in human fetuses and newborns: A longitudinal MEG study. *Clinical Neurophysiology*, *116*, 1949–55.

Hossain, Z., Field, T., Gonzalez, J., Malphurs, J., DelValle, C. & Pickens, J. (1994). Infants of depressed mothers interact better with their nondepressed fathers. *Infant Mental Health Journal, 15,* 348–57.

Howell, C.S. (2001). Mothers' speech with 12-month-old infants: Influences on the amount and complexity of infants' vocalizations. *Dissertation Abstracts International: Section A: Humanities and Social Sciences, 61,* 4751.

Hsu, H.C. (2001). Infant vocal development in a dynamic mother–infant communication system. *Infancy, 2,* 87–109.

Hsu, H.C., Fogel, A. & Messinger, D.S. (2001). Infant non-distress vocalization during mother–infant face-to-face interaction: Factors associated with quantitative and qualitative differences. *Infant Behavior & Development, 24,* 107–28.

Huffman, L.C., Bryan, Y.E., del Carmen, R., Pedersen, F.A., Doussard-Roosevelt, J.A. & Porges, S.W. (1998). Infant temperament and cardiac vagal tone: Assessments at twelve weeks of age. *Child Development, 69,* 624–35.

Hui-Chin, H. & Fogel, A. (2003). Stability and transitions in mother–infant face-to-face communication during the first 6 months: A microhistorical approach. *Developmental Psychology, 39,* 1061–82.

Huizink, A.C., Robles de Medina, P.G., Mulder, E.J., Visser, G.H. & Buitelaar, J.K. (2002). Psychology measures of prenatal stress as predictors of infant temperament. *Journal of American Academic Child Adolescent Psychiatry, 41,* 1078–85.

Huizink, A.C., Robles de Medina, P.G., Mulder, E.J., Visser, G.H. & Buitelaar, J.K. (2003). Stress during pregnancy is associated with developmental outcome in infancy. *Journal of Child Psychology and Psychiatry, 44,* 810–18.

Humphrey, T. (1972). Central representation of the oral and facial areas of human fetuses. In J.F. Bosma (Ed.), *Third symposium on oral sensation and perception: The mouth of the infant.* Springfield, IL: Charles C. Thomas.

Hunnius, S. & Geuze, R.H. (2004). Developmental changes in visual scanning of dynamic faces and abstract stimuli in infants: A longitudinal study. *Infancy, 6,* 231–55.

Hunsley, M. & Thoman, E.B. (2002). The sleep of co-sleeping infants when they are not co-sleeping: Evidence that co-sleeping is stressful. *Developmental Psychology, 40,* 14–22.

Huntington, N.L. (2001). Infant behavior during a social interaction: the interrelationship of gaze fluctuations, arousal and cyclic motor activity. *Dissertation Abstract International: Section B: The Sciences and Engineering, 61,* 5028.

Huot, R.L., Brennan, P.A., Stowe, Z.N., Plotsky, P.M. & Walker, E.F. (2004). Negative affect in offspring of depressed mothers is predicted by infant cortisol levels at 6 months and maternal depression during pregnancy, but not postpartum. *Abdominal Aortic Aneurysm: Genetics, Pathophysiology, and Molecular Biology, 1032,* 234–6.

Innis, S.M., Gilley, J. & Werker, J. (2001). Are human milk long-chain polyunsaturated fatty acids related to visual and neural development in breast-fed term infants? *Journal of Pediatrics, 139,* 532–8.

Israelian, M.K. (2000). Prenatal patterns of movement and habituation as predictors of obstetric complications, anthropometric measures, and neurobehavioral outcomes. *Dissertation Abstracts International: Section B: The Sciences and Engineering, 61,* 2203.

Jacklin, C.N., Snow, M.E. & Maccoby, E.E. (1981). Tactile sensitivity and muscle strength in newborn boys and girls. *Infant Behavior and Development, 4,* 261–8.

James, D.K., Spencer, C.J. & Stepsis, B.W. (2002). Fetal learning: A prospective randomized controlled study. *Ultrasound Obstetrics & Gynecology, 20,* 431–8.

James-Roberts, I.S., Goodwin, J., Peter, B., Adams, D. & Hunt, S. (2003). Individual differences in responsivity to a neurobehavioural examination predict crying patterns of 1-week-old infants at home. *Developmental Medicine and Child Neurology, 45,* 400–7.

Jenni, O.G., Fuhrer, H.Z., Iglowstein, I., Molinari, L. & Largo, R.H. (2005). A longitudinal study of bed sharing and sleep problems among Swiss children in the first 10 years of life. *Pediatrics, 115,* 233–40.

Johnson, A.N. (2005). Kangaroo holding beyond the NICU. *Pediatric Nursing, 31,* 53–6.

Jones, N.A., Field, T., Davalos, M. & Hart, S. (2004). Greater right frontal EEG asymmetry and nonemphatic behavior are observed in children prenatally exposed to cocaine. *International Journal of Neuroscience, 114,* 459–80.

Jones, N.A., Field, T., Hart, S., Lundy, B. & Davalos, M. (2001). Maternal self-perceptions and reactions to infant crying among intrusive and withdrawn depressed mothers. *Infant Mental Health Journal, 22,* 576–86.

Jones, N.A., McFall, B.A. & Diego, M.A. (2004). Patterns of brain electrical activity in infants of depressed mothers who breastfeed and bottle feed: The mediating role of infant temperament. *Biology and Psychology, 67,* 103–24.

Jones-Molfese, V.J. (1977). Responses of neonates to colored stimuli. *Child Development, 48,* 1092–5.

Jonsson, C.O., Clinton, D.N., Fahrman, M., Mazzaglia, G., Novak, S. & Sorhus, K. (2001). How do mothers signal shared feeling-states to their infants? An investigation of affect attunement and imitation during the first year of life. *Scandinavian Journal of Psychology, 42,* 377–81.

Jouen, F., Lepecq, J.C., Gapenne, O. & Bertenthal, B.I. (2000). Optic flow sensitivity in neonates. *Infant Behavior and Development, 23,* 271–84.

Kanazawa, S., Shirai, N., Ohtsuka, Y. & Yamaguchi, M.K. (2006). Perception of opposite-moving dots in 3- to 5-month-old infants. *Vision Research, 46,* 346–56.

Kaplan, P.S., Bachorowski, J.A., Smoski, M.J. & Hudenko, W.J. (2002). Infants of depressed mothers, although competent learners, fail to learn in response to their own mothers' infant-directed speech. *Psychological Science, 13,* 268–71.

Kaplan, P.S., Dungan, J.K. & Zinser, M.C. (2004). Infants of chronically depressed mothers learn in response to male, but not female, infant-directed speech. *Developmental Psychology, 40,* 140–8.

Kawakami, K., Takai, K.K., Okazaki, Y., Kurihara, H., Shimizu, Y. & Yanaihara, T. (1997). The effect of odors on human newborn infants under stress. *Infant Behavior and Development, 20,* 531–5.

Keen, R. (1964). The effects of auditory stimuli on sucking behavior in the human neonate. *Journal of Experimental Child Psychology, 1,* 348–54.

Keenan, K., Grace, D. & Gunthorpe, D. (2003). Examining stress reactivity in neonates: Relation between cortisol and behavior. *Child Development, 74,* 1930–42.

Keller, M.A. & Goldberg, W.A. (2004). Co-sleeping: Help or hindrance for young children's independence? *Infant and Child Development, 13,* 369–88.

Kelmanson, I.A. (2000). Snoring, noisy breathing in sleep and daytime behaviour in 2–4-month-old infants. *European Journal of Pediatrics, 159,* 734–9.

Kelmanson, I.A., Erman, L.V. & Litvina, S.V. (2002). Maternal smoking during pregnancy and behavioral characteristics in 2–4-month-old infants. *Klinische Pädiatrie, 214,* 359–64.

Kilbride, H.W., Thorstad, K. & Daily, D.K. (2004). Preschool outcome of less than 801-gram preterm infants compared with full-term siblings. *Pediatrics, 113,* 742–7.

Kisilevsky, B.S. & Muir, D.W. (1991). Human fetal and subsequent newborn responses to sound and vibration. *Infant Behavior and Development, 14,* 1–26.

Kitamura, C., Thanavishuth, C., Burnham, D. & Luksaneeyanawin, S. (2002). Universality and specificity in infant-directed speech: Pitch modifications as a function of infant age and sex in a tonal and non-tonal language. *Infant Behavior and Development, 24,* 372–92.

Klassen, A.F., Lee, S.K., Raina, P., Chan, H.W., Matthew, D. & Brabyn, D. (2004). Health status and health-related quality of life in a population-based sample of neonatal intensive care unit graduates. *Pediatrics, 113,* 594–600.

Klein, D., Lewinsohn, P., Rohde, P., Seeley, J. & Olino, T. (2005). Psychopathology in the adolescent and young adult offspring of a community sample of mothers and fathers with major depression. *Psychological Medicine, 35,* 353–65.

Kokkinaki, T. (2003). A longitudinal, naturalistic and cross-cultural study on emotions in early infant–parent imitative interactions. *British Journal of Developmental Psychology, 21,* 243–58.

Kooijman, V., Hagoort, P. & Cutler, A. (2005). Electrophysiological evidence for prelinguistic infants' word recognition in continuous speech. *Cognitive Brain Research, 24,* 109–16.

Kosugi, D. & Fujita, K. (2001). Infants' recognition of causality: Discrimination between inanimate objects and people. *Psychologia: An International Journal of Psychology in the Orient, 44,* 31–45.

Kuhn, C.M., Schanberg, S.M., Field, T., Symanski, R., Zimmerman, E.,

Scafidi, F. & Roberts, J. (1991). Tactile-kinesthetic stimulation effects on sympathetic and adrenocortical function in preterm infants. *Journal of Pediatrics, 119,* 434–40.

Kujala, A., Huotilainen, M., Hotakainen, M., Lennes, M., Parkkonen, L., Fellman, V. & Näätänen, R. (2004). Speech sound discrimination in neonates as measured with MEG. *Neuroreport: For Rapid Communication of Neuroscience Research, 15,* 2089–92.

Kurihara, H., Chiba, H., Shimizu, Y., Yanaihara, T., Takeda, M., Kawakami, K. & Takai, K.K. (1996). Behavioral and adrenocortical responses to stress in neonates and the stabilizing effects of maternal heartbeat on them. *Early Human Development, 46,* 117–27.

Kushnerenko, E., Ceponiene, R., Balan, P., Fellman, V., Huotilainen, M. & Näätänen, R. (2002a). Maturation of the auditory change detection response in infants: a longitudinal ERP study. *Neuroreport, 13,* 1843–8.

Kushnerenko, E., Ceponiene, R., Balan, P., Fellman, V., Huotilainen, M. & Näätänen, R. (2002b). Maturation of the auditory event-related potentials during the first year of life. *Neuroreport, 13,* 47–51.

LaGasse, L.L., Neal, A.R. & Lester, B.M. (2005). Assessment of infant cry: Acoustic cry analysis and parental perception. *Mental Retardation and Developmental Disabilities Research Reviews, 11,* 83–93.

Laine, K., Heikkinen, T., Ekblad, U. & Kero, P. (2003). Effects of exposure to selective serotonin reuptake inhibitors during pregnancy on serotonergic symptoms in newborns and cord blood monoamine and prolactin concentrations. *Archives of General Psychiatry, 60,* 720–6.

Lamb, M.E. & Sternberg, K.J. (1990). Do we really know day care affects children? *Journal of Applied Developmental Psychology, 11,* 351–79.

Langkamp, D.L., Kim, Y. & Pascoe, J.M. (1998). Temperament of preterm infants at 4 months of age: Maternal rating and perceptions. *Journal of Developmental & Behavioral Pediatrics, 19,* 391–6.

LaPlante, D.P. (1997). Effects of stimulus movement and post-habituation delay on newborn infants' ability to retain visual information. *Dissertation Abstracts International: Section B: The Sciences and Engineering, 57,* 4747.

LaPlante, D.P., Orr, R.R., Neville, K., Vorkapich, L., et al. (1996). Discrimination of stimulus rotation by newborns. *Infant Behavior and Development, 19,* 271–9.

Lattimore, K.A., Donn, S.M., Kaciroti, N., Kemper, A.R., Neal, C.R. & Vazquez, D.M. (2005). Selective serotonin reuptake inhibitor (SSRI) use during pregnancy and effects on the fetus and newborn: A meta-analysis. *Journal of Perinatology, 25,* 595–604.

Laudenslager, M.L. (2005). Of mice and men, corticosteroids, and vicarious participation. *Brain Behavior and Immunity, 18,* 414–15.

Leach, P. (1997). Infant care from infants' viewpoint: The views of some professionals. *Early Development and Parenting, 6,* 47–58.

Lebib, R., Baudonniere, P., Papo, D. & de Bode, S. (2003). Evidence of a visual-to-auditory cross-modal sensory gating phenomenon as reflected by the human P50 event-related brain potential modulation. *Neuroscience Letters, 341*, 185–8.

Lecanuet, J.P., Granier-Deferre, C. & Busnel, M.C. (1989). Differential fetal auditory reactiveness as a function of stimulus characteristics and state. *Seminars in Perinatology, 13,* 421–9.

Lecanuet, J.P., Granier-Deferre, C., Jacquet, A.Y. & Busnel, M.C. (1992). Decelerative cardiac responsiveness to acoustical stimulation in the near term fetus. *Quarterly Journal of Experimental Psychology, 44b,* 279–303.

Lecanuet, J.P., Granier-Deferre, C., Jacquet, A.Y. & DeCasper, A.J. (2000). Fetal discrimination of low-pitched musical notes. *Developmental Psychobiology, 36,* 29–39.

Ledebt, A. (2000). Changes in arm posture during the early acquisition of walking. *Infant Behavior and Development, 23,* 79–89.

Lee, S.I., Khang, Y.H., Yun, S. & Jo, M.W. (2000). Rising rates, changing relationships: Caesarean section and its correlates in South Korea, 1988–2000. *BJOG, 112,* 810–19.

Legendre, A. (2003). Environmental features influencing toddler's bio-emotional reactions in day care centers. *Environment and Behavior, 35,* 523–49.

LeGrand, R., Mondloch, C.J., Maurer, D. & Brent, H.P. (2003). Expert face processing requires visual input to the right hemisphere during infancy. *Natural Neuroscience, 6,* 1329.

Lehtonen, L. & Martin, R.J. (2004). Ontogeny of sleep and awake states in relation to breathing in preterm infants. *Seminars in Neonatology, 9,* 229–38.

Lewis, M. & Brooks, J. (1978). Self-knowledge in emotional development. In M. Lewis & L. Rosenblum (Eds.), *The Development of affect* (pp. 205–26). New York: Plenum.

Lewis, M., Feiring, C. & Rosenthal, S. (2000). Attachment over time. *Child Development, 71,* 707–20.

Lewis, M. & Ramsay, D. (2004). Development of self-recognition, personal pronoun use, and pretend play during the 2nd year. *Child Development, 75,* 1821–31.

Lewis, M. & Ramsay, D. (2005). Infant emotional and cortisol responses to goal blockage. *Child Development, 76,* 518–30.

Lewkowicz, D.J. (2000). Infants' perception of the audible, visible and bimodal attributes of multimodal syllables. *Child Development, 71,* 1241–57.

Lewkowski, M.D., Barr, R.G., Sherrard, A., Lessard, J., Harris, A.R. & Young, S.N. (2003). Effects of chewing gum on responses to routine painful procedures in children. *Physiology and Behavior, 79,* 257–65.

Lhote, M. & Streri, A. (1998). Haptic memory and handedness in 2-month-old infants. *Laterality, 3,* 173–92.

Light, K.C., Grewen, K.M., Amico, J.A., Boccia, M., Brownley, K.A. & Johns, J.M. (2004). Deficits in plasma oxytocin responses and increased negative affect, stress, and blood pressure in mothers with cocaine exposure during pregnancy. *Addictive Behavior, 29,* 1541–64.

Lipsitt, L.P. (2003). Crib Death: A biobehavioral Phenomenon?

Current Directions in Psychological Science, 12, 164–70.

Lipsitt, L.P. & Kaye, H. (1964). Conditioned sucking in the human newborn. *Psychonomic Science, 1*, 29–30.

Liszkowski, U., Carpenter, M., Henning, A., Striano, T. & Tomasello, M. (2004). Twelve-month-olds point to share attention and interest. *Developmental Science, 7*, 297–307.

Little, R.E. & Wendt, J.K. (1991). The effects of maternal drinking in the reproductive period: An epidemiologic review. *Journal of Substance Abuse, 3*, 187–204.

Liu, S., Heaman, M., Joseph, K., Liston, R., Huang, L., Suave, R. & Kramer, M. (2005). Risk of maternal postpartum readmission associated with mode of delivery. *Obstetrics and Gynecology, 105*, 836–42.

Lobel, M., DeVincent, C.J., Kaminer, A. & Meyer, B.A. (2000). The impact of prenatal maternal stress and optimistic disposition on birth outcomes in medically high-risk women. *Health Psychology, 19*, 544–53.

Love, J.M., Harrison, L., Sagi-Schwartz, A., van Ijzendoorn, M.H., Ross, C., Ungerer, J.A., Raikes, H., Brady-Smith, C., Boller, K., Brooks-Gunn, J., Constantine, J., Kisker, E.E., Paulsell, D. & Chazan-Cohen, R. (2003). Child care quality matters: How conclusions may vary within context. *Child Development, 74*, 1021–33.

Ludington-Hoe, S.M., Anderson, G.C., Swinth, J.Y., Thompson, C. & Hadeed, A.J. (2004). Randomized controlled trial of kangaroo care:

Cardiorespiratory and thermal effects on healthy preterm infants. *Neonatal Network, 23*, 39–48.

Ludman, E., McBride, C., Nelson, J., Curry, S., Grothaus, L., Lando, H. & Pirie, P. (2000). Stress, depressive symptoms, and smoking cessation among pregnant women. *Health Psychology, 19*, 21–7.

Lukowski, A.F., Wiebe, S.A., Haight, J.C., DeBoer, T., Nelson, C.A. & Bauer, P.J. (2005). Forming a stable memory representation in the first year of life: Why imitation is more than child's play. *Developmental Science, 8*, 279–98.

Lundy, B.L. (2000). Face recognition performance in one-year-olds: A function of stimulus characteristics? *Infant Behavior and Development, 23*, 125–35.

Lutchmaya, S. & Baron-Cohen, S. (2002). Human sex differences in social and non-social looking preferences, at 12 months of age. *Infant Behavior & Development, 25*, 319–25.

Maestro, S., Muratori, F., Cesari, A., Cavallaro, M.C., Paziente, A., Pecini Grassi, C., Manfredi, A. & Sommario, C. (2005). Course of autism signs in the first year of life. *Psychopathology, 38*, 26–31.

Maikranz, J.M., Colombo, J., Richman, W. & Frick, J.E. (2002). Autonomic correlates of individual differences in sensitization and look duration during infancy. *Infant Behavior and Development, 23*, 137–51.

Main, M. & Hesse, E. (1990). Parents' unresolved traumatic experiences are related to infant disorganized attachment status. In M. Greenberg, D. Cicchetti & E. Cummings (Eds.),

Attachment in the preschool years: Theory, research and intervention (pp. 161–220). Chicago: University of Chicago Press.

Malloy, M.H. & MacDorman, M. (2005). Changes in the classification of sudden unexpected infant deaths: United States, 1992–2001. *Pediatrics, 115*, 1247–53.

Malphurs, J., Field, T., Larraine, C.M., Pickens, J., Pelaez-Nogueras, M., Yando, R. & Bendell, D. (1996). Altering withdrawn and intrusive interaction behaviors of depressed mothers. *Infant Mental Health Journal, 17*, 152–60.

Mäntymaa, M., Puura, K., Luoma, I., Salmelin, R.K. & Tamminen, T. (2004). Early mother–infant interaction, parental mental health and symptoms of behavioral and emotional problems in toddlers. *Infant Behavior and Development, 27*, 34–49.

Maratos, O. (1998). Neonatal, early and later imitation: Same order phenomena? In F. Simion (Ed.), *The development of sensory, motor and cognitive capacities in early infancy: From perception to cognition*. Hove, UK: Psychology Press/Erlbaum (UK) Taylor & Francis.

Marlier, L. & Schaal, B. (2005). Human newborns prefer human milk: Conspecific milk odor is attractive without postnatal exposure. *Child Development, 76*, 155–68.

Marmorstein, N.R., Malone, S.M. & Iacono, W.G. (2004). Psychiatric disorders among offspring of depressed mothers: Associations with paternal psychopathology. *American Journal of Psychiatry, 161*, 1588–94.

Marshall, P.J., Bar-Haim, Y. & Fox, N.A. (2002). Development of the EEG from 5 months to 4 years of age. *Clinical Neurophysiology, 113*, 1199–208.

Marshall, P.J., Fox, N.A. & Bucharest Early Intervention Project Core Group. (2004). A comparison of the electroencephalogram between institutionalized and community children in Romania. *Cognitive Neurosciences, 16*, 1327–38.

Martin, G.B. & Clark, R.D. (1982). Distress crying in neonates: Species and peer specificity. *Developmental Psychology, 18*, 3–9.

Martin, J.A., Hamilton, B.E., Sutton, P.D., Ventura, S.J., Menacker, F. & Munson, M.L. (2005). Births: Final data for 2003. *National Vital Statistics Report, 54*, 1–116.

Martin, R.P., Noyes, J., Wisenbaker, J. & Huttunen, M.O. (1999). Prediction of early childhood negative emotionality and inhibition from maternal distress during pregnancy. *Merrill Palmer Quarterly, 45*, 370–91.

Mastropieri, D.P. (1996). The influence of prenatal experience on differential responsiveness to vocal expressions of emotion in newborns. *Dissertation Abstracts International: Section B: The Sciences and Engineering, 7*, 3433.

Matsuyama, K. (2005). Correlation between musical responsiveness and developmental age among early age children as assessed by the Non-Verbal Measurement of the Musical Responsiveness of Children. *Medical Science Monitor, 11*, 485–92.

Matthey, S., Barnett, B., Kavanagh, D.J. & Howie, P. (2001). Validation of the Edinburgh postnatal depression scale for men, and comparison of items endorsement with their partners. *Journal of Affective Disorders, 64(2–3)*, 175–84.

Maxted, A.E., Dickstein, S., Miller-Loncar, C., High, P., Spritz, B., Liu, J. & Lester, B.M. (2005). Infant colic and maternal depression. *Infant Mental Health Journal, 26*, 56–68.

Mayes, L. (2002). A behavioral teratogenic model of the impact of prenatal cocaine exposure on arousal regulatory systems. *Neurotoxicology and Teratology, 24*, 385–95.

Mayes, L. (2003). Genetics of childhood disorders: LV. Prenatal drug exposure. *Journal of American Academy of Child and Adolescent Psychiatry, 42*, 1258–61.

Mayor, S. (2005). 23% of babies in England are delivered by caesarean section. *British Medical Journal, 330*, 806.

McAdams, S. & Bertoncini, J. (1997). Organization and discrimination of repeating sound sequences by newborn infants. *Journal of the Acoustical Society of America, 102*, 2945–53.

McCarty, M.E., Clifton, R.K. & Collard, R.R. (2001). The beginnings of tool use by infants and toddlers. *Infancy, 2*, 233–56.

McDade, T.W. (2001). Parent–offspring conflict and the cultural ecology of breast-feeding. *Human Nature, 12*, 9–25.

McGlaughlin, A. & Grayson, A. (2001). Crying in the first year of infancy: Patterns and prevalence. *Journal of Reproductive and Infant Psychology, 19*, 47–59.

Mears, K., McAuliffe, F., Grimes, H. & Morrison, J.J. (2004). Fetal cortisol in relation to labour, intrapartum events and mode of delivery. *Journal of Obstetric and Gynaecology, 24*, 129–32.

Mehl, M. & Lewis, F. (2004). Hypnosis to facilitate uncomplicated birth. *American Journal of Clinical Hypnosis, 46*, 299–312.

Meltzoff, A.N. (1995). What infant memory tells us about infantile amnesia: Long-term recall and deferred imitation. *Journal of Experimental Child Psychology, 59*, 497–515.

Meltzoff, A.N. (2004). The case for a developmental cognitive science: Theories of people and things. In G. Bremner & A. Slater (Eds.), *Theories of infant development* (pp. 145–73). Oxford: Blackwell.

Meltzoff, A.N. & Decety, J. (2003). What imitation tells us about social cognition: A rapprochement between developmental psychology and cognitive neuroscience. *Philosophical Transactions of the Royal Society B: Biological Science, 358*, 491–500.

Meltzoff, A.N. & Moore, M. (1977). Imitation of facial and manual gestures by human neonates. *Science, 198*, 74–8.

Meltzoff, A.N. & Moore, M.K. (1984). Newborn infants imitate adult gestures. *Child Development, 54*, 702–9.

Mennella, J. (2001). Regulation of milk intake after exposure to alcohol in mother's milk. *Alcoholism: Clinical and Experimental Research, 25*, 590–3.

Mennella, J.A., Johnson, A. & Beauchamp, G.K. (1995). Garlic ingestion by pregnant women alters the odor of amniotic fluid. *Chemical Senses, 20*, 207–9.

Messinger, D.S., Fogel, A. & Dickson, K.L. (2001). All smiles are positive, but some smiles are more positive than others. *Developmental Psychology*, 37, 642–53.

Metcalfe, J.S. & Clark, J.E. (2000). Sensory information affords exploration of posture in newly walking infants and toddlers. *Infant Behavior and Development*, 23, 391–405.

Mezulis, A.H., Hyde, J.S. & Clark, R. (2004). Father involvement moderates the effect of maternal depression during a child's infancy on child behavior problems in kindergarten. *Journal of Family Psychology*, 18, 575–88.

Mikel-Kostyra, K., Mazur, J. & Boltruszko, I. (2002). Effect of early skin-to-skin contact after delivery on duration of breastfeeding: a prospective cohort study. *Acta Paediatrica*, 91, 1288–9.

Milgrom, J., Westley, D.T. & Gemmil, A.W. (2004). The mediating role of maternal responsiveness in some longer term effects of postnatal depression on infant development. *Infant Behavior and Development*, 27, 441–54.

Milligan, K., Atkinson, L., Trehub, S.E., Benoit, D. & Poulton, L. (2003). Maternal attachment and the communication of emotion through song. *Infant Behavior and Development*, 26, 1–13.

Minnes, S., Singer, L., Arendt, R. & Satayanthum, S. (2005). Effects of prenatal cocaine/polydrug use on maternal–infant feeding interactions during the first year of life. *Journal of Developmental Behavior and Pediatrics*, 26, 194–200.

Miranda, J., Siddique, J., Belin, T.R. & Kohn-Wood, L.P. (2005). Depression prevalence in disadvantaged young black women: African and Caribbean immigrants compared to US-born African Americans. *Social Psychiatry and Psychiatry of Epidemiology*, 40, 253–8.

Mirmiran, M., Maas, Y.G. & Ariagno, R.L. (2003). Development of fetal and neonatal sleep and circadian rhythms. *Sleep Medicine Reviews*, 7, 321–34.

Misri, S., Oberlander, T., Fairbrother, N., Carter, D., Ryan, D., Kuan, A. & Reebye, P. (2004). Relation between prenatal maternal mood and anxiety and neonatal health. *Canadian Journal of Psychiatry*, 49, 684–9.

Mitchell, R.W. (2001). Americans' talk to dogs: Similarities and differences with talk to infants. *Research on Language and Social Interaction*, 34, 183–210.

Mizuno, K., Mizuno, N., Shinohara, T. & Noda, M. (2004). Mother–infant skin-to-skin contact after delivery results in early recognition of own mother's milk odour. *Acta Paediatrica*, 93, 1640–5.

Mizuno, K. & Ueda, A. (2005). Neonatal feeding performance as a predictor of neurodevelopmental outcome at 18 months. *Developmental Medicine of Children Neurology*, 47, 299–304.

Molfese, D.L. & Molfese, V.J. (1997). Discrimination of language skills at five years of age using event-related potentials recorded at birth. *Developmental Neuropsychology*, 13, 135–56.

Molina, M. & Jouen, F. (2004). Manual cyclical activity as an exploratory tool in neonates. *Infant Behavior and Development*, 27, 42–53.

Mondschein, E.R., Adolph, K.E. & Tamis-LeMonda, C.S. (2000). Gender bias in mothers' expectations about infant crawling. *Journal of Experimental Child Psychology*, 77, 304–16.

Monk, C., Fifer, W.P., Myers, M.M., Sloan, R.P., Trien, L. & Hurtado, A. (2000). Maternal stress responses and anxiety during pregnancy: effects on fetal heart rate. *Developmental Psychobiology*, 36, 67–77.

Montague, D.R. & Walter-Andrews, A.S. (2002). Mothers, fathers, and infants: The role of familiarity and parental involvement in infants' perception of emotion expressions. *Child Development*, 73, 1339–52.

Moon, C., Cooper, R.P. & Fifer, W.P. (1993). Two-day-olds prefer their native language. *Infant Behavior and Development*, 16, 495–500.

Moon, C. & Fifer, W.P. (1990). Syllables as signals for 2-day-old infants. *Infant Behavior and Development*, 13, 377–90.

Moore, C. & D'Entremont, B. (2001). Developmental changes in pointing as a function of attentional focus. *Journal of Cognition and Development*, 2, 109–29.

Moore, G.A. & Calkins, S.D. (2004). Infants' vagal regulation in the still-face paradigm is related to dyadic coordination of mother–infant interaction. *Development in Psychology*, 40, 1068–80.

Moore, R., Vadeyar, S., Fulford, J., Tyler, D., Gribben, C., Baker, P., James, D. & Gowland, P. (2001). Antenatal determination of fetal brain activity in response to an acoustic stimulus using functional magnetic resonance imaging. *Human Brain Mapping*, 12, 94–9.

Moore, V. & Davies, M. (2005). Diet during pregnancy neonatal outcomes and later health. *Reproduction, Fertility and Development*, 17, 341–8.

Morgan, B., Finan, A., Yarnold, R., Petersen, S., Horsfield, M., Rickett, A. & Wailoo, M. (2002). Assessment of infant physiology and neuronal development using magnetic resonance imaging. *Child: Care, Health and Development*, 28, 7–10.

Morrell, J. & Steele, H. (2003). The role of attachment security, temperament, maternal perception, and care-giving behavior in persistent infant sleeping problems. *Infant Mental Health Journal*, 24, 447–68.

Morrongiello, B.A., Fenwick, K.D. & Chance, G. (1998). Crossmodal learning in newborn infants: Inferences about properties of auditory-visual events. *Infant Behavior and Development*, 21, 543–53.

Morrow, C., Bandstra, E., Anthony, J., Ofir, A., Xue, L. & Reyes, M. (2003). Influence of prenatal cocaine exposure on early language development: longitudinal findings from four months to three years of age. *Journal of Developmental Behavior and Pediatrics*, 24, 39–50.

Morse, C.A., Buist, A. & Durkin, S. (2000). First-time parenthood: Influences on pre- and postnatal adjustment in fathers and mothers. *Journal of Obstetrics and Gynecology*, 2, 109–20.

Moses-Kolko, E.L., Bogen, D., Perel, J., Bregar, A., Uhl, K., Levin, B. & Wisner, K.L. (2005). Neonatal signs after late in utero exposure to serotonin reuptake inhibitors: Literature review and implications for clinical applications. *JAMA, 293*, 2372–83.

Mundy, P., Fox, N. & Card, J. (2003). Joint attention, EEG coherence and early vocabulary development. *Developmental Science, 6*, 48–54.

Nadel, J., Revel, A. & Andy, P. (2005). Toward communication: first imitations in infants, children with autism and robots. *Interdisciplinary Journal of Interaction Studies, 1*, 45–75.

Nagy, E., Loveland, K.A., Kopp, M., Hajnalka, O., Pal, A. & Molnar, P. (2001). Different emergence of fear expressions in infant boys and girls. *Infant Behavior & Development, 24*, 189–94.

Nagy, E. & Molnar, P. (2004). Homo imitans or homo provocans? Human imprinting model of neonatal imitation. *Infant Behavior & Development, 27*, 54–63.

Nakata, T. & Trehub, S.E. (2004). Infants' responsiveness to maternal speech and singing. *Infant Behavior & Development, 27*, 455–64.

Needham, A., Barrett, T. & Peterman, K. (2002). A pick-me-up for infants' exploratory skills: Early stimulated experiences reaching for objects using "sticky mittens" enhances young infants' object exploration skills. *Infant Behavior and Development, 25*, 279–95.

Nelson, M., Clifton, R., Dowd, J. & Field, T. (1978). Cardiac responding to auditory stimuli in newborn infants: Why pacifiers should not be used when heart rate is the major dependent variable. *Infant Behavior and Development, 1*, 277–90.

Nesheim, B., Kinge, R., Berg, B., Alfredsson, B., Allgot, E., Hove, G., Johnsen, W., Jorsett, I., Skei, S. & Solberg, S. (2003). Acupuncture during labor can reduce the use of meperidine: A controlled clinical study. *Clinical Journal of Pain, 19*, 187–91.

Newnham, J., Doherty, D., Kendall, G., Zubrick, S., Laudau, L. & Stanley, F. (2004). Effects of repeated prenatal ultrasound examinations on childhood outcome up to 8 years of age: Follow-up of a randomized controlled trial. *Lancet, 364*, 2038–44.

NICHD Early Child Care Research Network (2003). Early child care and mother–child interaction from 36 months through first grade. *Infant Behavior & Development, 26*, 345–70.

NICHD Early Child Care Research Network (2004). Type of child care and children's development at 54 months. *Early Childhood Research Quarterly, 19*, 203–30.

NICHD Early Child Care Research Network (2006). Child-care effect size for the NICHD Study of early Child Care and Youth Development. *American Psychologist, 61*, 99–116.

Niederhofer, H. & Reiter, A. (2004). Prenatal maternal stress, prenatal fetal movements and perinatal temperament factors influence behavior and school marks at the age of 6 years. *Fetal Diagnosis and Therapy, 19(2)*, 160–2.

Nielsen, M. & Dissanayake, C. (2003). Pretend play, mirror self-recognition and imitation: A longitudinal investigation through the second year. *Infant Behavior & Development*, 27, 342–65.

Nielsen, M., Dissanayake, C. & Kashima, Y. (2002). A longitudinal study of self–other discrimination and the emergence of mirror self-recognition. *Infant Behavior & Development*, 26, 213–26.

Niwano, K. & Sugai, K. (2003). Pitch characteristics of speech during mother–infant and father–infant vocal interactions. *Japanese Journal of Special Education*, 40, 663–74.

Noland, J., Singer, L., Short, E., Minnes, S., Arendt, R., Kirchner, H. & Bearer, C. (2005). Prenatal drug exposure and selective attention in preschoolers. *Neurotoxology and Teratology*, 17, 429–38.

Novosad, C., Freudigman, K. & Thoman, E.B. (1999). Sleep patterns in newborns and temperament at eight months: A preliminary study. *Journal of Developmental and Behavioral Pediatrics*, 20, 99–105.

Novosad, C. & Thoman, E.B. (2003). The breathing bear: An intervention for crying babies and their mothers. *Journal of Developmental Behavior and Pediatrics*, 24, 89–95.

Oddy, W.H., Scott, J.A., Graham, K.I. & Binns, C.W. (2006). Breastfeeding influences on growth and health at one year of age. *Breastfeeding Review*, 14, 15–23.

Ohgi, S., Fukuda, M., Moriuchi, H., Kusumoto, T., Akiyama, T., Nugent, J.K., Brazelton, T.B., Arisawa, K., Takahashi, T. & Saitoh, H. (2002). Comparison of kangaroo care and standard care: Behavioral organiza-tion, development, and temperament in healthy, low-birth-weight infants through 1 year. *Journal of Perinatology*, 22, 374–9.

Olko, C. & Turkewitz, G. (2001). Cerebral asymmetry of emotion and its relationship to olfaction in infancy. *Laterality: Asymmetries of Body, Brain and Cognition*, 6, 29–37.

Oller, D.K. & Eilers, R.E. (1982). The role of audition in infant babbling. *Child Development*, 59, 441–9.

Oller, D.K., Eilers, R.E., Neal, A.R. & Cobo-Lewis, A.B. (1998). Late onset canonical babbling: A possible early marker for abnormal development. *America Journal on Mental Retardation*, 103, 249–63.

Orekhova, E.V., Stroganova, T.A., Posikera, I.N. & Malykh, S.B. (2003). Heritability and "environmentability" of electroencephalogram in infants: The twin study. *Psychobiology*, 40, 727–41.

Owen, C.G., Martin, R.M., Whincup, P.H., Smith, G.D. & Cook, D.G. (2005). Effect of infant feeding on the risk of obesity across the life course: a quantitative review of published evidence. *Pediatrics*, 115, 1367–77.

Papaeliou, C.F. & Trevarthen, C. (2006). Prelinguistic pitch patterns expressing "communication" and "apprehension." *Journal of Child Language*, 33, 163–78.

Papousek, M. & von Hofacker, N. (1998). Persistent crying in early infancy: A non-trivial condition of risk for the developing mother–infant relationship. *Child Care, Health & Development*, 24, 395–424.

Parker, S.J. & Barret, D.E. (1992). Maternal Type A behavior during pregnancy, neonatal crying, and early infant temperament: Do Type A women have type A babies? *Pediatrics*, *89*, 474–9.

Pascalis, O., de Schonen, S., Morton, J., Deruelle, C. & Fabre-Grenet, M. (1995). Mother's face recognition by neonates: A replication and an extension. *Infant Behavior and Development*, *18*, 79–85.

Pascalis, O., Scott, L.S., Kelly, D.J., Shannon, R.W., Nicholson, E., Coleman, M. & Nelson, C.A. (2005). Plasticity of face processing in infancy. *Proceedings of the National Academy of Science of the United States of America*, *102*, 5297–300.

Patterson, M.L. & Werker, J.E. (2002). Infants' ability to match dynamic phonetic and gender information in the face and voice. *Journal of Experimental Child Psychology*, *81*, 93–115.

Pedersen, F., Huffman, L., del Carmen, R. & Bryan, Y. (1996). Prenatal maternal reactivity to infant cries predicts postnatal perceptions of infant temperament and marriage appraisal. *Child Development*, *67*, 2541–52.

Preti, A., Cardascia, L., Zen, T., Pellizzari, P., Marchetti, M., Favaretto, G. & Miotto, P. (2000). Obstetric complications in patients with depression – a population-based case-control study. *Journal of Affective Disorders*, *61*, 101–6.

Petrogiannis, K. (2002). Greek day care centres' quality, caregivers' behavior and children's development. *International Journal of Early Years Education*, *10*, 137–48.

Pierroutsakos, S.L. & Troseth, G.L. (2003). Video Verité: Infants' manual investigation of objects on video. *Infant Behavior & Development*, *26*, 183–99.

Pinette, M., Wax, J. & Wilson, E. (2004). The risks of underwater birth. *American Journal of Obstetrics & Gynecology*, *190*, 1211–15.

Poehlmann, J. & Fiese, B.H. (2001). Parent–infant interaction as a mediator of the relation between neonatal risk status and 12-month cognitive development. *Infant Behavior and Development*, *24*, 171–88.

Polizzi, J., Byers, J.F. & Kiehl, E. (2003). Co-bedding versus traditional bedding of multiple-gestation infants in the NICU. *Journal of Healthcare Quality*, *25*, 5–10.

Pomerleau, A., Malcuit, G. & Sequin, R. (1992). Five-month-old girls' and boys' exploratory behaviors in the presence of familiar and unfamiliar toys. *Journal of Genetic Psychology*, *153*, 47–61.

Pool, M.M., Bijleveld, C.C.J.H. & Tavecchio, L.W.C. (2000). The effect of same-age and mixed-age grouping in day care on parent–child attachment security. *Social Behavior and Personality*, *28*, 595–602.

Porges, S.W. (1996). Orienting in a defensive world: Mammalian modifications of our evolutionary heritage. A polyvagal theory. *Psychophysiology*, *32*, 301–18.

Porter, C.L. (2003). Coregulation in mother–infant dyads: Links to infants' cardiac vagal tone. *Psychological Reports*, *92*, 307–19.

Porter, C.L., Wouden-Miller, M., Silva, S.S. & Porter, A.E. (2003). Marital harmony and conflict: Links to infants' emotional regulation and cardiac vagal tone. *Infancy*, *4*, 297–307.

Poulson, C.L., Kyparissos, N., Andreatos, M., Kymissis, E. & Parnes, M. (2002). Generalized imitation within three response classes in typically developing infants. *Journal of Experimental Child Psychology*, *81*, 341–57.

Puchalski, M. & Hummel, P. (2002). The reality of neonatal pain. *Advances in Neonatal Care*, *2*, 233–44.

Pullarkat, R. & Azar, B. (1992). Retinoic acid, embryonic development and alcohol-induced birth defects, *Alcohol Research & Health*, *6*, 317–23.

Purphonen, M., Kilpelainen-Lees, R., Valkonen-Korhonen, M., Karhu, J. & Lehtonen, J. (2004). Cerebral processing of mother's voice compared to unfamiliar voice in 4-month-old infants. *International Journal of Psychophysiology*, *52*, 257–66.

Quinn, P.C., Eimas, P.D. & Tarr, M.J. (2001). Perceptual categorization of cat and dog silhouettes by 3- to 4-month-old infants. *Journal of Experimental Child Psychology*, *79*, 78–94.

Quinn, P.C., Slater, A.M., Brown, E. & Hayes, R.A. (2001). Developmental changes in form categorization in early infancy. *British Journal of Developmental Psychology*, *19*, 207–18.

Quinn, P.C., Yahr, J., Kuhn, A., Slater, A.M. & Pascalis, O. (2002). Representation of the gender of human faces by infants: A preference for female. *Perception*, *31*, 1109–21.

Radzyminski, S. (2005). Neurobehavioral functioning and breastfeeding behavior in the newborn. *Journal of Obstetrics and Gynecology of Neonatal Nursing*, *34*, 335–41.

Ragan, P.E. (1996). Neonatal response to the dichotic presentation of distress cry in another infant. *Dissertation Abstracts International: Section B: The Sciences and Engineering*, *56*, 4608.

Räihä, H., Lehtonen, L., Huhtala, V., Saleva, K. & Korvenranta, H. (2002). Excessively crying infant in the family: Mother–infant, father–infant and mother–father interaction. *Child: Care, Health and Development*, *28*, 419–29.

Raikes, H. (1993). Relationship duration in infant care: Time with highability teacher and infant–teacher attachment. *Early Childhood Research Quarterly*, *8*, 309–25.

Räikkönen, K., Pesonen, A.K., Järvenpää, A.L. & Strandberg, T.E. (2004). Sweet babies: Chocolate consumption during pregnancy and infant temperament at six months. *Early Human Development*, *76*, 139–45.

Rambaud, C. & Guilleminault, C. (2004). "Back to sleep" and unexplained death in infants. *Sleep: Journal of Sleep and Sleep Disorders Research*, *27*, 1359–66.

Ramchandani, P., Stein, A., Evans, J., O'Connor, T.G. & ALSPAC Study Team. (2005). Paternal depression in the postnatal period and child development: A prospective population study. *Lancet*, *365*, 2201–5.

Ramsay, D., Langlois, J.H., Hoss, R.A., Rubenstein, A.J. & Griffin, A.M. (2004). Origins of a stereotype: Categorization of facial attractiveness by 6-month-old infants. *Developmental Science*, *7*, 201–11.

Ramsay, D. & Lewis, M. (2003). Reactivity and regulation in cortisol and behavioral responses to stress. *Child Development, 74*, 456–64.

Ransjö-Arvidson, A., Matthiesen, A., Lilja, G., Nissen, E., Widström, A. & Uvnäs-Moberg, K. (2001). Maternal analgesia during labor disturbs newborn behavior: Effects on breastfeeding, temperature, and crying. *Birth: Issues in Perinatal Care, 28*, 5–12.

Rasmussen, L.B. (2001). Relationship between acute procedural pain and the immune status in newborn infants. *Dissertation Abstracts International: Section B: The Sciences and Engineering, 61*, 4652.

Rattaz, C., Goubet, N. & Bullinger, A. (2005). The calming effect of a familiar odor on full-term newborns. *Journal of Development Pediatrics, 26*, 86–92.

Reardon, P. & Bushnell, E. (1988). Infants' sensitivity to arbitrary pairings of color and taste. *Infant behavior & Development, 11*, 245–50.

Receveur, C., Lenoir, P., Desombre, H., Roux, S., Barthelemy, C. & Malvy, J. (2005). Interaction and imitation deficits from infancy to 4 years of age in children with autism: A pilot study based on videotapes. *Autism, 9*, 69–82.

Reijneveld, S.A., Lanting, C.I., Crone, M.R. & Van Wouwe, J.P. (2005). Exposure to tobacco smoke and infant crying. *Acta Paediatrica, 94*, 217–21.

Reissland, N., Shepherd, J. & Herrera, E. (2003). The pitch of maternal voice: A comparison of mothers suffering from depressed mood and non-depressed mothers reading books to their infants. *Journal of Childhood Psychology and Psychiatry, 44*, 255–61.

Richards, J. & Cronise, K. (2000). Extended visual fixation in the early preschool years: Look duration, heart rate changes, and attentional inertia. *Child Development, 71*, 602–20.

Richards, M., Hardy, R. & Wadsworth, M.E. (2002). Long-term effects of breast-feeding in a national birth cohort: educational attainment and midlife cognitive function. *Public Health Nursing, 5*, 631–5.

Rieser, J., Yonas, A. & Wikner, K. (1976). Radial localization of odors by human newborns. *Child Development, 47*, 856–9.

Riley, E.P. & McGee, C.L. (2005). Fetal alcohol spectrum disorders: An overview with emphasis on changes in brain and behavior. *Experimental Biology and Medicine, 230*, 357–65.

Rivera-Gaxiola, M., Silva-Pereyra, J. & Kuhl, P.K. (2005). Brain potentials to native and non-native speech contrasts in 7- and 11-month-old American infants. *Developmental Science, 8*, 162–72.

Roberts, I. (1996). Out-of-home day care and health. *Archives of Disease in Childhood, 74*, 73–6.

Robinson, A.J. & Pascalis, O. (2004). Development of flexible visual recognition memory in human infants. *Developmental Science, 7*, 527–33.

Rodrigues, M.C., Mello, R.R. & Fonseca, S.C. (2006). Learning difficulties in schoolchildren born with very low birth weight. *Jornal de Pediatria*, *82*, 6–14.

Roggman, L.A., Langlois, J.H., Hubbs-Tait, T.L. & Rieser-Danner, L.A. (1994). Infant day-care, attachment, and the "file drawer problem." *Child Development*, *65*, 1429–43.

Rose, S.A., Feldman, J.F. & Jankowski, J.J. (2003). Infant visual recognition memory: Independent contributions of speed and attention. *Developmental Psychology*, *39*, 563–71.

Rosenstein, D. & Oster, H. (1997). Differential facial responses to four basic tastes in newborns. In P. Ekman, E.L. Rosenberg, et al. (Eds.), *What the face reveals: Basic and applied studies of spontaneous expression using the Facial Action Coding System (FACS)*. Series in affective science. New York: Oxford University Press, pp. 302–27.

Rovee-Collier, C., Adler, S.A. & Borza, M.A. (1994). Substituting new details for old? Effects of delaying postevent information on infant memory. *Memory & Cognition*, *22*, 644–56.

Rovee-Collier, C., Hartshorn, K. & DiRubbo, M. (1999). Long-term maintenance of infant memory. *Developmental Psychobiology*, *35*, 91–102.

Rubin, G.B., Fagen, J.W. & Caroll, M.H. (1998). Olfactory context and memory retrieval in 3-month-old infants. *Infant Behavior and Development*, *21*, 641–58.

Rubin, K.H., Burgess, K.B. & Hastings, P.D. (2002). Stability and social-behavioral consequences of toddlers' inhibited temperament and parenting behaviors. *Children Development*, *73*, 483–95.

Ruusuvirta, T., Huotilainen, M., Fellman, V. & Naatanen, R. (2003). The newborn human brain binds sound features together. *Neuroreport*, *14*, 2117–19.

Ruusuvirta, T., Huotilainen, M., Fellman, V. & Naatanen, R. (2004). Newborn human brain identifies repeated auditory feature conjunctions of low sequential probability. *European Journal of Neurosciences*, *20*, 2819–21.

Ryan, K., Schnatz, P., Greene, J. & Curry, S. (2005). Change in cesarean section rate as a reflection of the present malpractice crisis. *Connecticut Medicine*, *69*, 139–41.

Saffran, J.R., Loman, M.M. & Robertson, R.R.W. (2000). Infant memory for musical experiences. *Cognition*, *77*, 15–23.

Sagi, A. & Hoffman, M.L. (1976). Empathetic distress in the newborn. *Developmental Psychology*, *12*, 175–6.

Sagi, A., Koren-Karie, N., Gini, M., Ziv, Y. & Joels, T. (2002). Shedding further light on the effects of various types and quality of early child care on infant–mother attachment relationship: The Haifa Study of Early Child Care. *Child Development*, *73*, 1166–86.

Sahni, R., Schulze, K.F., Kashyap, S., Ohira-Kist, K., Fifer, W.P. & Myers, M.M. (2005). Sleeping position and electrocortical activity in low birth-weight infants. *Archives of Disease in Childhood Fetal and Neonatal Edition*, *90(4)*, F311–15.

Salisbury, A., Minard, K., Hunsley, M. & Thoman, E.B. (2001). Audio recording of infant crying: comparison with maternal cry logs. *International Journal of Behavioral Development*, 25, 458–65.

Salisbury, A.L. (2001). Sleep and cry behavior in excessively crying infants: A system perspective. *Dissertation Abstract International: Section B. The Sciences and Engineering*, 61, 4469.

Sameroff, A.J. (1967). Nonnutritive sucking in newborns under visual and auditory stimulation. *Child Development*, 38, 443–52.

Sanders, C., Diego, M., Fernandez, M., Field, T., Hernandez-Reif, M. & Roca, A. (2002). EEG asymmetry responses to lavender and rosemary aromas in adults and infants. *International Journal of Neuroscience*, 112, 1305–20.

Sangrigoli, S. & de Schonen, S. (2004). Recognition of own-race and other-race faces by three-month-old infants. *Journal of Child Psychology and Psychiatry*, 45, 1219–27.

Santos, D., Gabbard, C. & Gonçalves, V. (2001). Motor development during the first year: A comparative study. *Journal of Genetic Psychology*, 162, 143–53.

Saudino, K.J. & Eaton, W.O. (1991). Infant temperament and genetics: an objective twin study of motor activity level. *Child Development*, 62, 1167–74.

Scher, A. & Cohen, D. (2005). Locomotion and nightwaking. *Child: Care, Health and Development*, 31, 685–91.

Schieche, M. & Spangler, G. (2005). Individual differences in biobehavioral organization during problem-solving in toddlers: The influence of maternal behavior, infant–mother attachment, and behavioral inhibition on the attachment–exploration balance. *Developmental Psychobiology*, 46, 293–306.

Schuetze, P. & Zeskind, P.S. (2001a). Relation between women's depressive symptoms and perceptions of infant distress signals varying in pitch. *Infancy*, 2, 450.

Schuetze, P. & Zeskind, P.S. (2001b). Relation between maternal cigarette smoking during pregnancy and behavioral and physiological measures of autonomic regulation in neonates. *Infancy*, 2, 371–83.

Schuetze, P., Zeskind, P.S. & Eiden, R.D. (2003). The perceptions of infant distress signals varying in pitch by cocaine-using mothers. *Infancy*, 4, 65–83.

Schweinle, A. & Wilcox, T. (2004). Intermodal perception and physical reasoning in infancy. *Infant Behavior and Development*, 27, 246–65.

Seifer, R., Sameroff, A., Dickstein, S., Schiller, M. & Hayden, L. (2003). Your own children are special: Clues to the sources of reporting bias in temperament assessments. *Infant Behavior and Development*, 27, 323–41.

Seifritz, E., Esposito, F., Neuhoff, J.G., Lüthi, A., Mustovic, H., Dammann, G., von Bardeleben, U., Radue, E.W., Cirillo, S., Tedeschi, G. & Di Salle, F. (2003). Differential sex-independent amygdala response to infant crying and laughing in parents versus nonparents. *Biological Psychiatry*, 54, 1367–5.

Serbin, L.A., Poulin-Dubois, D., Colburne, K.A., Sen, M.G. & Eichstedt, J.A. (2001). Gender stereotyping in infancy: Visual preferences for and knowledge of gender-stereotyped toys in the second year. *International Journal of Behavioral Development*, *25*, 7–15.

Severi, F., Prattichizzo, D., Casarosa, E., Barbagli, F., Ferretti, C., Altomare, A., Vicino, A. & Petraglia, F. (2005). Virtual fetal touch through a haptic interface decreases maternal anxiety and salivary cortisol. *Journal of Society for Gynecological Investigations*, *12*, 37–40.

Sharps, P.W., El-Mohandes, A.A., Nabil El-Khorazaty, M., Kiely, M. & Walker, T. (2003). Health beliefs and parenting attitudes influence breast-feeding patterns among low-income African-American women. *Journal of Perinatology*, *23*, 414–19.

Sheiner, E., Levy, A., Katz, M. & Mazor, M. (2005). Short stature – An independent risk factor for Cesarean delivery. *European Journal of Obstetric Gynecology and Reproductive Biology*, *120*, 175–8.

Shi, R., Werker, J.F. & Morgan, J.L. (1999). Newborn infants' sensitivity to perceptual cues to lexical and grammatical words. *Cognition*, *72*, 11–21.

Shute, B. & Wheldall, K. (2001). How do grandmothers speak to their grandchildren? Fundamental frequency and temporal modifications in the speech of British grandmothers to their grandchildren. *Educational Psychology*, *21*, 493–503.

Silvén, I.A. (2002). Comparative characteristic of early vocalisations of Russian and Finnish infants. *Journal of the Sensory System*, 1.

Simos, P.G. & Molfese, D.L. (1997). Electrophysiological responses from a temporal order continuum in the newborn infant. *Neuropsychologia*, *35*, 89–98.

Singer, L.T., Arendt, R., Minnes, S., Salvator, A., Siegel, A.C. & Lewis, B.A. (2001). Developing language skills of cocaine-exposed infants. *Pediatrics*, *107*, 1057–64.

Singh, L., Morgan, J.L. & Best, C.T. (2002). Infants' listening preferences: Baby talk or happy talk. *Infancy*, *3*, 365–94.

Skari, H., Skreden, M., Malt, U., Dalholt, M., Ostensen, A., Egeland, T. & Emblem, R. (2002). Comparative levels of psychological distress, stress symptoms, depression and anxiety after childbirth: A prospective population-based study of mothers and fathers. *International Journal of Obstetrics and Gynaecology*, *109*, 1154–63.

Slaney, M. & McRoberts, G. (2003). Baby ears: A recognition system for affective vocalizations. *Speech Communication*, *39*, 367–84.

Slater, A., et al. (1999). Intermodal perception at birth: Intersensory redundancy guides newborn infants' learning of arbitrary auditory–visual pairings. *Developmental Science*, *2*, 333–8.

Slater, A., Bremner, G., Johnson, S.P., Sherwood, P., Hayes, R. & Brown, E. (2000). Newborn infants' preference for attractive faces: The role of internal and external facial features. *Infancy*, *1*, 265–74.

Slater, A., Brown, E. & Badenoch, M. (1997). Intermodal perception at birth: Newborn infants' memory for arbitrary auditory–visual pairings. *Early Development and Parenting*, *6*, 99–104.

Slater, A., Morison, V. & Rose, D. (1983). Perception of shape by the newborn baby. *British Journal of Developmental Psychology*, 1, 135–42.

Slater, A., Von der Schulenburg, C., Brown, E., Badenoch, M., Butterworth, G., Parsons, S. & Samuels, C. (1998). Newborn infants prefer attractive faces. *Infant Behavior and Development*, 21, 345–54.

Slaughter, V. & Boh, W. (2001). Decalage in infants' search for mothers versus toys demonstrated with a delayed response task. *Infancy*, 2, 405–13.

Smith, M.N., Durkin, M., Hinton, V.J., Bellinger, D. & Kuhn, L. (2003). Influence of breastfeeding on cognitive outcomes at age 6–8 years: Follow-up of very low birth weight infants. *American Journal of Epidemiology*, 158, 1075–82.

Soltis, J. (2004). The signal functions of early infant crying. *Behavioral and Brain Sciences*, 27, 443–90.

Sood, B., Delaney-Black, V., Covington, C., Nordstrom-Klee, B., Ager, J., Templin, T., Janisse, J., Martier, S. & Sokol, R.J. (2001). Prenatal alcohol exposure and childhood behavior at age 6 to 7 years: I. Dose-response effect. *Pediatrics*, 108, E34.

South, M.M., Strauss, R.A., South, A.P., Boggess, J.F. & Thorp, J.M. (2005). The use of non-nutritive sucking to decrease the physiologic pain response during neonatal circumcision: A randomized controlled trial. *American Journal of Obstetrics and Gynecology*, 193, 537–42.

Spangler, G. & Schieche, M. (1994). Biobehavioral organization in one-year-olds: Quality of mother–infant attachment and immunological and adrenocortical regulation. *Psychologische Beiträge*, 36, 30–5.

Spelke, E.S. (2005). Sex differences in intrinsic aptitude for mathematics and science? A critical review. *American Psychologist*, 60, 950–8.

Spence, M.J. & Freeman, M.S. (1996). Newborn infants prefer the maternal low-pass filtered voice, but not the maternal whispered voice. *Infant Behavior and Development*, 19, 199–212.

St James-Roberts, I. & Halil, T. (1991). Infant crying patterns in the first year: Normal community and clinical findings. *Journal of Child Psychology & Psychiatry*, 32(6), 951–68.

St James-Roberts, I., Goodwin, J., Peter, B., Adams, D. & Hunt, S. (2003). Individual differences in responsivity to a neurobehavioural examination predict crying patterns of 1-week-old infants at home. *Developmental Medicine & Child Neurology*, 45, 400–7.

Starc, T.J., Langston, C., Goldfarb, J., Colin, A.A., Cooper, E.R., Easley, K.A., Sunkle, S. & Schluchter, M.D. (1999). Unexpected non-HIV causes of death in children born to HIV-infected mothers. Pediatric pulmonary and cardiac complications of vertically transmitted HIV infection study group. *Pediatrics*, 104(6).

Steiner, J.E. (1979). Human facial expressions in response to taste and smell stimulation. In H.W. Reese and L.P. Lipsitt (Eds.), *Advances in child development and behavior*, vol. 13. New York: Academic Press.

Steiner, J.E., Glaser, D., Hawilo, M. & Berridge, K.C. (2001). Comparative expression of hedonic impact: Affective reactions to taste by human infants and other primates. *Neuroscience and Biobehavioral Reviews*, 25, 53–74.

Stepakoff, S.A. (2000). Mother–infant tactile communication at four months: Effects of infant gender, maternal ethnicity, and maternal depression. *Dissertation Abstracts International: Section B: The Sciences and Engineering*, 60, 5793.

Stettler, N., Stallings, V.A., Troxel, A.B., Zhao, J., Schinnar, R., Nelson, S.E., Ziegler, E.E. & Strom, B.L. (2005). Weight gain in the first week of life and overweight in adulthood: A cohort study of European American subjects fed infants formula. *Circulation*, 111, 1897–903.

Stifter, C. & Fox, N. (1990). Preschool children's ability to identify and label emotions. *Journal of Nonverbal Behavior*, 11, 43–54.

Stifter, C.A. & Spinrad, T.L. (2002). The effect of excessive crying on the development of emotion regulation. *Infancy*, 3, 133–52.

Stormark, K.M. & Braarud, H.C. (2003). Infant's sensitivity to social contingency: A "double video" study of face-to-face communication between 2- and 4-month-olds and their mothers. *Infant Behavior and Development*, 27, 195–203.

Strandberg, T.E., Järvenpää, A.L., Vanhanen, H. & McKeigue, P.M. (2001). Birth outcome in relation to licorice consumption during pregnancy. *American Journal of Epidemiology*, 153, 1085–8.

Streri, A. (2003). Cross-modal recognition of shape from hand to eyes in human newborns. *Somatosensory and Motor Research*, 20, 13–18.

Streri, A. & Gentaz, E. (2003). Cross-modal recognition of shape from hand to eyes and handedness in human newborns. *Neuropsychologia*, 42, 1365–9.

Striano, T. & Bertin, E. (2004). Contribution of facial and vocal cues in the still-face response of 4-month-old infants. *Infant Behavior and Development*, 27, 499–508.

Striano, T. & Liszkowski, U. (2004). Sensitivity to the context of facial expression in the still face at 3, 6, and 9 months of age. *Infant Behavior and Development*, 28, 10–19.

Striano, T. & Rochat, P. (2000). Emergence of selective social referencing in infancy. *Infancy*, 1, 253–64.

Sullivan, J.R. (1999). Development of father–infant attachment in fathers of preterm infants. *Neonatal Network*, 18, 33–9.

Sullivan, M.W. & Lewis, M. (2003). Contextual determinants of anger and other negative expressions in young infants. *Developmental Psychology*, 39, 693–705.

Swanson, K., Beckwith, L. & Howard, J. (2000). Intrusive caregiving and quality of attachment in prenatally drug-exposed toddlers and their primary caregivers. *Attachment Human Development*, 2, 130–48.

Swanson, M.W., Streissguth, A.P., Sampson, P.D. & Olson, H.C. (1999). Prenatal cocaine and neuromotor outcome at four months: Effect of duration of exposure. *Journal of Developmental & Behavioral Pediatrics*, 220, 325–34.

Taanila, A., Murray, G.K., Jokelainen, J., Isohanni, M. & Rantakallio, P. (2005). Infant developmental milestones: a 31-year follow-up. *Devel-*

opmental Medicine and Child Neurology, 47, 581–6.

Tafuri, J. & Villa, D. (2002). Musical elements in the vocalisations of infants aged 2 to 8 months. British Journal of Music Education, 19, 73–88.

Tamis-LeMonda, C.S., Bornstein, M.H. & Baumwell, L. (2001). Maternal responsiveness and children's achievement of language milestones. Child Development, 72, 748–67.

Tan, U., Ors, R., Kurkcuoglu, M., Kutlu, N., Cankaya, A. (1992). Lateralization of the grasp reflex in male and female human newborns. Internal Journal of Neuroscience, 62, 155–63.

Taylor, A., Atkins, R., Kumar, R., Adams, D. & Glover, V. (2005). A new mother-to-infant bonding scale: links with early maternal mood. Archives of Women Mental Health, 8, 45–51.

Thase, M.E. (2000). Treatment issues related to sleep and depression. Journal of Clinical Psychiatry, 61, 46–50.

Thelen, E. (1990). Coupling perception and action in the development of skill: A dynamic approach. In H. Bloch & B.I. Bertenthal (Eds.), Sensory-motor organizations and development in infancy and early childhood (pp. 39–56). Norwell, MA: Kluwer Academic.

Thelen, E., Jensen, J.L., Kamm, K., Corbetta, D., Schneider, K. & Zernicke, R.F. (1991). Infant motor development: Implications for motor neuroscience. In J. Requin & G.E. Stelmach (Eds.), Tutorials in motor neuroscience (pp. 43–57). Norwell, MA: Kluwer Academic.

Thelen, E. & Spencer, J. (1998). Postural control during reaching in young infants: A dynamic system approach. Neuroscience Biobehavior Reviews, 22, 507–14.

Therien, J.M., Worwa, C.T., Mattia, F.R. & de Regnier, R.A. (2004). Altered pathways for auditory discrimination and recognition memory in preterm infants. Developmental Medicine for Children and Neurology, 46, 816–24.

Thierry, G., Vihman, M. & Roberts, M. (2003). Familiar words capture the attention of 11-month-olds in less than 250ms. Neuroreport, 14, 2307–10.

Thomas, K.A. & Foreman, S.W. (2005). Infant sleep and feeding pattern: effects on maternal sleep. Journal of Midwifery Women Health, 50, 399–404.

Thomasson, M.A. & Teller, D. (2000). Infant color vision: Sharp chromatic edges are not required for chromatic discrimination in 4-month-olds. Vision Research, 40, 1051–7.

Thompson, L.A., Madrid, V., Westbrook, S. & Johnston, V. (2001). Infants attend to second-order relational properties of faces. Psychonomic Bulletin Review, 8, 769–77.

Thoni, A., Zech, N. & Moroder, L. (2005). Water birth and neonatal infections. Experience with 1575 deliveries in water. Minerva Ginecologica, 57, 199–206.

Tirosh, E., Harel, J., Abadi, J., Berger, A. & Cohen, A. (1992). Relationship between neonatal behavior and subsequent temperament. Acta Paediatrica, 81, 829–31.

Togari, H., Kato, I., Saito, N. & Yamaguchi, N. (2000). The healthy human infant tends to sleep in the prone rather than the supine position. *Early Human Development*, 59, 151–8.

Tomasello, M. (1995). Joint attention as social cognition. In C. Moore & P.Dunham (Eds.), *Joint attention: Its origins and role in development* (pp. 103–30). Hillsdale, NJ: Lawrence Erlbaum.

Tornek, A., Field, T., Hernandez-Reif, M., Diego, M. & Jones, N. (2003). Music effects on EEG in intrusive and withdrawn mothers with depressive symptoms. *Psychiatry*, 66, 234–43.

Trainor, L.J., Austin, C.M. & Desjardins, R.N. (2000). Is infant-directed speech prosody a result of the vocal expression of emotion? *Psychology Science*, 11, 188–95.

Trainor, L.J. & Desjardins, R.N. (2002). Pitch characteristics of infant-directed speech affect infants' ability to discriminate vowels. *Psychonomic Bulletin and Review*, 9, 335–40.

Trainor, L.J., Wu, L. & Tsang, C. (2004). Long-term memory for music: Infants remember tempo and timbre. *Developmental Science*, 7, 289–96.

Trehub, S.E. (2001). Musical predispositions in infancy. *Annals New York Academy of Science*, 930, 1–16.

Trinder, J., Newman, N.M., LeGrande, M., Whitworth, F., Kay, A., Pirkis, J. & Jordan, K. (1990). Behavioral and EEG responses to auditory stimuli during sleep in newborn infants and in infants aged 3 months. *Biological Psychology*, 3, 213–27.

Tronick, E. (1990). Emotions and emotional communication in infants. *American Psychologist*, 44, 112–19.

Tuladhar, R., Harding, R., Cranage, S.M., Adamson, T.M. & Horne, R.S.C. (2003). Effects of sleep position, sleep state and age on heart rate responses following provoked arousal in term infants. *Early Human Development*, 71, 157–69.

Turati, C., Sangrigoli, S., Ruel, J. & de Schonen, S. (2004). Evidence of the face inversion effect in 4-month-old infants. *Infancy*, 6, 275–97.

Turati, C. & Simion, F. (2002). Newborns' recognition of changing and unchanging aspects of schematic faces. *Journal of Experimental Child Psychology*, 83, 239–61.

Tzourio-Mazoyer, N., DeSchonen, S., Crivello, F., Reutter, B., Aujard, Y. & Mazoyer, B. (2002). Neural correlates of woman face processing by 2-month-old infants. *Neuroimage*, 15, 454–61.

Umiltà, C., Simion, F. & Valenza, E. (1996). Newborn's preference for faces. *European Psychologist*, 1, 200–5.

UNICEF. (2001). *Global data base*. Retrieved from http://www.unicef.org

Urizar, G., Milazzo, M., Le, H., Delucchi, K., Sotelo, R. & Munoz, R. (2004). Impact of stress reduction instructions on stress and cortisol levels during pregnancy. *Biological Psychology*, 67, 275–82.

Vaish, A. & Striano, T. (2004). Is visual reference necessary? Contributions of facial versus vocal cues in 12-month-olds' social referencing behavior. *Developmental Science*, 7, 261–9.

van Bakel, H.J. & Riksen-Walraven, J.M. (2004). Stress reactivity in 15-

month-old infants: Links with infant temperament, cognitive competence, and attachment security. *Developmental Psychobiology*, *44*, 157–67.

Van Egeren, L.A., Barratt, M.S. & Roach, M.A. (2001). Mother–infant responsiveness: Timing, mutual regulation, and interactional context. *Development Psychology*, *37*, 684–97.

von Kries, R., Kalies, H. & Papousek, M. (2006). Excessive crying beyond 3 months may herald other features of multiple regulatory problems. *Archives of Pediatrics & Adolescent Medicine*, *160*, 508–11.

Wadhwa, P. (2005). Psychoneuroendocrine processes in human pregnancy influence fetal development and health. *Psychoneuroendocrinology*, *30*, 724–43.

Wadhwa, P.D., Porto, M., Garite, T.J., Chicz-DeMet, A. & Sandman, C.A. (1998). Maternal corticotropin-releasing hormone levels in the early third trimester predict length of gestation in human pregnancy. *American Journal of Obstetrics and Gynecology*, *179*, 1079–85.

Wake, M., Morton-Allen, E., Poulakis, Z., Hiscock, H., Gallagher, S. & Oberklaid, F. (2006). Prevalence, stability, and outcomes of cry-fuss and sleep problems in the first 2 years of life: Prospective community based study. *Pediatrics*, *117*, 836–42.

Walton, G.E., Armstrong, E.S. & Bower, T.G.R. (1997). Faces as forms in the world of the newborn. *Infant Behavior and Development*, *20(4)*, 537–43.

Warren, S.I., Gunnar, M.R., Kagan, J., Anders, T.F., Simmens, S.J., Rones, M., Wease, S., Aron, E., Dahl, R.E.

& Sroufe, L.A. (2003). Maternal panic disorder: Infant temperament, neurophysiology, and parenting behaviors. *Journal of American Academy Childhood and Adolescent Psychiatry*, *42*, 814–25.

Wasserman, M.D. (2000). The effects of compound contextual stimuli on infant memory. *Dissertation Abstracts International: Section B: The Sciences and Engineering*, *61*, 1107.

Watamura, S.E., Donzella, B., Kertes, D.A. & Gunnar, M.R. (2004). Developmental changes in baseline cortisol activity in early childhood: Relations with napping and effortful control. *Developmental Psychobiology*, *45*, 125–33.

Webb, S.J. & Nelson, C.A. (2001). Perceptual priming for upright and inverted faces in infants and adults. *Journal of Experimental Child Psychology*, *79*, 1–22.

Weiner, L. & Morse, B.Q. (1990). Alcohol, pregnancy, and fetal development. In R.C. Engs (Ed.), *Alcohol and drug problems association* (pp. 61–8). Dubuque, IA: Kendall/Hunt Publishing.

Weinstock, M. (2005). The potential influence of maternal stress hormones on development and mental health of the offspring. *Brain, Behavior and Immunity*, *19*, 296–308.

Wells, J.C., Stanley, M., Laidlaw, A.S., Day, J.M., Stafford, M. & Davies, P.S. (1997). Investigation of the relationship between infant temperament and later body composition. *International Journal of Obesity & Related Metabolic Disorders*, *21*, 400–6.

Weppelman, T.L., Bostow, A., Schiffer, R., Elbert-Perez, E. & Newman,

R.S. (2003). Children's use of the prosodic characteristics of infant-directed speech. *Language and Communication*, 23, 63–80.

Whipple, J. (2000). The effect of parenting in music and multimodal stimulation on parent–neonate interactions in the neonatal intensive care unit. *Journal of Music Therapy*, 37, 250–68.

White, B.P., Gunnar, M.R., Larson, M.C., Donzella, B. & Barr, R.G. (2000). Behavioral and physiological responsivity, sleep, and patterns of daily cortisol. *Child Development*, 71, 862–77.

White, M.A., Wilson, M.E., Elander, G. & Persson, B. (1999). The Swedish family: Tradition to parenthood. *Scandinavian Journal of Caring Sciences*, 13, 171–6.

Willford, J.A., Richarson, G.A., Leech, S.L. & Day, N.L. (2004). Verbal and visuaspatial learning and memory function in children with moderate prenatal alcohol exposure. *Alcohol Clinical Experimental Research*, 28, 497–507.

Wilson, M.E., Megel, M.E., Fredrichs, A.M. & McLaughlin, P. (2003). Physiologic and behavioral responses to stress, temperament, and incidence of infection and atopic disorders in the first year of life: A pilot study. *Journal of Pediatrics Nurses*, 18, 257–66.

Winkler, I., Kushnerenko, E., Horváth, J., Ceponiene, R., Fellman, V., Huotilainen, M., Näätänen, R. & Sussman, E. (2003). Newborn infants can organize the auditory world. *Proceedings of the National Academy of Science of the United States of America*, 100, 11812–15.

Wolf, R., Lawson, R., Dryden, C. &

Davies, F. (1996). Recovery after desflurane anaesthesia in the infant: Comparison with isoflurane. *British Journal of Anaesthesia*, 76, 362–4.

Wolff, P.H. (1966). The causes, controls and organization of behavior in the neonate. *Psychological Issues*, 5, 1.

Wolfson, A.R., Crowley, S.J., Answer, U. & Basset, J.L. (2003). Changes in sleep patterns and depressive symptoms in first-time mothers: Last trimester to 1-year postpartum. *Behavioral Sleep Medicine*, 1, 54–67.

Wolke, D., Rizzo, P. & Woods, P. (2002). Persistent infant crying and hyperactivity problems in middle childhood. *Pediatrics*, 109, 1054–60.

Wood, R.D. & Spear, L.P. (1998). Prenatal cocaine alters social competition of infant, adolescent, and adult rats. *Behavioral Neuroscience*, 112, 419–31.

Woodward, A.L. & Guajardo, J.J. (2002). Infants' understating of the point gesture as an object-directed action. *Cognitive Development*, 17, 1061–84.

Worku, B. & Kassir, A. (2005). Kangaroo mother care: A randomized controlled trial on effectiveness of early kangaroo mother care for the low birthweight infants in Addis Ababa, Ethiopia. *Journal of Tropical Pediatrics*, 51, 93–7.

Xu, F. (2003). Numerosity discrimination in infants: Evidence for two systems of representations. *Cognition*, 89, B15–25.

Yamada, H., Sadato, N., Konishi, Y., Muramoto, S., Kimura, K., Tanaka, M.A., Yonekura, Y., Ishii, Y., & Itoh, H. (2000). Milestone for normal development of the infantile brain detected by functional MRI. *Neurology*, *55*, 218–23.

Yamaguchi, M.K. (2000). Discriminating the sex of faces by 6- and 8-month-old infants. *Perceptual Motor Skills*, *91*, 653–64.

Yehuda, R., Engel, S.M., Brand, S.R., Seckl, J., Marcus, S.M. & Berkowitz, G.S. (2005). Transgenerational effects of posttraumatic stress disorder in babies of mothers exposed to the World Trade Center attacks during pregnancy. *Journal of Clinical Endocrinology and Metabolism*, *90(7)*, 4115–18.

Zayas, L.H., Cunnigham, M., McKee, M.D. & Jankowski, K.R. (2002). Depression and negative life events among pregnant African-American and Hispanic women. *Women's Health Issues*, *12*, 16–22.

Zelazo, P.R., Zelazo, N.A. & Kolb, S. (1972). "Walking" in the newborn. *Science*, *176*, 314–15.

Zeskind, P.S. & Field, T. (1984). Neonatal cry thresholds and heart rate variability. *Infant Behavior and Development, Developmental Psychobiology*, *24(6)*, 51–60.

Zeskind, P.S. & Gingras, J.L. (2005). Maternal cigarette-smoking during pregnancy disrupts rhythms in fetal heart rate. *Journal of Pediatric Psychology*, *31(1)*, 5–14.

Zwaigenbaum, L., Bryson, S., Rogers, T., Roberts, W., Brian, J. & Szatmari, P. (2005). Behavioral manifestations of autism in the first year of life. *International Journal of Developmental Neuroscience*, *23*, 143–52.

Index

317